Issues in Progress
    Intragroup Conflict and Cooperation
        Alexander Chizhik, Robert Shelly, & Lisa Troyer
    Immigrants and Hosts: Perceptions, Interactions, and Transformations
        Kay Deaux, Victoria Esses, Richard Lalonde, & Rupert Brown
    The Social and Psychological Dynamics of Collective Action:
        From Theory and Research to Policy and Practice
        Aarti Iyer & Martijn van Zomeren
    The Changing Landscape of Intergroup Relations in South Africa
        Gillian Finchilescu & Colin Tredoux
    New Perspectives on Human-Animal Interactions: Theory, Policy,
        and Research
        Sarah Knight & Harold A. Herzog
    International Perspectives on Gender and Political Socialization
        Hans-Peter Kuhn, Connie Flanagan, Lonnie Sherrod, & Angela Ittel
    Democracy and Disenfranchisement
        Kevin Lanning
    Young People's Perspectives on the Rights of the Child: Implications for Theory,
        Research, and Practice
        Martin D. Ruck & Stacey S. Horn
    The Landscape of the Multiracial Experience
        Diana Sanchez & Margaret Shih

Editorial Advisory Board
    Harold L. Arnold, Jr., Temple University, United States
    B. Ann Bettencourt, University of Missouri, United States
    Herbert H. Blumberg, Goldsmiths College, University of London,
        United Kingdom
    Marcella H. Boynton, University of Connecticut, United States
    Heather E. Bullock, University of California, Santa Cruz, United States
    Gillian Finchilescu, University of the Witwatersrand, South Africa
    I-Ching Lee, National Chengchi University, Taiwan
    Susan Clayton, College of Wooster, United States
    Sara McClelland, City University of New York, United States
    Rupert W. Nacoste, North Carolina State University, United States
    Noraini M. Noor, International Islamic University, Malaysia
    Louis A. Penner, Wayne State University, United States
    Stephanie Rowley, University of Michigan, United States
    Johanna Vollhardt, University of Massachusetts, Amherst, United States

Reviewers of Selected Articles, This Issue
    Jost Stellmacher, University of Marburg, Germany
    Bernd Six, University of Halle-Wittenberg, Germany

Past JSI Editors
  Irene Hanson Frieze (2001–2005)
  Phyllis Katz (1997–2000)
  Daniel Perlman (1993–1996)
  Stuart Oskamp (1988–1992)
  George Levinger (1984–1987)
  Joseph E. McGrath (1979–1983)
  Jacqueline D. Goodchilds (1974–1978)
  Bertram H. Raven (1970–1973)
  Joshua A. Fishman (1966–1969)
  Leonard Solomon (1963)
  Robert Chin (1960–1965)
  John Harding (1956–1959)
  M. Brewster Smith (1951–1955)
  Harold H. Kelley (1949)
  Ronald Lippitt (1944–1950)

2008 Vol. 64, No. 2

Ethnic Prejudice and Discrimination in Europe
Issue Editors: Andreas Zick, Thomas F. Pettigrew, and Ulrich Wagner

INTRODUCTION

Ethnic Prejudice and Discrimination in Europe 233
Andreas Zick, Thomas F. Pettigrew, and Ulrich Wagner

RESEARCH AND THEORY

Everyday Racism as Predictor of Political Racism in Flemish Belgium 253
Jaak Billiet and Hans de Witte

More than Two Decades of Changing Ethnic Attitudes
in the Netherlands 269
*Marcel Coenders, Marcel Lubbers, Peer Scheepers,
and Maykel Verkuyten*

Black Immigrants in Portugal: Luso–Tropicalism and Prejudice 287
Jorge Vala, Diniz Lopes, and Marcus Lima

Postconflict Reconciliation: Intergroup Forgiveness and Implicit
Biases in Northern Ireland 303
*Tania Tam, Miles Hewstone, Jared B. Kenworthy, Ed Cairns,
Claudia Marinetti, Leo Geddes, and Brian Parkinson*

Types of Identification and Intergroup Differentiation
in the Russian Federation 321
Anca Minescu, Louk Hagendoorn, and Edwin Poppe

Anti-Semitic Attitudes in Europe: A Comparative Perspective 343
Werner Bergmann

The Syndrome of Group-Focused Enmity: The Interrelation
of Prejudices Tested with Multiple Cross-Sectional and Panel Data 363
*Andreas Zick, Carina Wolf, Beate Küpper, Eldad Davidov,
Peter Schmidt, and Wilhelm Heitmeyer*

Relative Deprivation and Intergroup Prejudice 385
*Thomas F. Pettigrew, Oliver Christ, Ulrich Wagner,
Roel W. Meertens, Rolf van Dick, and Andreas Zick*

Prejudice and Group-Related Behavior in Germany 403
Ulrich Wagner, Oliver Christ, and Thomas F. Pettigrew

COMMENTARY
Viewing Intergroup Relations in Europe through Allport's Lens Model
of Prejudice   417
  Walter G. Stephan

ERRATUM   430

Ethnic Prejudice and Discrimination in Europe

Andreas Zick*
University of Bielefeld

Thomas F. Pettigrew
University of California

Ulrich Wagner
Philipps-University

This article provides an introduction to research on European prejudice and discrimination. First, we list the distinctive characteristics of a European perspective and provide a short sketch of European immigration and ethnic groups. Europe has become a multicultural community. Nevertheless, public opinion and the continent's politics often do not reflect this empirical fact. Prejudice and discrimination directed at immigrants are a widespread phenomena across Europe. Several cross-European surveys support this conclusion, although theoretically driven surveys on prejudice and discrimination in Europe remain rare. Cross-European research studies classical and modern theories of prejudice and discrimination and attempts to uncover the psychological mechanisms that explain individual readiness to exclude ethnic groups. A brief sketch of recent European research is presented. This issue offers both important cross-national perspectives as well as needed comparisons with the more studied case of racial prejudice and discrimination in the United States.

Why an Issue Focusing on Intergroup Relations in Europe?

Scholars who study ethnic group relations have repeatedly shown the dependence of ethnic relations on the societal context (Trickett, Watts, & Birman,

---

*Correspondence concerning this article should be addressed to Dr. Andreas Zick, University of Bielefeld, Institute for Interdisciplinary Research of Conflict and Violence, Universitaetsstr. 25, 33615 Bielefeld, Germany [e-mail: zick@uni-bielefeld.de].

1994). Yet social psychological research on ethnic intergroup relations has been dominated by a North-American perspective, focusing in particular on the unique case of Black–White relations. The present issue on prejudice and discrimination addresses this problem by presenting research on the great variety of intergroup relations throughout Europe.

But why focus on Europe for the needed comparisons? First, as this issue demonstrates, recent years have witnessed a belated outpouring of research on intergroup relations throughout the continent. This literature has not been widely available to North American social scientists. Thus, we hope this issue will serve to make this expanding and important research literature more widely known and available.

Second, the apparent similarities between Europe and North America are more superficial than their deep differences. Focusing on European ethnic research not only means an extension from one cultural context to another but also taps vastly different historical backgrounds that shape even current debates on interethnic relations. Europe has had a longer and deeper history of colonization than the United States. In turn, the United States had slavery—an institution unknown in Europe as a mass phenomenon since the Middle Ages. Additionally, Europe never had a comparable civil rights movement primarily driven by ethnic minorities as the United States did in the 1960s. One critical consequence of this is that European ethnic minorities typically have severely limited political influence (ERCOMER, 1997).

Moreover, 20th century Europe had two horrific wars on its soil, with a total renewal of the political system in many countries after World War II. Thus, in many European countries the end of the war, the polarization between the Eastern Block and the Western N.A.T.O. coalition, and the establishment of the European Community (now the European Union [E.U.]) are significant milestones that shaped interethnic relations and set the context for the migration between different European countries and the immigration of millions of non-Europeans. Still another factor is that the holocaust significantly influences the current debate on ethnic intergroup relations in Europe—especially in Germany.

There are other crucial differences between the continents. Compared to Canada and the United States, European states still do not consider themselves to be countries of in-migration. Many nations, such as Germany, regard the new immigration as a novel event and ignore that they have actually experienced in-migration for centuries. This fact helps to explain the often-arbitrary categorization of European ethnicities. Thus, the children and grandchildren of the immigrants of the 1960s and 1970s are still often considered foreigners. This perception affects citizenship policy (Martiniello, 1995). In some nations, such as Germany, most immigrants and their progeny have never received citizenship, even if they were born and raised in the country. In other states, such as the United Kingdom and France, immigrants of the third generation still are often considered to be foreigners despite their citizenship.

Third, parts of Europe in between are unified in European Union. Nevertheless, Europe is still extremely heterogeneous, as can be seen from Table 1, delivering some selected demographic, economic, and social background variables for different European countries.[1]

In addition, even the E.U. is sharply different from the governance structures of Canada and the United States. Not surprisingly, Europe does not yet offer a widely adopted common identity. National identities remain strong. Characteristically, the basic identity is Greek, Swedish, Irish, or French—not European. One consequence of this regional identification involves group comparisons. Typically, Europeans not only distinguish themselves from non-Europeans, as U.S. citizens distinguish themselves from noncitizens but also compare themselves with other European countries (Breakwell & Lyons, 1996). Thus, regionalization and differentiation affects ethnic relations more than in North America—with the exception of the Deep South in the United States.

For these many reasons, research on European ethnic relations provides a rich array of social contexts with which to test how societal processes shape social psychological processes of ethnic intergroup relations (see also Pettigrew, Wagner, & Christ, in press). Before discussing the individual articles, we turn next to a sketch of European immigration.

Immigration and Emigration in Europe

Europe has become a multicultural patchwork with millions of new immigrants. After World War II, Europe received significant labor migration from its former colonies as well as major internal migration from the south and east to the north and west of Europe. In the 1950s and 1960s, rapidly industrializing Europe recruited millions of misnamed "guest workers." Although Western European countries stopped this recruitment during later economic crises in the 1970s, immigrants from all over the world kept coming (Jackson, Brown, & Kirby, 1998). Southern European countries began to record significant immigration flows in the 1970s when migrants could no longer get direct access to Western Europe.

Most of the world's immigrants live in Europe (about 56 million), Asia (50 million), and North America (42 million) (United Nations, 2002; see also Table 1 for net migration rates). Since 1990, all European countries save Lithuania, Poland, Romania, and Iceland have experienced more immigration than emigration. It is difficult to obtain solid ethnicity data in Europe because of differences in official statistics and ethnic definitions. For example, resettlers of German

---

[1] Several demographic, social, and economic indicators are available by data set of Eurostat, the Statistical Office of the European Commission, the European Foundation for the Improvement of Living and Working Conditions, and the OECD (see also Atkinson, Cantillon, Marlie & Nolan, 2002). The most important free access surveys on attitudes and opinions of European citizens are the Eurobarometer (European Commission), the European Community Household Panel (Eurostat), the European Value Study, and the European Social Survey.

Table 1. Selected Demographic Facts and Estimations of Welfare and Living Conditions Across Europe

	Population in 2003	Net migration in 2002	Gross domestic product (GDP) (2006)[d]	Unemployment quota (% in 2005)	At-risk-of-poverty rate after social transfers[g]	Welfare of country is (very) good %[h]	Satisfaction with living standard 2003[i]
Austria	8.082.0	32.2	128.7	5.2	12	75	7.9
Belgium	10.355.8	35.2	123.3	8.4	16[a]	79	7.6
Bulgaria	7.845.8	0.0	37.1				4
Czech Republic	10.203.3	25.8	79.3	7.9	10[f]	25	6.1
Denmark	5.383.5	7.0	126.6	4.8	12	83	8.3
Germany	82.536.7	144.9	113.6	9.5	13[f]	52	7.3
Estonia	1.356.0	−.04[b]	67.9	7.9	18	17	5.7
Ireland	3.963.6	28.3	142.8	4.3	20	59	7.6
Greece	11.006.4	35.0	96.9[e]	9.8	20	23	
Spain	41.550.6[a]	594.3	102.4	9.2	20	46	6.6
France	59.635.0	55.0	112.8	9.5	13	69	6.8
Italy	57.321.1	511.2	103.7	7.6	19	30	7.1
Cyprus	715.1	12.9[b]	93.2	5.3	16[f]	65	6.9
Latvia	2.331.5	−.08	55.8	8.2	19[f]	9	5.7
Lithuania	3.462.6	−6.3[b]	57.7	9.0	21[f]	21	5.1
Luxembourg	448.3	2.1	278.6	5.3	13	86	7.9
Hungary	10.142.4	15.5	65.3	7.2	13[f]	18	5.8
Malta	397.3	1.7	75.5	7.3	15[f]	60	7.5
Netherlands	16.921.6	2.8	132.1	4.7	11[f]	57	7.5
Poland	38.218.5	−13.8	52.9	17.7	21[b]	10	5.5
Portugal	10.407.5	63.5	74.4[e]	7.6	20[b]	10	5.9
Romania	21.722.8	−7.4	37.6[e]		18		6.1
Slovenia	1.995.0	3.4	88.8	6.3	12[f]	48	6.5
Slovakia	5.379.2	1.4	62.7	16.4	13[f]	9	5.1
Finland	5.206.3	5.8	116.3	8.4	12	92	7.5

(continued).

Table 1. Continued.

	Population in 2003	Net migration in 2002	Gross domestic product (GDP) (2006)[d]	Unemployment quota (% in 2005)	At-risk-of-poverty rate after social transfers[g]	Welfare of country is (very) good %[h]	Satisfaction with living standard 2003[i]
Sweden	8.940.8	28.7	120.3	7.8	9	61	7.6
United Kingdom	59.328.9	103.0	119.1	4.7	18[f]	46	7.2
Croatia	4.442.2	8.6[c]	49.9[e]				5.5[j]
Macedonia, the former Yugoslav Republic of	2.023.7	−24.8[c]	27.6[e]				
Turkey	70.173.0	100.0	29.4				
Iceland	288.5	−0.2[b]	135.8		10		4.6
Norway	4.552.3	11.2	186.9				
Switzerland	7.317.9[b]	41.2	135.8				

Note. (a) Eurostat estimate; (b) Provisional; (c) 2002, Eurostat; (d) Measure for the economic activity: defined as the value of all goods and services produced less the value of any goods or services used in their creation. The volume index of GDP per capita in Purchasing Power Standards (PPS) is expressed in relation to the European Union (U-27) average set to equal 100. If the index of a country is higher than 100, this country's level of GDP per head is higher than the EU average and vice versa. Basic figures are expressed in PPS, that is, a common currency that eliminates the differences in price levels between countries allowing meaningful volume comparisons of GDP between countries; (e) forecast; (f) break in series; (g) The share of persons with an equivalized disposable income below the risk-of-poverty threshold, which is set at 60% of the national median equivalized disposable income (after social transfers) (data by Eurostat); (h) Eurostat estimate; (i) Eurobarometer 62.1, 2004; (j) European Foundation for the Improvement of Living and Working Conditions, survey 2003; Mean value on a scale of 1 "very dissatisfied" to 10 "very satisfied" with the own present standard of living (see also European Foundation for the Improvement of Living and Working Conditions, 2004); (k) 2002.

origin from Romania and Russia are not counted as immigrants in Germany (Zick, Wagner, van Dick, & Petzel, 2001). Nonetheless, Eurostat, the Statistical Office of the European Commission, calculated that in 2001 Germany had the highest level of immigration both from within the E.U. (879,217) as well as from non-E.U.-countries (564,669), followed by Spain (414,772/343,960), U.K. (372,206/209,234), Italy (226,968/182,034), The Netherlands (133,404/72,095), and non-E.U. Switzerland (122,494/80,079). Eastern European countries probably have far less in-migration—though those that have recently entered the E.U. may now experience higher rates.

The mean amount of 5% non-European immigrants in the continent's total population may seem small compared to such multicultural societies as Canada, the Russian Federation, the United States, or even Rwanda (see Dovidio & Esses, 2001). But the Organization for Economic Development and Cooperation (O.E.C.D.; 2003) reported an annual and substantial inflow of migrants into the E.U. (1,310,600)—a figure larger than that of the United States (849,800), Canada (227,200), Australia (92,300), and New Zealand (38,300) combined.

But to grasp fully the larger immigration picture, one must also consider emigration. The O.E.C.D. notes that emigration rates are quite high in Germany (562,400), Switzerland (55,800), Austria (44,400), and Belgium (35,600). Table 2 delivers a comparison of national immigration and emigration numbers.

Table 2. Population and Migration Indicators for the Continents in Thousands and Percentage of Population

	Population		Migration stock		Net migration[a]	
	1990	2000	1990	2000	1990–1995	1995–2000
Europe	721,981	727,304	48,437 6.7%	56,100 7.7%	1.120	769
Eastern Europe	310,770	304,172	23,017 7.4%	24,812 8.2%	274	124
Northern Europe	92,478	95,076	6,774 7.3%	7,453 7.8%	92	134
Southern Europe	142,643	144,935	3,418 2.4%	4,999 3.4%	−6	229
Western Europe	176,091	183,121	15,229 8.6	18836 10.3%	760	282
Latin America & Caribbean	440,354	518,809	7,014 1.6	5,944 1.1	−580	−494
Northern America	282,598	314,113	27,597 9.8	40,844 13.0	1,189	1,394
Asia	3,164,081	3,672,342	49,986 1.6%	49,948 1.4%	−1,460	−1,311
Africa	619,477	793,627	16,221 2.6%	16,277 2.1%	−372	−447
Oceania	26,330	30,521	4,751 18.0%	5,835 19.1%	103	90

Note. An annual average for 1990–1995 and 1995–2000; Public data by United Nations (2002).

In addition to first-generation immigrants, millions of the descendents of immigrants now live in Europe, and millions of Europeans are crossing the open E.U. borders. A vast array of diverse groups—from asylum seekers, refugees, and legal and illegal workers to sojourners, tourists, international students, resettlers, descendents of the second- and third-generation immigrants and many others—make up modern Europe today. This picture became even more multicultural with the 2004 inclusion into the E.U. of eight Eastern European countries, Malta, and Cyprus. And the diversity will increase even further when there is additional E.U. expansion.

Public Reactions and Cross-European Studies

Europe has responded to this sweeping change in diverse ways ranging from full acceptance to prejudice, discrimination, and violence (Pettigrew, 1998a, 1998b; Pettigrew et al., 1998). The media, governmental institutions, and social science research all report severe and continuing discrimination of minorities in Europe. Immigrants are particular targets of prejudice and discrimination (Wagner, Christ, & Heitmeyer, in press). Especially during economic recessions in Western Europe, foreign workers are often blamed for economic and social problems. And there is scant recognition that immigration made Western Europe's remarkable postwar economic recovery possible.

There have been no uniform European immigration practices (Noiriel, 1994). And from the beginning, immigration was constructed and framed as a problem and often perceived as a threat by the native population. Indeed, the very term "guest worker" implies a temporary, low-status position in society. Surveys document the continuing effects of these policies on public opinion. The Eurobarometer 48 showed that in 1997, 45% of E.U. Europeans thought that there were "too many" foreigners living in their country (Greece 71%, Belgium 60%, Italy 53%, Germany 52%, Austria 50%, France 46%, Denmark 46%, U.K. 42%, the Netherlands 40%, Sweden 38%, Luxembourg 33%, Portugal 28%, Spain 20%, Ireland 19%, and Finland 10%). In 2002, the Eurobarometer 57 showed that 15% of the respondents did not find ethnic discrimination of immigrants to be unjustified (Marsh & Sahin-Dikmen, 2003). The European Social Survey in 2002 confirmed that ethnic prejudice and discrimination are widespread, but it also revealed sharp differences among European countries. Figure 1 shows the mean agreement that "Immigrants make [home country] a worse or better place" on an 11-point rating scale.

These surveys, limited to one point in time, offer just a snapshot of opinions. Longitudinal surveys on prejudice and discrimination are needed but still rare. Most available data on European prejudice derives from unrelated studies in various European countries using different measures and target groups. Cross-European research on prejudice, exemplified by the E.U.'s Eurobarometer and the European Social Survey, is relatively recent. And it has largely lacked theoretical frameworks

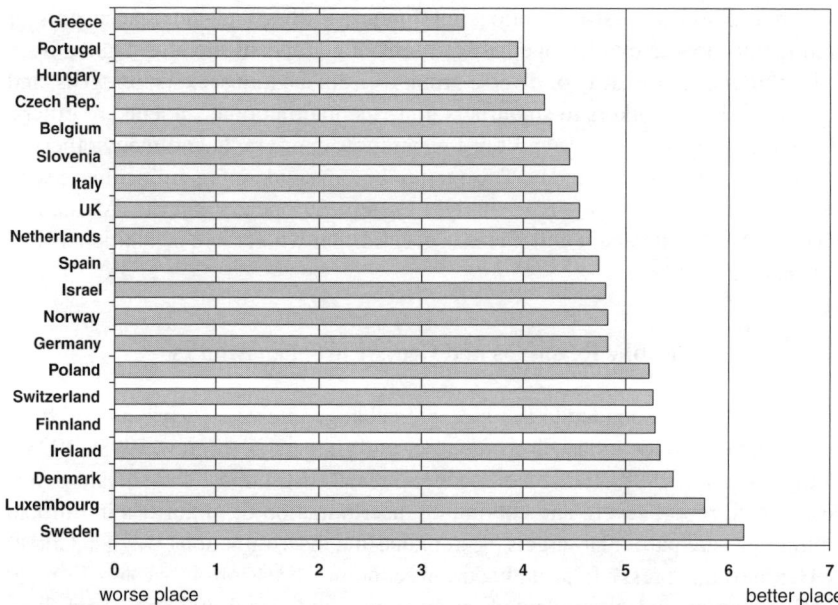

Fig. 1. Mean (dis)agreement with the item "Immigrants make (country of respondents) a worse or better place" in the European Social Survey 2002 (0 = *worse place*, 10 = *better place*).

for cross-cultural comparisons. Consequently, unique European contributions are only now emerging.

As in the North America, European cross-national research demonstrates that different expressions of prejudice and discrimination must be considered. In particular, the distinction between old-fashioned and modern racism has shaped recent work (Macmaster, 2001; Pettigrew et al., 1998). Using the 1988 Eurobarometer 30, Pettigrew and Meertens (1995) developed two different measures of prejudice. The Blatant Prejudice Scale consists of two components—one a threat and rejection factor (e.g., "West Indians have jobs the British should have."), the other an intimacy factor (e.g., "I would not mind if a Turk who had a similar economic background as mine joined my close family by marriage.").

Thus, blatant prejudice is the more traditional form—close, hot, and direct. By contrast, subtle prejudice is the modern form—distant, cool, and indirect. This new form has been widely studied and validated throughout the Western world. The Subtle Prejudice Scale has three components that share an ostensibly nonracial focus. The first consists of a traditional values factor (e.g., "Asians living here teach their children values and skills different from those required to be successful in France."). The second component concerns views of the outgroup as extremely different culturally from the ingroup. The Subtle Scale's final component involves the denial of sympathy and admiration for the outgroup. Note this component tests for the denial of positive emotions rather than the expression of negative emotions—fear, envy, hatred—that are associated with blatant prejudice.

Researchers have successfully employed these two scales and their adaptations in a great variety of European nations and intergroup situations—including Australia, Belgium, France, Germany, Great Britain, Italy, the Netherlands, Norway, Portugal, Spain, and the United States (Arcuri & Boca, 1999; Hamberger & Hewstone, 1997; Hightower, 1997; Pedersen & Walker, 1997; Pettigrew, 1997; Pettigrew et al., 1998; Rattazzi & Volpato, 2001; Rise, Haugen, Klinger, & Bierbrauer, 2000; Rueda & Navas, 1996; Six & Wolfradt, 2000; Vala, Brito, & Lopes, 1999; Villano, 1999; Volpato & Rattazzi, 2000; Wagner & Zick, 1995; Zick et al., 2001). Several articles in this issue use these blatant and subtle prejudice scales.

Another major topic of European work concentrates on the links between social structural, political, and individual determinants of prejudice (Wagner et al., in press). This research highlights the potential threat raised by immigration and the resulting prejudice generated by this perceived threat. For instance, Hello, Scheepers, and Mérove (2002) analyzed data from the cross-national survey on religious and moral pluralism in 11 European countries. Their analyses show that in Hungary ethnic prejudice is highest (mean = 3.94; max = 7) followed by Poland (3.56), Italy (3.22), and Belgium (3.11). More interesting are their findings concerning the link between education and prejudice. Research throughout the world has repeatedly found the poorly educated to be more prejudiced (Wagner & Zick, 1995). However, these investigators show that this education effect is weaker in the new democracies of Eastern Europe than in the longstanding democracies of Western Europe (see Coenders & Scheepers, 2003; and Hjerm, 2001, for comparable results from the International Social Survey Programme—the ISSP.). Furthermore, the more religiously heterogeneous a country is, the smaller the differences between educational groups. Neither unemployment rate nor the percentage of nonnationals affected the relation between education and prejudice. These results suggest that cross-cultural differences in the transmission of tolerant values explain in part education's effects on prejudice.

Coenders and Scheepers (1998) emphasize ethnic competition theory. They assume that social groups compete for such scarce resources as jobs and housing. Perceived ethnic competition is then predicted to be positively related to an increasing number of people from different ethnic groups who compete for the same scarce resources, or a decreasing amount of scarce resources for which the same number of people compete. This theory holds that even with a stable level of scarce resources the relative number of people from ethnic minorities can initiate the perception of threat. Ethnic competition theory, with its hypothesis that prejudice is a direct expression of realistic group conflicts, is quite popular in European political debates.

Kunovich (2002, 2004) tested group-threat theory's predictions that the effects of social structural variables are stronger in countries with larger immigrant populations and poorer economic conditions. The rival hypothesis is that the effects of social structural variables are weaker in countries with larger immigration populations and poorer economic conditions. Kunovich reanalyzed the ISSP of 1995 using data from 17 Eastern and Western European countries as well as the nations of North America, Oceania, and Southeast Asia. For individual respondents, he developed an anti-immigrant prejudice scale and measured such social location variables as labor market position, education, and income. On the country level, he built an index of relative group size of immigrants and controlled for economic conditions. Kunovich showed that social structural variables, except for poverty, have a more powerful influence on prejudice in Western than in Eastern Europe. According to group-threat theory, nations with larger immigration populations should show greater prejudice. But if the other country-level variables are included in the analyses, the effect of the size of the immigration-population relationship disappears. Contrary to threat theory, countries with poor economic conditions yield significantly lower effects of immigration population. Economic conditions are much more important than the number or ratio of immigrants. Moreover, poor economic conditions have a much stronger effect on prejudice in Eastern than in Western Europe.

Further research helps to explain this apparent falsification of threat theory. A recent study using the German General Social Survey of 1996 measured the actual immigrant proportion in small districts, the perceived immigrant proportion, the perceived threat from immigrants, and exclusionary attitudes toward immigrants (Semyonov, Raijman, Tov, & Schmidt, 2004). No relationship was uncovered between the actual immigrant proportion and either perceived threat or anti-immigrant attitudes. But perceived immigrant proportion did correlate with both perceived threat and exclusionary attitudes. Surprisingly, the actual immigrant percentage in the area and the perceived percentage were essentially unrelated. Note that threat, as sociological theory asserts, mediates the effect between the perceived proportion and prejudice. But it is the perceived—and not the actual—proportion of immigrants that is the critical predictor of threat and anti-immigrant opinions.

Through increased contact, larger immigrant population ratios can even reduce prejudice. For example, Wagner, Christ, Pettigrew, and Wolf (2006) demonstrated that with larger foreigner populations in a German district, the frequency and intensity of intergroup contacts also increase. And this intergroup contact in turn reduces ethnic outgroup rejection. Similar results have been presented by Hamberger and Hewstone (1997) and Pettigrew (1997) who showed with European survey data that having close friends of another cultural group reduces the prejudice of dominant group members. McLaren (2003) similarly finds in his cross-European research that contact and perceived group threat predict European prejudice.

Beyond the role of threat, other cross-European research focuses on social identity. Several European studies indicate that citizens with strong national identity are more prone to prejudice and discrimination (Billiet, Maddens, & Beerten, 2003; Kirch, Kirch, Pettai, & Tuisk, 1997; Maddens, Billiet & Beerten, 2000; Triandafyllidou, 2000; Verkuyten & Hagendoorn, 1998; Weiss, 2003). But other forms of identification relate to intergroup acceptance. Thus, those respondents who "feel" European and often think of themselves as European are less prejudiced against immigrants (Becker, Wagner, & Christ, 2007). Moreover, a universalistic identification that involves respondents expressing pride in their nation's democratic institutions also is associated with greater acceptance of immigrants (Heyder & Schmidt, 2002).

The often-replicated finding that individuals who are highly identified with their nation express prejudice against nonnationals is closely connected to the social identity theory (Tajfel & Turner, 1979). This most prominent European intergroup theory defines prejudice and discrimination as processes of intergroup differentiation. Expanding on this basic work, several articles that follow treat this issue.

This Issue

Although research in Europe has a special focus on immigration, prejudice and discrimination are not limited to these new minorities. Right-wing activity also relates to increasing anti-Semitism in Europe. Since September 11, 2001, growing hostility toward Muslims is also apparent (Allen & Nielsen, 2002). And recent surveys also have uncovered widespread prejudice against such nonethnic minorities as the homeless, handicapped, homosexuals, persons with AIDS, Gypsies, and other groups. The many changing processes—migration, political transformations, the European unification process, and widespread negative opinions toward ethnic and social minorities—underline the importance of social context for prejudice and discrimination. These sweeping changes call for increased attention to the links between the macro- and micro-determinants of prejudice and discrimination. This perspective connects the articles of this issue.

New perspectives and questions are raised by the entry into the E.U. of eight nations of Eastern Europe. Research on intergroup prejudice and discrimination in the East is sparse. The influence of national identity in Eastern European countries is especially intriguing. The sudden transformation from old to new political systems should have consequences for both the self-definition of the dominant society and its relation to minorities. Early research suggests that strong national identity is closely connected to prejudice and discrimination of ethnic minorities. Another focus concerns the rise of far-right-wing political parties—phenomena observed throughout Europe since the early 1990s. Open hostility against ethnic minorities shocked much of the public. Austria, Belgium, France, Germany, Italy, and even the Netherlands all witnessed increasing political support and mass media attention to extreme right-wing groups. This political movement obviously affects the analysis of European prejudice and discrimination.

The following articles demonstrate in detail that the rejection of ethnic and social groups is approaching dangerously high levels in both Western and Eastern Europe. All the articles concentrate on empirical findings throughout Europe as well as cross-national comparisons. This research reveals both consistent patterns and intriguing differences across countries. The studies test for differences between traditional prejudices, such as anti-Semitism, and prejudices against the new immigrants and other target groups. This focus allows comparisons between Eastern and Western European patterns of prejudice as well as between Europe, North America, and other areas of the world. The authors represent three social science disciplines—political science, sociology, and social psychology. Thus, this issue will propose diverse perspectives, theoretical approaches, and levels of analysis.

The issue starts with a look at the "extreme pole" of prejudices and discrimination. Survey results repeatedly demonstrate that Belgians on average evince greater prejudice, racism, and right-wing opinions than most E.U. countries. By contrast, Belgium's neighbor, the Netherlands, is known as one of the most tolerant European countries with, until recently, a long liberal immigration and integration history. Billiet and de Witte (2008) consider the case of racism in Flanders (Belgium) in detail. They note that cross-European studies reveal Belgium as one of the most anti-immigrant. Yet these Belgian attitudes toward immigrants have over recent decades been quite stable, while the support of the right-wing, anti-immigration Flemish Vlaams Blok political part has steadily increased over the past generation. The article discusses the historical, political, and social reasons of this striking discrepancy. Billiet and de Witte show that prejudice is closely related to political movements and political reasoning in Belgium. Their analysis of election and opinion surveys underline the importance of the distinction between attitude direction and attitude strength, structural changes in society, and the emergence of such issues as "fear of crime."

Coenders, Lubbers, Scheepers, and Verkuyten (2008) critically consider the widespread reputation of the Netherlands for tolerance toward ethnic minorities. They compare Dutch public opinion with that of their neighbors and utilize the distinction between blatant and subtle prejudice. The authors argue that the Dutch norm of tolerance grew out of its distinctive political system over the centuries. In Dutch history, separate communities retained a high level of autonomy and separation but compromised and cooperated through their elites. The authors discuss different historical and sociological explanations for the rise of this system; and they add their psychological focus on the analysis of attitudes and values. Coenders, Lubbers, Scheepers, and Verkuyten (2008) believe that the impact of multiculturalism, political correctness, and social dominance can explain the nation's low level of blatant prejudice as well as its high level amount of subtle prejudice.

The next article discusses specific cultural cases of ethnic prejudice in a postcolonial country. The article by Vala, Lopes, and Lima (2008) concentrates on prejudice against Africans in Portugal. Though widely distributed in the E.U., due to geographical closeness, Africans have come in greater numbers to Portugal in recent years. Vala and coworkers argue that due to Portugal's specific colonial history the social representation of luso-tropicalism has developed which still contributes to weaken the traditional association between national identity and overt prejudice which can be observed in many other countries. Thus, luso-tropicalism seems to protect against the expression of overt prejudice. However, their data also show that despite luso-tropicalism that Portugese express covert negative evaluations of cultural differences attributed to immigrants.

Tam et al. (2008) focus on the tragic violent conflict in Northern Ireland and means to overcome it. They argue, that in Northern Ireland identifying as "Catholic" and "Protestant" is an intergroup process and is as much ethnic and political as it is religious. Their article addresses psychological processes crucial to moving beyond such a history of violent sectarian conflict. In their research, they present intergroup forgiveness, changes in intergroup emotions, infrahumanization, increase in empathy, and trust as possible means to reduce intergroup bias. The results are discussed in terms of their implications for postconflict reconciliation in Northern Ireland.

Minescu, Hagendoorn, and Poppe (2008) extend the discussion beyond Western Europe with results of a recent survey of the ethnic prejudices of both majority and minority peoples in 10 republics of the Russian Federation measuring Russians' and titulars' identifications with their ethnic group, their republic, and the Russian Federation as well as the effects of these identification on intergroup stereotypes. They show that identification at various inclusiveness levels is differently reflected in the positive/negative stereotypes about ingroups and outgroups. While ingroup stereotypes are positively affected by all types of identification, outgroup stereotypes become negative by high ethnic identification and more positive by republican and federal identification. The authors propose a model of intergroup differentiation that takes into account social identification at different inclusiveness levels.

Can we generalize these findings from ethnic groups to other social groups in Europe that have long been target groups of prejudice and discrimination? The next two articles focus on different target groups of prejudice in Europe. Consistent with the social psychological literature over the past seven decades, they reveal that prejudices against different groups are positively intercorrelated. The first article, by Werner Bergmann (2008), investigates modern anti-Semitism. It presents comparative data and the history of European opinion about Jews. Adopting a social identity assumptions of intergroup processes (Tajfel & Turner, 1979), Bergmann assumes that European anti-Semitism, both currently and historically, is closely tied to issues and crises of national self-identification. Attitudes toward Jews are determined less by concrete experiences of cultural differences, or conflicts over scarce resources, than by a perceived threat to the national self-image, which leads to an accentuation of those pertinent prejudices, which categorize Jews as being responsible for it.

Zick et al., (2008) present their interdisciplinary approach to the syndrome of group-focused enmity. The syndrome is compounded of diverse types of prejudice: racism, sexism, xenophobia, homophobia, anti-Semitism, Islamophobia, and antinewcomer (e.g., special rights for the already established). Data from three probability surveys as well as a three-wave panel study have so far been conducted. The authors' primary contention is that prejudices are linked by a syndrome of group-focused enmity, which rests upon a generalized ideology of inequality. By cross-sectional and longitudinal probability survey data from Germany, Zick et al. show that a syndrome of group-focused enmity exists. Additionally, the same predictors, such as right-wing authoritarianism and relative deprivation, trigger the syndromatic devaluation of outgroups, and this devaluation influences the same discriminatory behavioral intentions.

The remaining articles explore specific issues concerning ethnic prejudice. First, the influence of relative deprivation is studied. The next article analyzes a basic question of research on prejudice: When do individuals and groups act out their prejudice?

Pettigrew et al. (2008) analyze the relationships between relative deprivation and ethnic prejudice. They utilize both macro- and micro-data from three European surveys. Pettigrew and his colleagues demonstrate how the individual (IRD) and group (GRD) forms of relative deprivation relate to each other. Next they show that GRD relates directly and positively with prejudice, but IRD does not. Moreover, GRD mediates the effects of IRD on prejudice. Thus, individual relative deprivation influences prejudice only through its tendency to increase the sense of group relative deprivation. In addition, these investigators show that GRD also mediates in part the effects of social class and identity predictors of prejudice.

One of the central questions of prejudice research is the connection of prejudiced attitudes and behavior toward outgroups. Wagner, Christ, and Pettigrew (2008) analyze representative survey and panel data from Germany to ascertain the link between prejudice and discrimination. They show on the basis of longitudinal data that prejudice is in fact an important predictor of both avoiding of ethnic minorities as well as of aggressive behavior intentions against these outgroup members. In addition, the effect of prejudice on behavior remains substantial even after controlling for potential confounding variables. And finally, their data deliver evidence that intergroup contact and intergroup threat affect behavior intentions in relation to ethnic outgroups and that the influence of contact and threat is at least partially mediated by intergroup prejudiced attitudes, thus again supporting the authors' view that prejudice is an important predictor of intergroup behavior.

The concluding chapter, authored by Stephan (2008), summarizes the articles of this issue from the perspective of Allport's (1954) lens model of the multiple causes of prejudice. The lens model specifies that historical, sociocultural, situational, and personality factors all contribute to prejudice. Stephan comes to the conclusion that the articles in this issue examine numerous variables located at different levels of Allport's lens model. He recommends more comparative and multilevel studies. And he also demands comprehensive theories that both integrate the results from different levels of analyses and acknowledge different cultural backgrounds as moderators of known causes of prejudice. Stephan suggests that the social sciences should use all possible means to get an overview of intergroup relations in Europe and other parts of the world. This achievement, he maintains, would allow us to develop practical intervention programs to fight more effectively racism, prejudice, and discrimination.

To sum up, this issue provides a comprehensive overview of prejudice in Europe from an interdisciplinary viewpoint. All articles presented are based on survey data, many of them on large representative samples. This kind of data allows generalization for the populations from which they are drawn, thus giving the opportunity to come to scientific conclusions about intergroup situations in, for example, a national state. Other data, as those based on student samples, are very restricted in this respect. On the other hand, testing assumptions about relevant causal influences on prejudiced attitudes and analyzing the consequences of prejudice, for example, discriminatory behavior, is often not extremely difficult on these basis of cross-sectional survey data: Correlational data deliver information about the covariation of some preconditions and consequences with individuals' prejudice, however, they usually do not allow testing what is cause and what is effect. An exception is the analysis of longitudinal data, as shown by Wagner et al. (in press). On the other hand, covariation is also a precondition of causality, that is, if a hypothesis about relevant predictors and consequences of prejudice cannot be shown on the basis of correlational data, this is a clear falsification of the hypothesis. Thus, the data presented here are of extreme value for an international comparative perspective, they have to be added, however, in the future by additional studies based on alternative methods, such as experiments, to come to a more secure test of causal relations, and also more qualitative methods to get a deeper insight about the subjective and culturally bound interpretation of the intergroup encounter in consideration.

One journal issue cannot resolve the complexities of prejudice and discriminatory behavior. But the articles presented here do clarify which predictors and theories are important. They demonstrate the significance of the interaction between individual and contextual factors. And they supply valuable markers with which to compare European phenomena with the voluminous North American research literature on prejudice and discrimination.

Europe is currently undergoing a prolonged process of rapid intergroup changes. The responses to this sweeping transformation have included prejudice, discrimination, and violence as well as acceptance and cultural enrichment. Such a massive and important phenomenon deserves intensive social scientific study for what we can learn as well as for what we can contribute to the continent's future harmony and social justice.

References

Arcuri, L., & Boca, S. (1999). Posicionamentos politicos: Racismo subtil e racismo flagrante em Italia [Political positions: Subtle and blatant racism in Italy]. In J. Vala (Ed.), *Novos racismos: Perspectivas comparativas* [The new racisms: Comparative perspectives.]. Oeiras, Portugal: Celta Editora.
Allen, C., & Nielsen, J. S. (2001). *Summary report on Islamophobia in the EU after 11 September 2001*. Vienna: European Monitoring Centre on Racism and Xenophobia.
Allport, G. W. (1954). *The nature of prejudice*. Reading, MA: Addison-Wesley.
Atkinson, T., Cantillon, B., Marlier, E., & Nolan, B. (Eds.), (2002). *Social indicators: The EU and social inclusion*. Oxford: Oxford University Press.
Becker, J., Wagner, U., & Christ, O. (2007). Nationalismus und Patriotismus als Ursache von Fremdenfeindlichkeit [Nationalism and patriotism as cause of prejudice]. In W. Heitmeyer (Ed.), *Deutsche Zustände. Folge, 5* [The German issues, series 5 Part 1] (pp. 131–149). Frankfurt, Germany: Suhrkamp.
Bergmann, W. (2008). Anti-semitic attitudes in Europe: A comparative perspective. *Journal of Social Issues, 64*(2), 343–362.
Billet, J., & De Witte, H. (2008). "Everyday racism" as predictor of "political racism" in Flemish Belgium. *Journal of Social Issues, 64*(2), 253–267.
Billiet, J., Maddens, B., & Beerten, R. (2003). National identity and attitude toward foreigners in a multinational state: A replication. *Political Psychology, 24,* 241–257.
Breakwell, G., & Lyons, E. (Eds.), (1996). *Changing European identities*. London: Routledge.
Coenders, M., Lubbers, M., Scheepers, P., & Verkuyten, M. (2008). More than two decades of changing ethnic attitudes in the Netherlands. *Journal of Social Issues 64*(2), 269–285.
Coenders, M., & Scheepers, P. (1998). Support for ethnic discrimination in the Netherlands, 1979–1993: Effects of period, cohort, and individual characteristics. *European Sociological Review, 14,* 405–422.
Coenders, M., & Scheepers, P. (2003). The effect of education on nationalism and ethnic exclusionism: An international comparison. *Political Psychology, 24,* 313–343.
Dovidio, J. F., & Esses, V. M. (2001). Immigrants and immigration: Advancing the psychological perspective. *Journal of Social Issues, 57,* 375–387.
ERCOMER. (Ed.). (1997). *Interethnic relations and human rights in Europe: A survey of research*. Utrecht: ERCOMER.
European Foundation for the Improvement of Living and Working Conditions. (2004). *Perceptions of living conditions in an enlarged Europe*. Dublin: Author.
Hamberger, J., & Hewstone, M. (1997). Inter-ethnic contact as a predictor of blatant and subtle prejudice: Tests of a model in four West European nations. *British Journal of Social Psychology, 36,* 173–190.
Hello, E., Scheepers, P., & Mérove, G. (2002). Education and ethnic prejudice in Europe: Explanations for cross-national variances in the educational effect on ethnic prejudice. *Scandinavian Journal of Educational Research, 46,* 5–24.
Heyder, A., & Schmidt, P. (2002). Deutscher Stolz. Patriotismus waere besser (German pride. Patriotism is better.) In W. Heitmeyer (Ed.), *Deutsche Zustände. Folge 1* [The German issues, series 1] (pp. 71–82). Frankfurt/Main: Suhrkamp Verlag.
Hightower, E. (1997). Psychosocial characteristics of subtle and blatant racists as compared to tolerant individuals. *Journal of Clinical Psychology, 53,* 369–374.

Hjerm, M. (2001). Education, xenophobia and nationalism: A comparative analysis. *Journal of Ethnic and Migration Studies, 27*, 37–60.
Jackson, J. S., Brown, K. T., & Kirby, D. (1998). International perspectives on prejudice and racism. In Jennifer L. Eberhardt & Susan T. Fiske (Eds.), *Confronting racism: The problem and the response* (pp. 101–135). Thousand Oaks CA: Sage.
Kirch, A., Kirch, M., Pettai, V., & Tuisk, T. (1997). Changing ethnic and national identities in Estonia. In D. F. Halpern & A. E. Voiskounsky (Eds.), *States of mind: American and post-Soviet perspectives on contemporary issues in psychology* (pp. 306–314). London: Oxford University Press.
Kunovich, R. M. (2002). Social structural sources of anti-immigrant prejudice in Europe: The impact of social class and stratification position. *International Journal of Sociology, 32*, 39–57.
Kunovich, R. M. (2004). Social structural position and prejudice: An exploration of cross-national differences in regression slopes. *Social Science Research, 33*, 20–44.
Macmaster, N. (2001). *Racism in Europe 1870 – 2000*. Houndmills: Palgrave.
Maddens, B., Billiet, J., & Beerten, R. (2000). National identity and the attitude towards foreigners in multi-national states: The case of Belgium. *Journal of Ethnic and Migration Studies, 26*, 45–60.
Marsh, A., & Sahin-Dikmen, M. (2003). *Discrimination in the European Union*. Brussels: European Commission.
Martiniello, M. (Ed.). (1995). *Migration, citizenship and ethno-national identities in the European Union*. Avebury: Aldershot.
McLaren, L. M. (2003). Anti-immigrant prejudice in Europe: Contact, threat perception, and preferences for the exclusion of migrants. *Social Forces, 81*, 909–936.
Minescu, A., Hagendoorn, L., & Poppe, E. (2008). Types of identification and intergroup differentiation in the Russian Federation. *Journal of Social Issues, 64*(2), 321–342.
Noiriel, G. (1994). "Civil rights" policy in the United States and the policy of "integration" in Europe: Divergent approaches to a similar issue. *Journal of Policy History, 6*, 120–139.
Pedersen, A., & Walker, I. (1997). Prejudice against Aborigines: Old-fashioned and modern forms. *European Journal of Social Psychology, 25*, 561–587.
Pettigrew, T. F. (1997). Generalized intergroup contact effects on prejudice. *Personality and Social Psychology Bulletin, 23*, 173–185.
Pettigrew, T. F. (1998a). Intergroup contact theory. *Annual Review of Psychology, 49*, 65–85.
Pettigrew, T. F. (1998b). Reactions toward the new minorities of Western Europe. *Annual Review of Sociology, 24*, 77–103.
Pettigrew, T. F., Christ, O., Wagner, U., van Dick, R., & Zick, A. (2008). Relative deprivation and intergroup prejudice. *Journal of Social Issues, 64*(2), 385–401.
Pettigrew, T. F., Jackson, J. S., Ben Brika, J., Lemaine, G., Meertens, R. W., Wagner, U., & Zick, A. (1998). Outgroup prejudice in Western Europe. In W. Stroebe & M. Hewstone (Eds.), *European review of social psychology* (Vol. 8) (pp. 241–273). Chichester: Wiley & Sons.
Pettigrew, T. F., & Meertens, R. W. (1995). Subtle and blatant prejudice in Western Europe. *European Journal of Social Psychology, 25*, 57–75.
Pettigrew, T. F., Wagner, U., & Christ, O. (in press). Who opposes immigration? Comparing German with North American findings. *Du Bois Review: Social Science Research on Race*.
Rattazzi, A. M. M., & Volpato, C. (2001). Forme sottili e manifeste di pregiudizio verso gli immigrati. [Subtle and blatant forms of prejudice against immigrants.]. *Giornale italiano di psicologia, 2, giugno 2001*, 351–378.
Rise, J., Haugen, K., Klinger, E., & Bierbrauer, G. (2000). *Subtle and blatant prejudice in a Norwegian population*. Unpublished manuscript, University of Oslo, Oslo, Norway.
Rueda, J. F., & Navas, M. (1996). Hacia una evaluacion de las nuevas formas del prejuicio racial: Las actitudes sutiles del racismo. [Toward an evaluation of the new forms of racial prejudice: The subtle attitudes of racism.] *Revista de Psicologia Social, 11*, 131–149.
Semyonov, M., Raijman, R., Tov, A. Y., & Schmidt, P. (2004). Population size, perceived threat and exclusion: A multiple indicators analysis of attitudes toward foreigners in Germany. *Social Science Research, 44*, 681–701.
Six, B., & Wolfradt, U. (2000). *Authoritarianism and some more social psychological traits: Structures and contingencies*. Paper presented at the International Congress of Psychology Conference, Stockholm, Sweden, July 25, 2000.

Stephan, W. G. (2008). Viewing intergroup relations in Europe through Allport's lens model of prejudice. *Journal of Social Issues, 64*(2), 417–429.
Tajfel, H., & Turner, J. C. (1979). An integrative theory of intergroup conflict. In W. G. Austin & S. Worchel (Eds.), *The social psychology of intergroup relations* (pp. 33–47). Monterey, CA: Brooks/Cole.
Tam, T., Hewstone, M., Kenworthy, J. B., Cairns, E., Marinetti, C., Geddes, L., & Parkinson, B. (2008). Post-conflict reconciliation: Intergroup forgiveness and implicit biases in Northern Ireland. *Journal of Social Issues, 64*(2), 303–320.
Triandafyllidou, A. (2000). The political discourse on immigration in Southern Europe: A critical analysis. *Journal of Community and Applied Social Psychology, 10,* 373–389.
Trickett, E. J., Watts, R. J., & Birman, D. (Eds.). (1994). *Human diversity: Perspectives on people in context*. San Francisco, CA: Jossey-Bass.
United Nations. (2002). *International migration report 2002*. New York: United Nations.
Vala, J., Brito, R., & Lopes, D. (1999). O racismo flagrante e o racismo subtil em Portugal. [Blatant and subtle racism in Portugal.] In J. Vala (Ed.), *Novos racismos: Perspectivas comparativas*. Oeiras, Portugal: Celta Editora.
Vala, J., Lopes, D., & Lima, M. (2008). Black immigrants in Portugal: Luso-tropicalism and prejudice. *Journal of Social Issues, 64*(2), 287–320.
Verkuyten, M., & Hagendoorn, L. (1998). Prejudice and self-categorization: The variable role of authoritarianism and in-group stereotypes. *Personality and Social Psychology Bulletin, 24,* 99–110.
Villano, P. (1999). Anti-Semitic prejudice in adolescence: An Italian study on shared beliefs. *Psychological Reports, 84,* 1372–1378.
Volpato, C., & Rattazzi, A. M. M. (2000). Pregiudizio e immigrazione. Effecti del contatto sulle relazioni interetniche. [Prejudice and immigration: Effects of contact upon interethnic relations]. *Ricerche di Psicologia, 24,* 57–80.
Wagner, U., Christ, O., & Heitmeyer, W. (in press). Ethnocentrism and bias towards immigrants. In J. F. Dovidio, M. Hewstone, P. Glick, & V. M. Esses. (Eds.), *Handbook of prejudice, stereotyping, and discrimination*. Thousand Oaks CA: Sage.
Wagner, U., Christ, O., & Pettigrew, T. F. (2008). Prejudice and group related behaviour in Germany. *Journal of Social Issues, 64*(2), 303–320.
Wagner, U., Christ, O., Pettigrew, T. F., & Wolf, H. (2006). Prejudice and minority proportion: Threat vs. contact opportunity. *Social Psychological Quarterly, 69,* 380–390.
Wagner, U., Christ, O., Wolf, C., van Dick, R., Stellmacher, J., Schlüter, E., & Zick, A. (in press). Social and political context effects on intergroup contact and intergroup attitudes. In U. Wagner, L. R. Tropp, G. Finchilescu, & C. Tredoux. (Eds.), *Improving intergroup relations: Building on the legacy of Thomas F. Pettigrew*. New York: Wiley.
Wagner, U., & Zick, A. (1995). The relation of formal education to ethnic prejudice: Its reliability, validity, explanation. *European Journal of Social Psychology, 25,* 41–56.
Weiss, H. (2003). A cross-national comparison of nationalism in Austria, the Czech and Slovac Republics, Hungary, and Poland. *Political Psychology, 24,* 377–401.
Zick, A. (Ed.). (1999). Special issue: Authoritarianism, *politics, groups and the individual* Vol. 8, Nos. 1 and 2. Norderstedt, Germany: APP.
Zick, A., Wagner, U., van Dick, R., & Petzel, R. (2001). Acculturation and prejudice in Germany: Majority and minority perspectives. *Journal of Social Issues, 57,* 541–557.
Zick, A., Wolf, C., Küpper, B., Davidov, E., Schmidt, P., & Heitmeyer, W. (2008). The syndrome of group-focused enmity: The interrelation of prejudices tested with multiple cross-sectional and panel data. *Journal of Social Issues, 64*(2), 363–383.

ANDREAS ZICK received a call to become Professor of Socialization and Conflict Research at the University of Bielefeld in Germany. Additionally, he manages the "Group-Focused Enmity in Europe" project. He received his PhD at the University of Marburg in 1996, worked from 1998 to 2003 as Assistant Professor at the University of Wuppertal, from 2004 to 2006 at the University of Bielefeld, and headed the Chair of Social Psychology at the University of Dresden from 2006–2007 and Jena (2007–2008). His current research interests include migration as well as studies on prejudice, racism, and discrimination in Europe; right-wing extremism; social dominance and the self-concept in social identity. He has published numerous articles and a monograph on prejudice and racism in Western Europe. His recent research investigates the link between immigration ideologies, dominance orientations, and racism (see Zick, 1999).

THOMAS F. PETTIGREW is Research Professor of Social Psychology at the University of California, Santa Cruz. He received his PhD at Harvard University (1956) and taught there until 1980. From 1986 until 1991, he taught at the University of Amsterdam and conducted research on prejudice in the Netherlands. Pettigrew has published 10 books and more than 200 articles and reviews on prejudice and racism. His publications include *How to think like a social scientist* (1996) and chapters on intergroup relations in the *Annual Review of Psychology* (Pettigrew, 1998a) and the *Annual Review of Sociology* (Pettigrew, 1998b). He served as President of S.P.S.S.I. (1967–1968) and has twice been awarded the Society's Allport Prize for Intergroup Relations Research (with Joanne Martin in 1988 and Linda Tropp in 2003). He also received the Society for Experimental Social Psychology's Distinguished Scientist Award (2001), a Senior Fellowship at the Research Institute of Comparative Studies in Race and Ethnicity at Stanford University (2001), and a Fulbright New Century Scholar Fellowship for continued research on prejudice and discrimination against the immigrants of Western Europe (2003).

ULRICH WAGNER is Professor of Social Psychology and Director of the Center for Conflict Studies at Philipps-University Marburg in Germany. Dr. Wagner's research interests include intergroup relations, ethnic prejudice, and intergroup aggression. His publications include contributions to the analyses of survey data on ethnic prejudice and racism, as published in a special issue of the *Zeitschrift für Politische Psychologie [Journal of Political Psychology]* (eds. Wagner & van Dick, 2001), an overview paper in the *Zeitschrift für Sozialpsychologie [Journal of Social Psychology]* (Wagner, van Dick, & Zick, 2001) and original data analyses (e.g., Wagner, van Dick, Pettigrew, & Christ, 2003; Wagner, Christ, Pettigrew, Stellmacher, & Wolf, 2006). Wagner heads the special graduate school addressing Group Focused Enmity, sponsored by the Deutsche Forschungsgemeinschaft [German Science Foundation].]. For the academic year 2003–2004, Wagner was a Senior Fellow at the Research Institute of Comparative Studies in Race and Ethnicity at Stanford University.

Everyday Racism as Predictor of Political Racism in Flemish Belgium

Jaak Billiet[*] and Hans de Witte
Katholieke Universiteit Leuven

> Two aspects of research on racism in Flanders (Belgium) are discussed in this article based on results from large-scale surveys between 1991 and 2003. The first relates to the (negative) attitudes of the majority toward foreigners (everyday racism). The second relates to the vote for an extreme right-wing political party that emphasizes anti-immigrant viewpoints in its political program and propaganda (political racism). Our main research question is how both forms of racism are related. First, theories to explain political racism are reviewed. Some theories suggest an extreme right-wing vote to be motivated by a content-related agreement with (part of) the program of these parties (e.g., racism, nationalism, or authoritarianism). Other theories suggest that this vote represents an antipolitical protest vote. From these theories, hypotheses are derived regarding the background characteristics and attitudes that are associated with an extreme right-wing vote (e.g., the Vlaams Blok). These hypotheses are tested using data from election research in 1991, 1999, and 2003. The results suggest that the vote for the party Vlaams Blok is a rational vote. Of all theories, the theory suggesting that everyday racism plays a prominent role received most support. Everyday racism thus motivates political racism in the Flemish part of Belgium.

The topic of racism has been the focus of an extensive amount of research in the Flemish part of Belgium during the last few decades. Two aspects of this topic have been studied most intensively: the attitudes of the majority toward foreigners or immigrants and extreme right-wing voting behavior. In this article, both research lines will be combined.

---

[*]Correspondence concerning this article should be addressed to Jaak Billiet, Department of Sociology, Katholieke Universiteit Leuven, Parkstraat 45, Leuven 3000, Belgium [e-mail: Jaak.billliet@soc.kuleuven.be].

The data used in this article are compiled by the ISPO as part of the AGORA programme, supervised by the Belgian Science Policy.

In previous research in Belgium, a Likert-type scale was developed to measure negative attitudes toward migrants (Billiet & De Witte, 1995). Central to this negative attitude is the idea that foreigners' cultural habits are too deviant from those of the Belgians, for example, "Foreigners are a threat to our culture and habits," and that they represent economic competition, for example, "Migrant workers threaten the employment of Belgians." This attitude can be understood as a form of *everyday racism* (for an overview, see De Witte, 1999). In his extensive overview of Belgian opinion polls, De Baets concluded that the level of everyday racism has not been rising over the recent decades and has possibly even decreased since the decolonization of the Belgian Congo in 1960 (De Baets, 1994).

Political racism refers to the vote for a political party that strongly emphasizes anti-immigrant viewpoints in its political program and propaganda (see e.g., De Witte and Klandermans, 2000). In the Flemish context, the extreme right-wing party *Vlaams Blok* is commonly referred to as a political racist party by experts and the media. In the 1991 General Elections for the Federal Parliament, the Vlaams Blok obtained 9.3% of the Flemish vote. This number rose to 17.1% in the 2003 General Elections and 19% in the 2007 General Elections.[1] The party even obtained 22.8% of the Flemish vote in the 2004 elections for the Flemish Parliament and became the largest political party in Flanders (Fraeys, 2004). The Vlaams Blok did not emerge from a vacuum but was able to build on an existing network of individuals who were active on the radical fringe of the Flemish Movement. The militants needed to engage in party activities and were thus available, and they had already been active in the political struggle. This facilitated the development of a coherent party. The majority of Vlaams Blok representatives elected in 1991 had previously been active in organizations of ideologically trained activists who made it possible to extend the party structures further. Another factor facilitating this development was the highly organized and tightly centrally led character of the Vlaams Blok as a party (Spruyt, 1995).

A core issue in the ideology of the Vlaams Blok is the preference for a monocultural and monoracial national state, in which "nation" is conceived as a "biologically defined ethnic community" (De Witte & Klandermans, 2000). Partly as a consequence, the party was convicted of racism by a Belgian court in 2004. Over the past decades, and, in particular, since the parliamentary elections of November 24, 1991, the Vlaams Blok electorate has been the subject of thorough electoral research (e.g., Billiet and De Witte, 1995, 2001) and Swyngedouw and Billiet (2002). These studies were because of the large Flemish samples in the election

---

[1] The percentages are based on the number of voters that went to the polls (blank and invalid included). Suffrage in Belgium is based on the "one man, one vote" principle. Every Belgian national, male or female, who has reached the age of 18 has the duty to cast a vote. Belgium is characterized by a multiparty electoral system with proportional representation.

surveys of the Institute of Social and Political Opinion Research (ISPO) in 1991, 1995, 1999, and 2003.[2]

In this article, we will discuss the relationship between everyday and political racism by focusing on the attitudinal determinants of a vote for the extreme right-wing party Vlaams Blok. Our main research question is whether both forms of racism are related: does *everyday racism* constitute an important determinant for *political racism*? Stated otherwise, do people who hold racist attitudes vote for a party that advocates racism in its political platform and propaganda? The following overview of the literature on extreme right-wing voting behavior suggests that the answer to this question is less than obvious because racism appears to be just one of many possible motives discussed in these theories. Data of postelectoral voter surveys carried out by ISPO between 1991 and 2003 will be used to test hypotheses related to the background characteristics of the Vlaams Blok voters and to the typical social attitudes of this electorate. Because we analyze data for a period of over 10 years, we can also analyze whether the determinants of the Vlaams Blok vote changed over time.

Theoretical Explanations of Extreme Right-Wing Voting

Two broad and competing hypotheses are presented in the literature regarding the reasons for voting for an extreme right-wing party (e.g., Van der Brug, Fennema, & Tillie, 2000). These may be termed *the rational vote* versus *the protest vote*.

A Substantive, Rational Vote

In this view, the choice of an extreme right-wing party expresses a content-related agreement with (an aspect of) the program or political platform of this party. This view is in agreement with the rational choice model of voting behavior (Himmelweit, Humphreys, Jaeger, & Katz, 1981), in which issue voting and ideological reasons are emphasized as determinants of voting behavior. These content-related reasons can be derived from various theories. For a more detailed discussion, see Lubbers and Scheepers (2000) and Lubbers (2001).

Negative attitudes toward foreigners (everyday racism) play a crucial role in the theory of threatened economic interests (De Witte, 1999; Lubbers, 2001) because the economic threat attributed to foreigners is emphasized. The theory of threatened economic interests states that voters vote for the political party that claims to defend their economic interests. Voters who feel threatened in economic

---

[2] The election surveys of 1991, 1995, 1999, and 2003 were carried out by the Institute of Social and Political Opinion Research (ISPO). The research group consisted of J. Billiet, M. Swyngedouw, A. Carton, and R. Beerten. The election survey was financed by the former Federal Offices for Cultural and Technical Assistance (DWTC).

terms by immigrants develop, in this view, a preference for political parties that wish to reduce the presence of immigrants in society. Blue-collar workers and low-skilled individuals, in particular, hold positions in economically unstable sectors. This results in heightened feelings of job insecurity among these categories (Näswall & De Witte, 2003). As a consequence, they are more likely to vote for an extreme right-wing party.

The theory of symbolic interests (e.g., Lubbers & Scheepers, 2000) stresses the effects of disintegration caused by processes of modernization and social exclusion. This theory assumes that disintegrated individuals are more likely to be receptive to nationalism because nationalism constitutes a symbolic substitute for social integration by offering them new group bounds and an identity. According to this theory, alienated individuals vote for an extreme right-wing party because these parties proclaim nationalism. In this view, nonchurchgoers, young people, individuals not associated with the traditional "pillar" organizations, and voters who do not actively participate in organizational life will be more likely to vote for an extreme right-wing party because they are less socially integrated.

The theory of psychological compensation highlights the importance of authoritarianism (Adorno, Frenkel-Brunswik, Levinson, & Sanford, 1950). At present, authoritarianism is conceived as an attitude dimension with three basic components (Altemeyer, 1998): conventionalism (rigid conformism to conventional norms and strict moral codes), authoritarian submission (uncritical and full submission to ingroup authorities), and authoritarian aggression (fierce rejection and punishment of violators of conventional norms). According to this theory, voters feel attracted to extreme right-wing parties because of the authoritarian concepts embodied by these parties (Adorno et al., 1950). Blue-collar workers and low-skilled individuals score higher on authoritarianism (Meloen, 1994) and will thus be attracted by extreme right-wing parties.

An Antipolitical Protest Vote

The theory of protest voting opposes the rational vote view. In this theory, the vote for an extreme right-wing party is motivated by a rejection of the political system and of politicians (e.g., Van der Brug et al., 2000). The program of such a party thus becomes irrelevant because the choice of an extreme right-wing party is solely the expression of apolitical protest. The hypothesis of the antipolitical protest vote suggests that attitudes such as political dissatisfaction, powerlessness, and distrust are the most important determinants of an extreme right-wing vote. Social categories that are characterized by these attitudes are those with a higher probability of voting for such parties. Depending on the attitude selected, this relates to blue-collar workers, low-skilled individuals, young people, nonchurchgoers, individuals not associated with the traditional pillar organizations, and voters who do not actively participate in organizational life. Research shows that these social categories indeed score more highly in terms of political dissatisfaction, powerlessness, anomy, and mistrust (see e.g., Swyngedouw & Billiet, 2002).

Hypotheses

A first set of hypotheses relates to background characteristics that are supposed to be associated with the vote for an extreme right-wing party (the Vlaams Blok). A higher probability of a Vlaams Blok vote is expected among blue-collar workers, low-skilled individuals, nonchurchgoers, young people, respondents not associated with the traditional pillar organizations, and voters who do not actively participate in organizational life. Note, however, that the confirmation of these hypotheses often corroborates more than one theory at the same time because several theories lead to the prediction of the same association with background characteristics. The higher probability to vote Vlaams Blok among blue-collar workers and low-skilled individuals, for instance, will corroborate no less than three theories: the theory of threatened economic interests, the theory of psychological compensation, and the theory of protest voting.

Our second set of hypotheses relates to the social attitudes associated with a vote for the Vlaams Blok. This set enables us to discriminate between the four theories as each theory suggests specific attitudes to lead to the vote for an extreme right-wing party. This second set also enables us to answer our core research question: the relationship between everyday and political racism. A negative attitude toward ethnic minorities will be evidence in favor of the theory of threatened economic interests, Flemish nationalism for the theory of symbolic interests, authoritarian attitudes for the theory of psychological compensation, and political inefficacy and distrust for the theory of protest voting.

Method

Data

This study uses the general election surveys of ISPO of 1991, 1999, and 2003. The 1995 data are not presented because the 1995 sample of respondents is mostly identical to the sample of 1991 and because only minor differences were observed (see Billiet & De Witte, 2001). The face-to-face interviews of the 1991 and 1999 surveys were performed by trained interviewers of the ISPO interviewer network. The 1991 fieldwork started directly after the elections in December 1991 to March 1992 ($N = 2{,}691$; response rate of 66%). The 1999 survey was carried out by the ISPO interviewer network between September 1999 and March 2000 ($N = 2{,}178$; response rate also 66%). The fieldwork related to the 2003 elections took place in January 2004 to March 2004 and was carried out by interviewers of a commercial bureau (significant), but controlled by a researcher of ISPO ($N = 1{,}215$; response rate of 69%). As expected, the Vlaams Blok is somewhat underrepresented in the data file. This is partly related to the underrepresentation of low-skilled individuals in the surveys. In order to correct this underrepresentation, weighted data are analyzed.

Measurements

The ISPO election surveys gathered information about the level of education (four levels), age (five categories), professional category (seven categories), religious involvement (five categories), membership in a health insurance fund, membership in a trade union, and active membership in voluntary associations. These variables were measured in exactly the same way in all surveys. Apart from Catholics or those who describe themselves as Christian, few respondents of other religions were present in the sample. In consequence, categories are divided according to the extent of religious involvement. We distinguish between marginal Catholics (who attend church only on special family occasions), irregular churchgoers (who also attend church on religious holidays), and those who attend church services with great regularity (regular churchgoers). Among the nonbelievers, a distinction is made between explicit *free thinkers* (nonreligious humanists) and people who claim to have no religious beliefs. Membership in a trade union or professional association and affiliation with a health insurance fund are included in order to measure the association with the traditional pillar organizations. Gender was added to the analysis for exploratory reasons and as a control variable.

In order to explain voting behavior, a range of attitude scales or social attitudes was included in all electoral surveys. The exact phrasing of all items has been published elsewhere (Billiet, Swyngedouw, Depickere, & Meersseman, 2001). All scales were converted into 11-point scales, ranging from 0 (*minimum*) to 10 (*maximum*). The highest scores always indicate an agreement with the concept mentioned in the name of the scale. The sets of items were largely the same in the 1991 and 1999 surveys, but smaller sets with only the most relevant items were used in the survey of 2003. Relevant deviations in the scales are reported below.

To measure a negative attitude toward immigrants (or everyday racism) only four items that are identical across the three surveys are available. These items express feelings of being threatened by immigrants in the domains of culture, customs, and social security. A fourth item expresses distrust of immigrants. The internal consistency (Cronbach's α) of these scales varies between .76 (1991), .81 (1999), and .83 (2003). Multigroup structural equation modeling shows that the reduced 4-item scale is factorially invariant in the three samples, indicating that the measurements are equivalent over time (Billiet, Goffé, & Maddens, 2007).

In order to measure nationalism, five items were used that measure (sub)national identity and the support for Flemish autonomy. High scores indicate that the respondents are in favor of more autonomy for Flanders, support the division of social security, and regard themselves as more Flemish than Belgian. The scale thus refers to Flemish nationalism. The indicators are mixed because they measure aspects such as national identity, national awareness, and attitudes toward separatism. The reliability of this scale is fairly high ($\alpha = .80$). Multigroup structural equation modeling shows that the latent variable was factorially invariant in the 1991 and 1999 samples, indicating that the measurements are equivalent. However, the 2003 scale is no longer measurement equivalent because two items were changed. As a consequence, a strict comparison between the 2003 and the previous surveys is impossible.

The authoritarian attitudes measured refer to obedience and respect for authorities, strong leadership, and aggression toward those who do not conform to norms. The scale contained six items in 1991 and had moderate measurement quality ($\alpha_{1991} = .75$). In 1999, an attempt to construct a new scale with a balanced set of items failed. Only five items, worded in the direction of authoritarianism, measured the concept ($\alpha_{1999} = .69$). Due to changes in the item content, this scale is not completely comparable to the scale that was used in 1991. There is no comparable measurement of authoritarianism in the 2003 survey. However, one particular aspect of authoritarianism, severe repression against criminals, was included in both the 1999 and 2003 surveys. Four items, dealing with severe sanctioning of criminal behavior, measure the concept in a reliable way ($\alpha_{1999} = .81$; $\alpha_{2003} = .73$). From a theoretical point of view, one can argue that this attitude forms part of the authoritarian aggression dimension of authoritarianism (Adorno et al., 1950). This is also corroborated empirically as the correlation between the scales of authoritarianism and repression against criminals was .64 in the 1999 survey.

We combined distrust in politics and political inefficacy into one general concept, measured with five identical items in both the 1999 and 2003 surveys. The items express distrust in elections, in political parties, and in politicians. The latter are perceived as persons who do not listen to ordinary people, who are not interested in the opinions of the citizens, and who promise much, but do nothing. The scale is highly internally consistent ($\alpha_{1999} = .85$; $\alpha_{2003} = .81$). The scale that was used in 1991 had lower measurement quality ($\alpha_{1991} = .71$) and was smaller in scope. It contained three items measuring political inefficacy only. This scale is not equivalent with the scales that are used in 1999 and 2003.

In all surveys, a question was asked regarding the vote of the respondent during the elections that were held before the survey took place. This actual voting behavior will be the dependent variable in all analyses.

Analysis

In order to estimate the effect of background variables on the probability of a vote for the Vlaams Blok, a logistic regression via the CATMOD procedure of SAS is used. In this multinomial logit analysis, the dependent variable is not the probability of a Vlaams Blok vote, but the probability ratio, Vlaams Blok/other parties. The analysis is performed in a two-step procedure. The social background variables are included in the models in the first step. In doing so, we obtain information

Table 1. Net Effect of Background Characteristics on Voting for the Vlaams Blok in the Elections to the House of Representatives in Flanders in 1991, 1999, and 2003 Estimated Using a Logit Model[a]

Background Variable Grand Mean	Vlaams Blok'91 9.7 (Obs.%)	Vlaams Blok'99 14.7 (Obs.%)	Vlaams Blok'03 17.07 (Obs.%)
Professional category			
Professionals, managers	−1.5 (6.1)	−6.4* (6.3)	−4.5 (12.1)
White-collar workers	+.6 (9.5)	−.8 (12.9)	−5.6 (12.4)
Self-employed	−1.0 (8.3)	−5.0 (8.8)	−1.2 (17.2)
Skilled blue-collar workers	+3.7* (14.5)	+6.8* (19.8)	+6.7* (28.7)
Unskilled blue-collar workers	+3.7 (13.9)	+4.3* (20.6)	+3.9* (28.0)
Retired	−2.9 (7.8)	+2.6 (18.8)	−1.2 (17.1)
Nonactive	−.7 (9.3)	−1.8 (12.7)	−5.9* (13.2)
Education			
Primary	+2.8* (11.1)	+6.3*** (21.2)	+7.9** (23.8)
Lower secondary	−1.0 (9.2)	+.2 (15.9)	+3.4 (20.2)
Higher secondary	+1.5 (121)	−3.1* (12.0)	−1.1 (17.2)
Higher	3.9* (53)	−3.5**	9.3*** (7.4)
Religious involvement			
No religious beliefs	+7.9*** (18.3)	+9.3*** (22.7)	−2.2 (15.1)
Humanists (free thinkers)	+5.7* (14.7)	+.7 (12.8)	−2.0 (15.0)
Marginal Catholic	+.2 (10.0)	+2.8 (17.4)	+1.6 (19.5)
Irregular churchgoers	−2.4 (6.8)	−2.5 (12.9)	+3.6* (18.7)
Regular churchgoers	−5.1** (4.1)	−9.5*** (6.9)	−10.2** (6.4)
Age			
−24	+4.9* (16.9)	+2.1 (15.9)	+3.5 (17.0)
25–34	−.9 (10.9)	+2.0 (16.4)	+5.9* (16.8)
35–44	−.8 (9.1)	−3.3 (12.3)	−.2 (17.5)
45–54	−2.6 (7.6)	−5.0*** (10.2)	−2.7 (16.4)
55–64	−2.11 (6.0)	+1.6 (15.5)	−.7 (17.7)
+65	+4.1* (8.7)	+3.9* (18.6)	+4.0* (17.0)
Health insurance fund			
Christian	−.1 (8.5)	+1.2* (14.5)	−2.2 (15.1)
Socialist	+.2 (13.1)	−1.1 (17.6)	+2.9 (22.2)
Liberal	−3.5 (6.8)	−9.7*** (6.8)	+.4 (14.8)
Other	+2.5 (11.2)	+.1** (16.5)	+4.3 (17.8)
Trade Union membership			
Christian	−.7 (9.4)	+4.9* (19.7)	+4.5 (21.4)
Socialist	+2.1 (14.8)	+.2 (16.9)	+7.8* (24.7)
Other	−.0 (8.5)	−2.2 (12.4)	−7.9* (7.9)
None	−.2 (9.0)	−1.7. (12.9)	−2.0 (14.9)
Active membership			
Yes	+.6 (11.1)	−2.2* (11.6)	−.8 (13.8)
No	−.9 (7.5)	+1.5 (16.8)	+.5 (19.0)
N (sample sizes)	2,501	1,942	1,036

Note. [a]Blank and invalid votes included in calculations. Reference category in the model: all non-Vlaams Blok voters. The weighted observed percentages are given in brackets. These percentages are weighted in the sample for gender, education, level of education, and election result. All percentages are bivariate percentages.
* $p \leq .05$; ** $p \leq .01$; *** $p \leq .001$.

about the total effects of these background variables on the probability ratio. In Table 1, the effect parameters are expressed as deviations from the average percentage obtained by the Vlaams Blok in 1991, 1999, and 2003. The figures in Table 1 are the net effects of each predictor on the probability of a vote for the Vlaams Blok, after elimination of the effect of all other predictors in the statistical model.

Table 2. Direct Significant ($p < .05$) Net Effects of Attitudes on a Vote for the Vlaams Blok in the Elections to the House of Representatives in Flanders in 1991, 1999, and 2003[a]

Attitudes	β (1991)	β (1999)	β (2003)
Negative attitudes toward immigrants	1.520*** (89.61)	1600*** (82.41)	1461***(39.60)
Flemish nationalism	1.115*** (12.96)	1.236*** (33.52)	1.328***(28.82)
Authoritarian attitudes	1.005 (.01)	1.124* (3.82)	–
Severe repression of criminals	–	1.274*** (13.60)	1.043 (.34)
Political inefficacy and distrust	1.005 (.01)	1.154*** (9.01)	1.152* (4.34)
N	2,232	1,862	1,022

Note. [a]Multiplicative logistic regression parameters (β) controlled for social background variables (see Table 1). Chi-square (1 df) of maximum likelihood analysis of variance in the complete model between brackets.
* $p \leq .05$; ** $p \leq .01$; *** $p \leq .001$.

For example, an effect parameter of –3.9 in the category of the higher educated means that the mean likelihood of voting for Vlaams Blok (9.7%) is 3.9 percentage points lower as a consequence of belonging to the category of the higher educated. Controlled for the other variables in the model, the likelihood of voting for Vlaams Blok is 5.8% in this category.

In the second step of the analysis, the attitudinal variables are included in the models. Because these are metric variables, we do not express their effects as deviations in average percentages, but as multiplicative logistic regression parameters affecting the ratio proportion, Vlaams Blok/other party. This ratio is called *probability ratio* or, more simply, *odds*. The parameters express the amount of change in the odds Vlaams Blok/other party when the value of the attitudinal variable increases with one unit standard deviation (*SD*). Parameters with a value close to 1.0 do not have any effect on the odds; parameters significantly lower than 1.0 express a decrease in odds; and parameters significantly higher than 1.0 express an increase. The parameters of the attitudinal variables are shown in Table 2. A parameter of 1.52 for the attitudinal variable negative attitude toward immigrants means that in 1991, the odds Vlaams Blok/all other voters increases with a factor of 1.52 when the score on the attitudinal variable increases with one unit *SD*. Table 2 is the main table of this article because it is directly related to our hypotheses. The effects of the social background variables change after including the attitudes. We do not report this, however, because we are not interested in a decomposition of the direct and indirect effects of the social background variables.

Results

Background Variables and the Vote for the Vlaams Blok

Table 1 contains the results relevant for the test of the hypotheses on background variables in 1991, 1999, and 2003. Gender did not make an independent contribution and was not included in Table 1. The results in Table 1 corroborate the hypothesis that blue-collar workers more strongly vote for the Vlaams Blok. This is especially true for the skilled blue-collar workers. This is in line with our expectations and with the findings in, for example, France and Austria (see Pettigrew, 1998). Voting for that party is less likely among the professionals since the 1999 elections and among white-collar workers in 2003. These findings complement the findings regarding the blue-collar workers. The results are also supportive of the hypothesis on the level of education. In all three election years, a vote for Vlaams Blok is more likely among voters who received less formal training (primary education), whereas the high-skilled voters (higher education) are clearly less likely to support this party.

The results concerning religious involvement are mostly in line with our expectations too. Respondents without any religious affiliation were more likely to vote for the Vlaams Blok in 1991 and 1999. Regular churchgoers were less likely to join the electorate of the extreme right-wing party in the three election years. In past research, we explained this effect of regular churchgoing by typical characteristics of Flemish Catholicism. This Catholicism is strongly organized around such values as justice, care, and solidarity, and the Christian Democratic Party was in the core of the organization network (Billiet, 1995). The estimated positive net effect of irregular churchgoers on a vote for the Vlaams Blok in 2003 (estimated 20.67%) seems to reject our hypothesis in 2003. This could indicate that more recently, new social categories of voters are joining the electorate of that party. It is possible that the steady growth of the electorate of the right-wing party realizes a shift in the social composition of its electorate.

The results regarding the age categories of the voters partly corroborate and partly refute our hypotheses. We note higher probabilities of voting for the Vlaams Blok among voters between 18 and 34 years of age in 1991 and 2003. The shift from the youngest age category in 1991 (mostly new voters) to the category of 25–34 years of age 10 years later in 2003 could indicate that the generation born in the 1970s remains more likely to vote for the extreme right. This is in harmony with the finding that voters for the Vlaams Blok are likely to stick to their previous choice in the future (see e.g., Swyngedouw & Billiet, 2002). Opposing our hypothesis, however, is the finding that the oldest category of voters is more likely to support the Vlaams Blok. This curvilinear relation with age seems present in all three elections. Voters in the age category of 45–54 years were least likely to vote for the extreme right in 1999. This was not predicted by our theories either.

We hypothesized that respondents not associated with the traditional pillar organizations and voters who do not actively participate in organizational life are more likely to vote for the Vlaams Blok. Our results mostly refute these hypotheses. Members of a nontraditional health insurance fund are only slightly more supportive for the Vlaams Blok in 1999, and the effect is rather modest. Trade union membership does not show the expected associations with a Vlaams Blok vote. Active membership in voluntary associations was only associated with a lower probability to vote Vlaams Blok in 1999.

Has the impact of the background variables changed compared to the beginning of the 1990s? The most striking finding relates to education. The effect of primary education only in 2003 has grown compared to 1991 (from +2.8 to +7.9). Note that also the effect of higher education grew during that period (from –3.9 to –9.3). This suggests that education became more important as a predictor of extreme right-wing voting behavior between 1991 and 2003. The proportions of both lower and higher educated in the electorate remained nearly the same during this period. The effect of professional category, and especially the category of the skilled blue-collar worker, also became more important during the same period (an increase from +3.7 in 1991 to +6.7 in 2003). Finally, the increase in effect of the regular churchgoers is also noticeable (from –5.1 in 1991 to –10.2 in 2003). This, however, does not affect substantially the grand mean of the Vlaams Blok since the marginal number of regular churchgoers in the electorate has been halved during the same period.

Attitudinal Determinants of a Vlaams Blok Vote

In a second step, attitudes are added to the background variables in the model. This allows us to examine the net effects of the attitudes on a vote for the Vlaams Blok, after controlling them for each other and for the background characteristics. The parameters of the significant attitude variables are given in Table 2. Two attitudes affect a vote for the Vlaams Blok in the three elections presented in Table 2. The most important attitude is undoubtedly a negative attitude toward immigrants. The odds Vlaams Blok/other party increases by 52% in 1991, by 60% in 1999, and by 46% in 2003 for an increase of one standard unit on the scale. These findings are in line with the theory of threatened economic interests. In addition, Flemish nationalism plays a role, thus corroborating the theory of symbolic interests. The odds Vlaams Blok/other party expanded by 11% in 1991 and by 33% in 2003, with an increase of one standard unit on the scale. The two remaining theories receive far less support. Authoritarian attitudes (and a severe approach to the issue of criminality) only play a role during the election of 1999, but seem irrelevant in 1991 and 2003. Political inefficacy and distrust have a modest effect on the Vlaams Blok vote in 1999 and 2003 only.

It is rather difficult to assess the evolution of the importance of the four attitudes because of different operationalizations across the three election studies. The scale measuring negative attitudes toward immigrants is factorially invariant over time. As a consequence, the parameters of this scale are comparable, even though changes in the strength and composition of the other scales affect these parameters too. Everyday racism seems to be roughly as important in 2003 as it was in 1991. This suggests that the importance of the theory of threatened economic interests in explaining the Vlaams Blok vote is stable over time. The results in Table 2 also seem to suggest that the importance of Flemish nationalism (and thus of the theory of symbolic interests) and of the protest motive increased slightly over time. This conclusion is not really justified, however, because the measurements of both attitudes are not completely comparable over time. The conclusion regarding the stability of the effect of everyday racism on the Vlaams Blok vote is more valid.

Conclusion and Discussion

Combining the results of both the background characteristics and the attitudinal determinants of voting behavior allows us to address our hypotheses in a more comprehensive way. In overall terms, our analyses confirm that the choice for the Vlaams Blok expresses a content-related preference for the political program of this extreme right-wing party. This is in line with the rational choice model of voting behavior (e.g., Himmelweit et al., 1981). Our results also suggest that the issue of everyday racism plays a prominent role in explaining this voting behavior because most evidence supports the theory of threatened economic interests. All the hypotheses derived from this theory are confirmed by our analyses. The preference for the Vlaams Blok is higher among blue-collar workers and low-skilled respondents, whereas a negative attitude toward immigrants strongly determines the vote for this party, as assumed in this theory. It should be noted, however, that categories that feel economically threatened by immigrants (blue-collar workers and low-skilled individuals) also adopt a more conservative sociocultural attitude (e.g., De Witte & Billiet, 1999). This also leads them to reject immigrants because immigrants differ in terms of customs and culture from the majority culture. As a consequence, the theory of threatened economic interests should be extended to threats related to economic and cultural issues and perhaps even to other topics such as criminality. This broadening aligns well with the notion of everyday racism, as developed elsewhere (De Witte, 1999). These results answer our core research question: everyday racism constitutes the most important attitudinal determinant of political racism in Flanders in the period between 1991 and 2003.

In addition to everyday racism, the analyses also suggest that the other three theories play a subordinate, additional role in explaining the preference for an extreme right-wing party. The theory of symbolic interests, which emphasizes nationalism as a determinant, is partly confirmed and partly refuted. In line with this theory are the results suggesting that nonchurchgoers (and especially those without religious beliefs) vote to a greater extent for the Vlaams Blok. The hypothesis that active members of a voluntary association are less likely to vote for the Vlaams Blok voters received only limited support. The prediction about the negative relationship between membership in traditional social organizations and the Vlaams Blok vote was not confirmed. Members of the socialist and Christian trade unions were even more likely to vote for this party during specific elections. The Flemish nationalist attitude of the respondents does play a role in predicting an extreme right-wing vote in Flanders. This finding corroborates the theory of symbolic interests.

The theory of psychological compensation is only partially corroborated by our results. Authoritarian attitudes were only relevant as voting determinants during the elections of 1999, but not in 1991 or 2003. The impact of this theory thus seems limited. The higher probability to vote Vlaams Blok among the blue-collar workers and lower educated is in line with this view. The findings concerning background characteristics can be interpreted in various ways, however, because they are also in line with the theory of threatened economic interests.

Finally, the Vlaams Blok vote also seems to reveal an undertone of apolitical protest, even though the results regarding the background characteristics are fairly ambivalent. In line with the protest hypothesis, we find a higher probability to vote the Vlaams Blok among blue-collar workers, low-skilled individuals, and nonchurchgoers. The results concerning active membership in organizational life are less convincing. The finding that the elderly are more likely to vote for the Vlaams Blok in 1991 and 1999 contradicts this hypothesis. The analysis of the attitudinal variables shows that political inefficacy and distrust play only a secondary role in determining the vote for this party in two of the three elections. This suggests that the preference for this extreme-right wing party reveals an undertone of political protest.

The conclusions discussed above all relate to the direct effects of the various attitudes on the vote for the Vlaams Blok. The multivariate analyses show that everyday racism is the main determinant of political racism. Nationalism, authoritarian, and apolitical protest all play an additional role. These three attitudes, however, also affect the Vlaams Blok voting in an indirect way because these three attitudes are also related to everyday racism. This has been shown regarding nationalism (Meloen, De Witte, & van der Linden, 1999), authoritarianism (Meloen, 1994), and expressions of apolitical protest (Billiet & De Witte, 1995). These three attitudes can, therefore, also be regarded as "underlying" determinants influencing the vote for an extreme right-wing party in an indirect way.

References

Adorno, T., Frenkel-Brunswik, E., Levinson, D., & Sanford, R. (1950). *The authoritarian personality.* New York: Harper & Row.

Altemeyer, B. (1998). The other "authoritarian personality." In L. Berkowitz (Ed.), *Advances in experimental social psychology* (Vol. 30, pp. 47–92). Orlando, FL: Academic Press.

Billiet, J. (1995). Church involvement, ethnocentrism and voting for a radical right wing party: Diverging behavioral outcomes of equal attitudinal dispositions. *Sociology of Religion, 56*, 303–326.

Billiet, J., & De Witte, H. (1995). Attitudinal disposition to vote for an extreme right-wing party—the case of "Vlaams Blok." *European Journal of Political Research, 27*, 181–202.

Billiet, J., & De Witte, H. (2001). Wie stemde in 1999 voor het Vlaams Blok en waarom? [Who voted Flemisch Blok and why?]. *Tijdschrift voor Sociologie, 21*, 5–36.

Billiet, J., Goffé, H., & Maddens, B. (2007). Een Vlaams-nationale identiteit en de houding tegenover allochtonen in een longitudinaal perspectief [translation]. In M. Swyngedouw, J. Billiet, & B. Goeminne (Eds.), *De kiezer onderzocht. De verkiezingen van 2003 en 2004 in Vlaanderen* (pp. 95–120). Louvain: Universitaire Pers Leuven.

Billiet, J., Swyngedouw, M., Depickere, A., & Meersseman, E. (2001). *Structurele determinanten van het stemgedrag en culturele kenmerken van de kiezerskorpsen in Vlaanderen. De verkiezingen van 1999* [Structural determinants of voting behaviour and cultural characteristics of the voters in Flanders: The elections of 1999]. Louvain: K.U. Leuven, ISPO.

De Baets, A. (1994). *De figuranten van de geschiedenis. Hoe het verleden van andere culturen wordt verbeeld en in herinnering gebracht* [The figurants of history. How the past of other cultures is divided and remembered]. Berchem: EPO.

De Witte, H. (1999). Everyday racism in Belgium: An overview of the research and an interpretation of its link with education. In L. Hagendoorn & S. Nekuee (Eds.), *Education and racism. A cross-national inventory of positive effects of education on ethnic tolerance* (pp. 47–74). Aldershot: Ashgate.

De Witte, H., & Billiet, J. (1999). Economic and cultural conservatism in Flanders: In search of concepts, determinants and impact on voting behavior. In H. De Witte & P. Scheepers (Eds.), *Ideology in the low countries. Trends, models and lacunae* (pp. 91–120). Assen: van Gorcum.

De Witte, H., & Klandermans, B. (2000). Political racism in Flanders and the Netherlands: Explaining differences in the electoral success of extreme-right wing parties. *Journal of Ethnic and Migration Studies, 26*, 699–717.

Fraeys, W. (2004). Les élections régionales et européennes du 13 juin 2004: Analyse des résultats [The regional and European elections of June 13 2004: Analysis of results]. *Res Publica, 46*, 357–376.

Himmelweit, H., Humphreys, P., Jaeger, M., & Katz, M. (1981). *How voters decide. A longitudinal study of political attitudes and voting extending over fifteen years*. London: Academic Press.

Lubbers, M. (2001). *Exclusionist electorates. Extreme right-wing voting in Western Europe*. Doctoral thesis, UNIVERSITY NAME, Nijmegen.

Lubbers, M., & Scheepers, P. (2000). Individual and contextual characteristics of the German extreme right-wing vote in the 1990s. A test of complementary theories. *European Journal of Political Research, 38*, 63–94.

Meloen, J. (1994). A critical analysis of forty years of authoritarianism research. In R. Farnen (Ed.), *Nationalism, ethnicity and identity: Cross-national and comparative perspectives* (pp. 127–165). New York: Transaction Books.

Meloen, J., De Witte, H., & Van Der Linden, G. (1999). Authoritarianism and voting for a racist party in Belgian Flanders. Politics, groups and the individual. *International Journal of Political Psychology and Political Socialization, 8*, 21–40.

Näswall, K., & De Witte, H. (2003). Who feels insecure in Europe? Predicting job insecurity from background variables. *Economic and Industrial Democracy, 24*, 189–215.

Pettigrew, T. F. (1998). Reactions towards the new minorities of Western Europe. *Annual Review of Sociology, 24*, 77–103.

Swyngedouw, M., & Billiet, J., Eds. (2002). *De kiezer heeft zijn redenen. 13 juni 1999 en de politieke opvattingen van Vlamingen* [The voter has his reasons. June 13 1999 and the political opinions of the Flamish]. Louvain: Acco.

Van Der Brug, W., Fennema, M., & Tillie, J. (2000). Anti-immigrant parties in Europe: Ideological or protest vote? *European Journal of Political Research, 37*, 77–102.

JAAK BILLIET, PhD in the Social Sciences, is Professor in Social Methodology at the Katholieke Universiteit Leuven, Belgium. He is head of the Centre for Sociological Research (CESO) and a member of the central coordination team of the European Social Survey (EC FP6). His main research interest in methodology deals with validity assessment, interviewer and response effects, and the modeling of measurement error in social surveys. His substantial research covers longitudinal and comparative research in the domains of ethnocentrism, political attitudes, and religious orientations. He also plays a central role in the implementation of the fourth wave of the European Value Study in 2008.

HANS DE WITTE, PhD in Psychology, is Professor in Work Psychology at the Department of Psychology of the Katholieke Universiteit Leuven, Belgium. His research interests include psychological consequences of work and unemployment (including job insecurity, temporary employment, and downsizing), attitudes toward work, the impact of job characteristics on social and political attitudes, racism, and right-wing extremism.

More than Two Decades of Changing Ethnic Attitudes in the Netherlands

Marcel Coenders and Marcel Lubbers
Utrecht University

Peer Scheepers
Radboud University Nijmegen

Maykel Verkuyten[*]
Utrecht University

This article uses data from three studies to examine changing reactions toward ethnic minority groups in the Netherlands (1979–2002). Using realistic conflict theory, Study 1 focuses on support for discrimination of immigrant groups in general. The findings indicate that this support is more widespread in times of high levels of immigration, when the unemployment level has recently risen strongly, and among cohorts that grew to maturity in times of large immigration waves or high unemployment rates. Studies 2 and 3 focus on changing feelings toward different ethnic out-groups in an ideological context (2001–2004) marked by a shift from multiculturalism toward assimilation. Study 2 showed that the shift toward assimilation negatively affected Dutch participants' feelings toward Islamic outgroups, but not to other minority groups. Study 3 used an experimental design, and the results showed that ethnic attitudes are more negative in an assimilation compared to a multicultural context. It is concluded that the structural and ideological social context is important for understanding people's changing reactions.

In the early 1960s, Dutch industry started recruiting migrant labor on a large scale. Most of these migrant workers were Turkish and Moroccan men who were either single or had left their families behind in their home country. At first, all parties concerned imagined that these migrants would remain in the Netherlands

---

[*]Correspondence concerning this article should be addressed to Maykel Verkuyten, Faculty of Social Sciences, Utrecht University, Heidelberglaan 2, 3584 CS Utrecht, The Netherlands [e-mail: M.Verkuyten@fss.uu.nl].

for only a limited period of time. Events proved otherwise, however, and in the mid-1970s, a process of family reunification began, as first the Turks and later the Moroccans were joined by their wives and children. At the same time, large numbers of Dutch nationals from the former colony of Suriname settled in the Netherlands.

In the 1990s many refugees and asylum seekers who had fled former East European countries but also countries such as Iraq, Iran, Sudan, Ghana, Somalia, and Ethiopia sought refuge in the Netherlands. In 2000, around 130,000 people came with the intention of settling in the Netherlands. In 2004, there were approximately 1.7 million non-Western immigrants resident in the Netherlands: 10% of total population, of which the Turks formed the largest single group (358,000), followed by the Surinamese (328,000), the Moroccans (315,000), and the Antilleans (135,000). More than half of these ethnic minorities live in the four largest cities, and in many neighborhoods in these cities the majority of the population are members of ethnic minorities (Wittebrood, Latten, & Nicolaas, 2005).

In terms of housing, schooling, and the labor market, the position of most ethnic minority groups is worse than that of the ethnic Dutch. Studies indicate that ethnic minority group students consistently perform less well in school and have the poorest academic results, irrespective of how academic performance is defined (Zorlu & Traag, 2005). Ethnic minorities also have higher unemployment rates (Dagevos & Bierings, 2005). The Turks and Moroccans, for example, have the highest unemployment rates and are around 3 to 4 times as likely to be unemployed as the Dutch. They perform more often (un-) skilled manual work, whereas there has been a strong increase in the number of immigrants starting up small enterprises as self-employed people (Dagevos & Bierings, 2005).

The ethnic minorities policy adopted in the early 1980s in response to the increased influx of foreigners has gradually been replaced by a policy of civic integration (Entzinger, 2003). In public debates in recent years, multiculturalism has been described as a "drama" and a "failure," and assimilation has been proposed as the only viable option (e.g., Schnabel, 2000). Although the retreat of multiculturalism is going on for quite some years (Joppke, 2004), it became more prominent and accepted with the rise of right-wing parties and politicians, in particular the populist Pim Fortuyn who was murdered a few days before the general elections of May 2002. In only a few years' time, the political and social climate changed considerably from a more multicultural perspective to one that emphasizes Dutch national identity and the need for assimilation of minority groups. This change is most evident among political parties on the right of the political spectrum but also involves left-wing parties such as the social democrats. As a result, in the so-called tolerant Dutch society, ethnic relations seem to have developed in a more negative direction.

In debates, two main explanations are being put forward for increasing antagonism toward immigrant groups: concerns over material and economic interests, and conflicting identities and values. These explanations correspond with realistic group conflict theories (e.g., Blalock, 1967; Sherif & Sherif, 1969) and social identity theory (Tajfel & Turner, 1979), respectively. In this article we will use the former theory for examining longitudinal changes in support for discrimination regarding ethnic outgroups in general (period 1979–2002; Study 1). The latter theory will be used for investigating changes in specific ethnic out-group feelings across time (period 2001–2004; Study 2) as well as experimentally (Study 3). Both theories emphasize the impact of social context characteristics on changing reactions toward ethnic minorities. In agreement with these theories, our findings suggest that the structural and ideological context is crucial for understanding people's changing reactions toward ethnic minorities.

Concerns over Realistic Conflicts

Realistic conflict theories argue that conflicts over material and economic group interests can result in negative out-group reactions. The core proposition is that (perceived) competition over scarce resources, such as houses and jobs, induces the desire to protect in-group interests, which is considered an underlying motivation for (the endorsement of) discriminatory behavior (cf. Coenders & Scheepers, 1998). In a situation where group interests are seen as incompatible, support for ethnic discrimination is more likely. However, material and economic concerns differ in salience depending on the social conditions people find themselves in. Realistic conflict theories lead to specific hypotheses on societal circumstances, which induce changes in the support for ethnic discrimination (i.e., historical societal conditions), as well as to hypotheses on cohort effects (i.e., societal conditions during individual's formative years).

First, the level of support for ethnic discrimination depends on contemporary competitive circumstances. There are at least two factors that may increase ethnic competition. One is immigration, which creates a situation in which there are more people who have to share a limited amount of resources (houses and jobs). The second factor is the level of unemployment, which creates a situation in which an equal number of people have to share diminished resources. Hence, these period factors may contribute to the explanation of the longitudinal changes in support for ethnic discrimination. We hypothesize therefore that the higher the level of ethnic immigration, and the higher the level of unemployment, the more widespread the support for ethnic discrimination is. Furthermore, the actual presence of non-Western minorities in the country might be a source contributing to the actual competition. Hence, we hypothesize that the larger the proportion of non-Western minorities in the country, the more widespread the support for ethnic discrimination is.

Apart from the effects of contemporary societal circumstances, we also anticipate that recent changes in these circumstances may have an additional influence on the perceptions of ethnic competition. A rapid rise of ethnic immigration will increase the perceived ethnic competition more strongly than a steady inflow of ethnic immigrants as shown, for example, by Olzak (1989) in the United States. Hence, we hypothesize that the larger the recent increase of ethnic immigration and the larger the recent increase of unemployment, the more widespread the support for ethnic discrimination will be.

Second, we propose that, similar to the proposition of period effects, cohort effects may also be operative. Karl Mannheim (1928/1964) argued that individuals within a birth cohort experience similar societal circumstances during their formative years. They may be marked by these circumstances in such a way that the attitudes acquired in these years remain relatively stable throughout the rest of their lives. This notion has been adopted, among others, by Inglehart (1990) in his work on the diffusion of postmaterialism. In his socialization hypothesis, Inglehart (1990, p. 68) stated that "to a large extent, one's basic values reflect the conditions that prevailed during one's preadult years." A similar argument has been put forward by Sears (1993) in his symbolic politics theory.

Combining the notion of formative years with realistic conflict theory leads to the hypothesis that the more ethnic competition a cohort has experienced during the formative years, the more widespread they will support ethnic discrimination. Using the aforementioned indicators of ethnic competition it can be predicted that the higher the level of ethnic immigration and the higher the level of unemployment during a cohort's formative years, the more widespread the support for ethnic discrimination is among these cohort members. This list of hypotheses will be tested in Study 1.

Group Identity Concerns

Ethnic relations involve competition not only over scarce resources but also concerns about group identities. These concerns depend on the perceived differences between ethnic groups and the threats that these groups pose to a positive and distinctive in-group identity. Identity issues have been found to underlie many ethnic conflicts around the world (Horowitz, 2000). Studying 17 European countries, McLaren (2003), for example, found that perceived threat to the national and cultural identity was related to anti-immigrant attitudes among majority groups.

In a recent study on exclusionary reactions to ethnic minorities in a representative sample of ethnically Dutch people, Sniderman, Hagendoorn, and Prior (2004) found that considerations of national identity overshadowed those of economic concerns. In the Netherlands, economic conditions are relatively good, whereas in the last 5 to 6 years cultural and religious differences and conflicts have become core issues in public and political debates. One aspect of this debate is the increased focus on Islamic groups, particularly Turks and Moroccans. Other minority groups are considered less problematic and a lesser threat to Dutch identity.

Hence, it seems important to examine evaluative reactions toward different ethnic outgroups.

Social identity accounts (Tajfel & Turner, 1979) argue that people are motivated to develop and maintain a positive and distinctive sense of their social self. Establishing favorable evaluative distinctiveness of one's group vis-à-vis other groups helps to achieve a positive and clear group identity. This can be done by evaluating the in-group positively, out-groups negatively or a combination of the two. In-group favoritism, however, is by no means an automatic product of group distinctions. The theory posits that the operation of cognitive and motivational processes depends on cultural and structural features of the social world: As Reicher (2004) stated "the social identity tradition forces us to turn toward the social world. It forces us to address the ideological and structural features of the world" (p. 921). The cognitive process of social categorization and the need for positive group identity that motivate intergroup strategies can explain why people show, for example, out-group negativity but do not explain when people show such negativity or rather adopt strategies of increased in-group orientation (Rubin & Hewstone, 2004). The implication is that the social identity processes should be examined in their political and ideological context.

In Study 2 and Study 3, we focused on the Dutch retreat of multiculturalism in favor of an increased emphasis on assimilation. Study 2 is concerned with 4-year changes (2001–2004) in ethnic out-group feelings, and Study 3 examines the experimental effects of multiculturalism and assimilation ideologies on these feelings.

In Study 2, we focused on the period 2001–2004 that was marked by dramatic political changes involving the political arrival of the charismatic Pim Fortuyn and his murder just 9 days before the general elections of 15 May 2002 (Van Praag, 2003). Despite his murder, the LPF (List Pim Fortuyn) gained 26 of the 150 seats in the May 2002 general election making it the second largest party of the 10 different parties in the newly elected Parliament. In the general elections of January 2003, the LPF lost heavily, retaining only eight seats. The party did not become part of the new coalition government and lost much of its attraction and popularity. However, the new right-wing government has adopted many of the anti-immigrant and anti-Muslim messages and policies of the LPF. Anti-Muslim sentiments have continued and have been fuelled further by the murder of the Dutch filmmaker, Theo van Gogh, in 2004, and by global tensions and divergences between the Islamic and the Western world.

Fortuyn's ideology combined various things, but above all he spoke against multiculturalism and attacked, what he called, the yoke of political correctness and the problems this had caused with ethnic minority groups. He explicitly rejected the idea of multiculturalism, pleading instead for assimilation and emphasizing national identity and pride. He argued that immigration and multiculturalism would eventually imply the abolishment of Dutch identity. This stance became very popular and attracted many votes (Van der Brug, 2003). Although not all political parties agreed with this, almost all started to accept and moreover incorporate the idea that multiculturalism had failed and that it had actually caused interethnic tensions and problems of social cohesion.

For Fortuyn, the problems of a multicultural society had mainly to do with Islam. He had a fiercely negative position on Islam, which, he argued, was a backward religion that seriously threatened Dutch society and culture. He argued that "a cold war against Islam is unavoidable" and labeled Muslims as a "fifth column." In the media, Islam became symbolic for problems related to ethnic minorities and immigration (Ter Wal, 2004). As a result, the public discussion almost completely focused on the Turks and Moroccans and the need to compel these two Islamic groups to assimilate. Other minority groups, such as ex-colonial ones, were hardly discussed and were not presented as a threat to Dutch values and identity. The political changes described led us to the prediction, tested in Study 2, which compared to 2001 in 2002–2004, the Dutch participants would be more negative about the Turks and Moroccans. In contrast, the evaluation of minority groups such as Surinamese and Antilleans was expected not to change much in this period. In Study 3, we expected that, compared to multiculturalism, an assimilation ideology is related to more negative ethnic out-group feelings, particularly toward Islamic outgroups (Turks and Moroccans).

Study 1

Sample and Measures

We used individual survey data on the support for ethnic discrimination and contextual data. The survey data were taken from 19 national samples collected by the Dutch Social and Cultural Planning Office (SCP) in the period 1979–2002. The data were collected as part of the Cultural Changes project. We combined the cross-sectional samples into one pooled data set containing 34,532 respondents, aged 16 to 74 years at the time of the interview.

Support for discrimination was measured by items that were explicitly about group competition for scare resources. The participants were presented with three fictional situations in which two persons or families, an ethnically Dutch and a non-Dutch, compete for a job, a job promotion, or a house. Participants were asked which of the two should get the scarce resource. In our analyses we combined these questions into an index of support for ethnic discrimination ($\alpha = .72$). We distinguished respondents who never supported ethnic discrimination from respondents who, in one or several cases, supported ethnic discrimination (for further details, see Coenders & Scheepers, 1998).

For the context indicators, we used national-level time-series data. The contemporary societal circumstances were operationalized by three indicators. First, we took the level of ethnic immigration. The country of origin was used as a criterion to specify ethnic immigration, as the longest available time series in the Netherlands are based on this criterion (CBS, 2005). Traditionally, large numbers of immigrants came from Surinam, the Netherlands Antilles, Morocco, and Turkey. The total number of ethnic immigrants consists of the total number of immigrants minus immigrants from countries of the European Union as well as countries that in the Dutch context are characterized as emigration countries (i.e., Australia, New Zealand, Canada, United States of America, and South Africa). Our second period indicator, the level of unemployment, is measured as the relative unemployment figure: the number of registered unemployed as a percentage of the labor force (CBS, 2005).

The changes in the historical societal conditions, that is, changes in the level of ethnic immigration and unemployment, are operationalized as the alteration compared to 5 years earlier. We also considered the percentage of the non-Western population present in the country. Here we followed the Statistics Netherlands' definition of first- and second-generation non-Western immigrants: all people who either themselves or one of their parents were born in a non-Western country. These figures were derived from CBS online database (CBS, 2005).

The societal circumstances during the formative years of the respondent (cohort characteristics) were operationalized by two indicators. The first one is the level of ethnic immigration during the formative years. We applied the same definition of ethnic immigration as explicated above (CBS, 2005). It was operationalized as the mean ethnic immigration level in the period when the respondent was between 16 and 20 years of age, that is, the age at which many respondents might enter the labor market. The second cohort variable is the level of unemployment during the formative years, measured as the mean relative unemployment figure over the period when the respondent was between 16 and 20 years of age (CBS, 1994, 2005).

Results

Changing support for ethnic discrimination. Applying pooled data from the 19 national surveys of the Dutch Social and Cultural Planning Office (SCP), Figure 1 displays the fluctuations in support for ethnic discrimination in the period from 1979 to 2002. The figure shows that nearly half (about 47%) of the Dutch respondents supported discrimination against ethnic minorities in 1979. Seven years later this percentage had dropped to about 25. However, from 1986 onward, the percentage of Dutch people in favor of ethnic discrimination has continually increased and ran up to about 40% in 1992. Thereafter, there was a slight drop in support until the year 1996, followed by a rather steep increase of support in the year 1998, particularly due to more support for discrimination in the housing market. In more recent years, the level of support appears to be stable at the (approximately same) level ascertained in the beginning of the nineties.

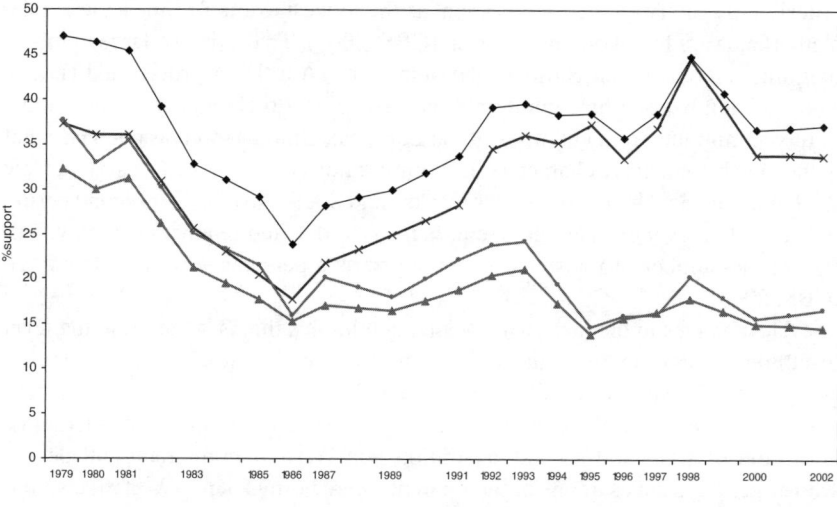

Fig. 1. Changes in support for ethnic discrimination in 1979–2002.

Table 1. Logistic Regression on Support for Ethnic Discrimination, 1979–2002

	b	Exp (b)
Intercept	−1.17***	0.31
Number ethnic immigrants (s)	0.06*	1.06
Unemployment rate (s)	−0.24***	0.78
% non-Western allochtonous people (s)	−0.10***	0.91
Changes in immigration (s)	−0.16***	0.86
Changes in unemployment rate (s)	0.10***	1.11
Cohort characteristics		
Unemployment rate (s)	0.11***	1.11
Number non-Western immigrants (s)	0.05*	1.05
N	34,532	
Model chi-square	2,322.48	
Degrees of freedom	35	
Nagelkerke R^2	0.089	

Note. (s) = standardized variable.
*$p < .05$; **$p < .01$; ***$p < .001$.

Societal conditions and support for ethnic discrimination. We used logistic regression models to predict for each individual the probability that he or she at least once supported ethnic discrimination. Table 1 shows the effects of period and cohort characteristics. Individual characteristics such as educational level, income, religiousness, and living conditions were included in the analysis as control variables but are not shown here.

The second column in Table 1 contains the parameter estimates, and the third column the exponents of these parameters, which can be interpreted as odds ratios. We will only describe the results for the context determinants of support for ethnic discrimination as referred to in the hypotheses.

We expected that support for ethnic discrimination is more widespread in times of relatively high levels of ethnic immigration or high levels of unemployment. As can be seen in Table 1, the effect of immigration was indeed positive. A higher level of ethnic immigration was related to more support for ethnic discrimination. However, the effect of the unemployment level was negative, which also holds for the presence of non-Western immigrants. Thus, in contrast to what was expected, support for ethnic discrimination was lower in times of relatively high unemployment and in times with higher percentages of non-Western immigrant residents.

Next, we proposed to test hypotheses on recent changes in ethnic competition that will have an effect on support for ethnic discrimination. The effect of changes in unemployment was in line with this expectation. A relatively large increase in unemployment in the previous 5 years turned out to be associated with more support for ethnic discrimination. However, in contrast to what we expected, a relatively strong increase in ethnic immigration was associated with less support for ethnic discrimination.

Cohorts and support for ethnic discrimination. We also stated hypotheses on support for ethnic discrimination that is considered to be more widespread among birth cohorts that perceived and experienced stronger ethnic competition in their formative years (16–20 years of age). Table 1 shows that there is indeed a positive effect of the number of immigrations during the formative period. The higher this number the more support there is for ethnic discrimination. Further, the level of national unemployment during the formative years also had a positive effect. Support for ethnic discrimination was stronger among birth cohorts that grew to maturity in times of high unemployment.

Discussion

For measuring ethnic discrimination, we used competitive situations concerning scare resources (housing, jobs). The results show that contemporary and formative societal conditions affect Dutch people's support for ethnic discrimination. The support is more widespread in times of high levels of immigration, when the unemployment level has increased recently, and among cohorts that grew to maturity in times of relatively large immigration waves or high unemployment. These findings are consistent with the idea that realistic conflicts and ethnic competition lead to stronger support for ethnic discrimination. The other results, however, are not consistent with this interpretation. It turned out that higher unemployment, stronger presence of non-Western immigrants, and increase in level of immigration were not positively related to support for ethnic discrimination.

Ethnic relations do not only involve competition over scarce resources and group discrimination, but also considerations about group identities and intergroup evaluations and feelings. In recent years, concerns about Dutch national identity and culture appear to have a stronger impact on ethnic attitudes and behaviors than economic concerns (Sniderman et al., 2004). National identity has emerged as the focus of immigration and diversity debates and Islam in particular is at the heart of what is perceived as a "crisis of multiculturalism" (Modood & Ahmad, 2007). Therefore, in Study 2 and Study 3, we examined the impact of the retreat of multiculturalism ideology in favor of assimilation on ethnic out-group feelings. Study 2 is concerned with changes in the years 2001–2004, and Study 3 adopts an experimental design to investigate the causal effects of these ideologies. In both studies, a stronger emphasis on assimilation (or a retreat of multiculturalism) was expected to lead to less positive out-group feelings toward ethnic minority groups, and Islamic outgroups (Turks and Moroccans) in particular.

Study 2

Samples and Measures

We used a cross-sectional design with four measure points (autumn of 2001, 2002, 2003, and 2004) assessing general affective group ratings among Dutch student participants ($N = 488$). The data were gathered at the same schools in all 4 years, and the samples were similar in crucial characteristics (see Verkuyten & Zaremba, 2005, for further details). In order to measure global ethnic group feelings, the participants were given the well-known feeling thermometer (scale 0 to 100 degrees) that has been successfully used in many studies, including in the Netherlands (e.g., Dijker, 1987). The participants were asked about their feelings toward four ethnic outgroups: Turks, Moroccans, Surinamese, and Antilleans.

We first examined whether the participants themselves perceived a change in the interethnic relations in Dutch society. In the 2003 sample, questions were asked on perceptions of the quality of interethnic relations in the society during the period 2001–2003. Using three questions, we asked the participants to assess the extent to which these relations were characterized by (respectively) equality, mutual respect, and tensions. These three questions were asked three times: "before Pim Fortuyn became popular" (2001), "during and directly after his popularity" (2002), and "now" (2003). For each period, the three questions were highly correlated ($r > .62$). Thus, for each year we computed a sum score in which a higher score indicated the perception of more negative interethnic relations. The correlation between the perceptions of the intergroup situation in 2001 and 2002 was .17 ($p > .05$), between 2001 and 2003, it was .31 ($p < .01$), and between 2002 and 2003 the correlation was .49 ($p < .001$).

Table 2. Thermometer Affect Ratings by Year

	Turks	Moroccans	Surinamese	Antilleans
2001 ($N = 104$)	57.0	47.9	63.7	52.8
2002 ($N = 104$)	42.5	35.4	59.8	49.6
2003 ($N = 104$)	49.8	36.5	61.9	48.7
2004 ($N = 139$)	46.9	36.2	60.1	52.7

Results

We used paired-sample tests to examine the 2003 participants' perception of interethnic relations during the 3 years. The mean score for perceived interethnic relations was 4.68 ($SD = 1.20$) in 2001, 5.54 ($SD = 1.19$) in 2002, and 5.15 ($SD = 1.07$) in 2003. The differences between all 3 years were significant ($ps < .01$). Thus, as a reflection of the political changes, the interethnic relations were perceived to be most negative in 2002, followed by those in 2003. The least problematic relations were perceived as existing in 2001. The decrease of the standard deviation might be interpreted as a growing consensus among participants in this respect.

To examine differences in in-group evaluations, we conducted a repeated-measures MANOVA with the four group evaluations (Turks, Moroccans, Surinamese, and Antilleans) as a repeated-measures factor. Year was the between-subjects factors. The analysis yielded a significant main effect for group evaluations, $F(4, 481) = 145.19, p < .001$. As shown in Table 2 and similar to previous studies on differential distances toward ethnic groups (Hagendoorn, 1995), the participants evaluated the Surinamese most positively, followed by Antilleans, the Turks, and the Moroccans. This main effect, however, was qualified by an interaction effect between group evaluation and year, $F(9, 481) = 6.03, p < .001$. Simple main-effect analyses indicated an effect for year for the Turks and Moroccans ($ps < .001$), but not for the Surinamese and the Antilleans ($ps > .05$). The pattern of results shown in the top three rows in Table 2 indicates a change in attitude toward the Turks and Moroccans between 2001 and the other 3 years. As expected, the feelings toward these two groups became more negative whereas the feelings toward the Surinamese and the Antilleans did not change over the 4 years.

Discussion

These results strongly suggest that a changing ideological context affects people's ethnic attitudes. However, we used cross-sectional data; and although the samples were very similar on background characteristics, it is always possible that other sample differences are partly responsible for the changes found. Hence, the methodology of this study leaves room for alternative explanations. Therefore, an additional study was conducted. This study has an experimental character in order to investigate the causal effects of multiculturalism and assimilation ideologies. Ethnic diversity raises all kinds of questions and raises much ambiguity for many people. Pratto and Lemieux (2001) showed that the meaning of immigration and the presence of ethnic minority groups can be manipulated through political discourse. Also, Wolsko, Park, Judd, and Wittenbrink (2000) successfully exposed participants experimentally to either a multicultural or color-blind ideological prompt condition (see also Richeson & Nussbaum, 2004).

Study 3

Samples and Measures

In Study 3 we examined the ethnic group feelings (thermometer question) of Dutch participants ($N = 114$) using an experimental questionnaire design. Multicultural and assimilation ideology was made salient in separate conditions. There were two different versions of a questionnaire that were divided randomly among the participants. One version focused on multiculturalism and another on assimilationism. The experimental manipulations were induced in the questionnaire first by its title, which was printed on the first page of the questionnaire and repeated in italics and in bold at the top of every page of the booklet, as well as by a short introduction, and 10 attitude statements (see Verkuyten, 2005, for details).

Here, we analyze whether these conditions have different effects on feelings toward different ethnic outgroups: Turks, Moroccans, Surinamese, and Antilleans. The Dutch participants were expected to show more negative out-group feelings in the assimilation condition than in the multicultural condition, particularly toward Islamic outgroups.

Results

An analysis of variance (general linear model) was performed with experimental condition as a between-subjects factor. The four out-group affective ratings served as multiple dependent variables. The multivariate effect for experimental condition was significant, $F(4, 110) = 6.12, p < .001$. As shown in Table 3, univariate analyses indicate that all ethnic outgroups were evaluated more

Table 3. Thermometer Affect Ratings for Four Ethnic Outgroups by Experimental Condition

	Turks	Moroccans	Surinamese	Antilleans
Experimental condition				
Multiculturalism	61.0	50.7	66.9	54.1
Assimilation	43.8	38.2	57.3	43.0
Univariate F-value	24.41***	9.72**	8.67**	7.26**

Note. **p < .01; ***p < .001.

negatively in the assimilation condition compared to the multicultural one. The greatest difference in mean scores between the two conditions was for the Turks as the target group, followed by the Moroccans, the Antilleans, and the Surinamese.

Discussion

The results of Study 3 clearly indicate that compared to a multicultural condition, in an assimilation condition, Dutch participants have more negative feelings toward ethnic out-groups, and particularly toward the two Islamic groups. This shows that ethnic attitudes, at least temporarily, are shaped by interethnic ideologies surrounding individuals as members of the society at large.

General Discussion

Ethnic attitudes are not static. Studies have shown, for example, positive historical changes in white Americans' racial stereotypes and prejudices (see Dovidio & Gaertner, 1986; Schuman, Steeh, Bobo, & Krysan, 1997). Despite considerable debate about whether these historical changes are more apparent than real (e.g., Crosby, Bromley, & Saxe, 1980; McConahay, Hardee, & Batts, 1981), it is often claimed that the sociostructural and ideological context influences (the expression of) group attitudes. Studies on historical changes, however, are not easy to interpret because of the many social, political, and economic differences between periods, as well as the differences in samples, methods, and measures (see Devine & Elliot, 1995).

In this article we have analyzed changing support for ethnic discrimination for the years 1979 to 2002 using national samples and the same measure, thereby avoiding some of the common pitfalls. In studying support for ethnic discrimination we focused on ethnic outgroups in general. In addition, we have examined changes in feelings toward specific and distinct ethnic outgroups using four measuring points (2001–2004). Theoretically, we have used realistic conflict theory and social identity theory for trying to understand these two changes, respectively.

The support for ethnic discrimination was measured with items presenting a competitive scenario involving the division of scarce goods (jobs and houses). For the years 1979–2002, a decrease in support for ethnic discrimination in the early 1980s was found, followed by an increase from the mid 1980s to higher levels at the end of the 1990s. Realistic conflict theory argues that competition over scarce resources between groups leads to more support for ethnic discrimination among the majority group. The implication is that more competitive contemporary structural circumstances (period effects) should lead to more support for ethnic discrimination. The results support this idea: support for ethnic discrimination was more widespread in times of high levels of ethnic immigration and when the unemployment level had recently risen strongly indicating an increase in ethnic competition in the labor market. In addition, not only contemporary circumstances but also specific competitive circumstances during the formative years (cohort effects) may lead to more support for ethnic discrimination. Cohorts that grew to maturity in times of large immigration waves or high unemployment rates were indeed found to display more widespread support for ethnic discrimination.

A shortcoming of this study was the neglect of changes in the political landscape that may have affected identity concerns and, in turn, over time changes in support for ethnic discrimination. People are not only concerned about their material and economic interests but also about conflicting identities and values. Identity issues have been found to underlie many ethnic conflicts and anti-immigrant attitudes around the world (Horowitz, 2000; McLaren, 2003), and when economic conditions are relatively good, considerations of group identity can overshadow those of economic concerns (Sniderman et al., 2004).

According to social identity theory, negative out-group evaluation is one strategy for establishing or maintaining a positive in-group identity. This strategy is more likely when one's group identity is considered to be under threat. In the last 5 to 6 years concerns about national identity have increased strongly in the Netherlands. Particularly, Islam has been publicly discussed as undermining Dutch identity and culture. Islam has increasingly become a symbol of problems perceived to be related to ethnic minorities and cultural diversity. Multiculturalism has been defined as a "drama" and is replaced by a public and political approach more strongly emphasizing assimilation. Considering these ideological and political changes, we expected over the years that the Dutch participants would evaluate the Islamic outgroups (Turks and Moroccans) more negatively. In contrast, their evaluations of other ethnic minority groups (Surinamese and Antilleans) were not expected to differ much during this period. Using cross-sectional data from 2001–2004, the results supported these expectations. Hence, the recent public and political retreat of multiculturalism in favor of assimilation seems to have led to more negative feelings toward ethnic outgroups, and toward Islamic groups in particular. This interpretation in terms of assimilationist ideas is supported by other survey research (e.g., Zick, Wagner, van Dick, & Petzel, 2001), and by our experimental work. In Study 3, in an assimilation ideological context, Dutch participants were found to evaluate ethnic outgroups more negatively than in a multicultural ideological context. These effects were strongest for the Turkish and Moroccan outgroups, but were also found in relation to the Surinamese and Antilleans.

Our analyses and findings support the idea that realistic conflict and social identity approaches do not have to be contradictory or mutually exclusive. The key explanatory mechanisms proposed by both theories differ, and depending on the circumstances, economic competition or rather identity concerns can be more or less prominent. Furthermore, concerns about interests seem especially relevant in situations of actual competition and discrimination, whereas identity considerations are probably more relevant in evaluative assessments. Both theories emphasize the critical role of social context for understanding ethnic attitudes and behaviors. In this article, we have focused on the level of society and in our analyses we have used national-level time-series data and descriptions of ideological changes. In addition, we examined the effects of different ideological experimental contexts. The results clearly indicate that social context characteristics are relevant for understanding people's changing reactions toward ethnic minority groups. Increased concerns over material and economic interests as well as conflicting identities and values can lead to more negative ethnic relations. Future studies should examine the independent and combined effects of both sets of determinants.

It is difficult, if not impossible, to predict what the future developments in the Netherlands will be. Ethnic group relations have moved into a negative direction and many people are worried about the increased "us–them" thinking. The importance of the social context implies, however, that relations can improve and that people can become more accepting or tolerant. Immigrants are also an economic asset and increasingly are making a contribution to public life and national culture, although these contributions are sometimes perceived as a threat, particularly by underprivileged social categories. In addition, developments in the Netherlands are not independent of what happens in other countries, at the level of the European Union and more globally. This makes it all the more difficult to make predictions about the future. It also makes it difficult to develop and implement policies that can lead to increased equality and harmonious social relations. Like most European countries, the Netherlands continues its struggle of finding productive ways for dealing with ethnic, cultural, and religious diversity.

References

Blalock, H. M. (1967). *Toward a theory of minority group relations*. New York: John Wiley and Sons.

Crosby, F., Bromley, S., & Saxe, L. (1980). Recent unobtrusive studies of black and white discrimination and prejudice: A literature review. *Psychological Bulletin, 87*, 546–563.

CBS. (1994). *1899–1994: Vijfennegentig jaren statistiek in tijdreeksen (1899–1994)* [Ninety-five years of statistics in periods]. SDU: The Netherlands: The Hague.

CBS. (2005). *CBS Statline. Online database of Statistics Netherlands (www.cbs.nl)*. Voorburg: Statistics Netherlands.

Coenders, M., & Scheepers, P. (1998). Support for ethnic discrimination in the Netherlands 1979–1993, effects of period, cohort and individual characteristics. *European Sociological Review, 14*, 405–422.

Dagevos, J., & Bierings, H. (2005). Arbeid en inkomen [Work and income]. In *Jaarrapport Integratie 2005*. The Hague: SCP/WODC/CBS.

Devine, P. G., & Elliot, A. J. (1995). Are racial stereotypes really fading? The Princeton trilogy revisited. *Personality and Social Psychology Bulletin, 21*, 1139–1150.

Dovidio, J. F., & Gaertner, S. L. (1986). Prejudice, discrimination, and racism: Historical trends and contemporary approaches. In J. F. Dovidio & S. L. Gaertner (Eds.), *Prejudice, discrimination, and racism* (pp. 1–34). Orlando: Academic Press.

Dijker, A. (1987). Emotional reactions to ethnic minorities. *European Journal of Social Psychology, 17*, 305–325.

Entzinger, H. (2003). The rise and fall of multiculturalism: The case of the Netherlands. In C. Joppke & E. Morawska (Eds.), *Toward assimilation and citizenship: Immigrants in liberal nation states* (pp. 59–86). London: Palgrave.
Hagendoorn, L. (1995). Intergroup biases in multiple group systems: The perception of ethnic hierarchies. *European Review of Social Psychology, 10*, 199–228.
Horowitz, D. (2000). *Ethnic groups in conflict* (2nd ed). Berkeley: University of California Press.
Inglehart, R. (1990). *Culture shift in advanced industrial society*. Princeton: Princeton University Press.
Joppke, C. (2004). The retreat of multiculturalism in the liberal state: Theory and policy. *British Journal of Sociology, 55*, 237–257.
Mannheim, K. (1964). Das Problem der Generationen [The problem of generations]. In K. Mannheim (Hrsg.), *Wissensoziologie*. Berlin: Hermann Luchterhand Verlag (Original work published 1928).
McConahay, J. B., Hardee, B. B., & Batts, V. (1981). Has racism declined in America? It depends on who is asking and what is asked. *Journal of Conflict Resolution, 25*, 563–579.
McLaren, L. M. (2003). Anti-immigrant prejudice in Europe: Contact, threat perception, and preferences for the exclusion of migrants. *Social Forces, 81*, 908–936.
Modood, T., & Ahmad, F. (2007). British Muslim perspectives on multiculturalism. *Theory, Culture and Society, 24*, 187–213.
Olzak, S. (1989). Labor unrest, immigration and ethnic conflict in urban America, 1880–1914. *American Journal of Sociology, 94*, 1303–1333.
Pratto, F., & Lemieux, A. F. (2001). The psychological ambiguity of immigration and its implications for promoting immigration policy. *Journal of Social Issues, 57*, 413–430.
Reicher, S. (2004). The context of social identity: Domination, resistance, and change. *Political Psychology, 25*, 921–945.
Richeson, J. A., & Nussbaum, R. J. (2004). The impact of multiculturalism versus color-blindness on racial bias. *Journal of Experimental Social Psychology, 40*, 417–423.
Rubin, M., & Hewstone, M. (2004). Social identity, system justification, and social dominance: Commentary on Reicher, Jost et al., and Sidanius et al. *Political Psychology, 25*, 823–844.
Schnabel, P. (2000). *De multiculturele illusie: Een pleidooi voor aanpassing en assimilatie*. [The multicultural illusion: A plea for accommodation and assimilation]. Utrecht: Forum.
Schuman, H., Steeh, C., Bobo, L., & Krysan, M. (1997). *Racial attitudes in America: Trends and interpretations*. Cambridge: Harvard University Press.
Sears, D. O. (1993). Symbolic politics: A socio-psychological theory. In S. Iyengar & W. J. McGuire (Eds.), *Explorations in political psychology* (pp. 113–149). Durham, NC: Duke University Press.
Sherif, M., & Sherif, C. W. (1969). *Social psychology*. New York: Harper & Row.
Sniderman, P. M., Hagendoorn, L., & Prior, M. (2004). Predisposing factors and situational triggers: Exclusionary reactions to immigrant minorities. *American Political Science Review, 98*, 35–49.
Tajfel, H., & Turner, J. (1979). An integrative theory of intergroup Conflict. In W. G. Austin & S. Worchel (Eds.), *The social psychology of intergroup relations* (pp. 33–47). Monterey, CA: Brooks/Cole.
Ter Wal, J. (2004). *Moslim in Nederland: Publieke discussie over de Islam in Nederland*. [Muslims in the Netherlands: Public discussion about the Islam in Netherlands]. The Hague: SCP.
Van Der Brug, W. (2003). How the LPF fuelled discontent: Empirical tests of explanations of LPF support. *Acta Politica, 38*, 89–106.
Van Praag, P. (2003). The winners and losers in a turbulent political year. *Acta Politica, 38*, 2–22.
Verkuyten, M. (2005). Ethnic group identification and group evaluation among minority and majority groups: Testing the multiculturalism hypothesis. *Journal of Personality and Social Psychology, 88*, 121–138.
Verkuyten, M., & Zaremba, K. (2005). Inter-ethnic relations in a changing political context. *Social Psychology Quarterly, 68*, 375–386.
Wittebrood, K., Latten, J., & Nicolaas, H. (2005). Wonen, leefbaarheid en veiligheid in concentratiewijken [Living, well-being and security in segregated neighborhoods]. In *Jaarrapport Integratie 2005*. The Hague: SCP/WODC/CBS.

Wolsko, C., Park, B., Judd, C. M., & Wittenbrink, B. (2000). Framing interethnic ideology: Effects of multicultural and color-blind perspectives on judgements of groups and individuals. *Journal of Personality and Social Psychology, 78*, 635–654.

Zick, A., Wagner, U., van Dick, R., & Petzel, T. (2001). Acculturation and prejudice in Germany: Majority and minority perspectives. *Journal of Social Issues, 57*, 541–557.

Zorlu, A., & Traag, T. (2005). Opleidingsniveau en taalvaardigheid [Educational level and language proficiency]. In *Jaarrapport Integratie 2005*. The Hague: SCP/WODC/CBS.

MARCEL COENDERS is an Associate Professor at the Faculty of Social and Behavioural Sciences at Utrecht University and a senior researcher of the ICS Graduate Research School. His research interests include comparative research on racism, discrimination, and ethnic relations.

MARCEL LUBBERS is an Associate Professor at the Faculty of Social and Behavioural Sciences at Utrecht University and a senior researcher of the ICS Graduate Research School. He is a recipient of the VENI grant (NWO) from 2003 to 2006 for the topic *Euroscepticism: its social determinants and political consequences*.

PEER SCHEEPERS was previously an Endowed Professor of Social Prejudice and currently is a Professor of Social Science Research Methodology in the Faculty of Social Sciences at University of Nijmegen, the Netherlands, Member of ICS, and Director of the Nijmegen Instituut voor Sociaal en Cultureel Onderzoek (NISCO). He is also the Dutch national coordinator (together with Rob Eisinga) for the European Social Survey and as such authorized representative for the Dutch Science Foundation (NWO). His research interests include the methodology of comparative social surveys as well as longitudinal and cross-national studies on political and religious attitudes and behavior, more in particular regarding ethnic exclusionism.

MAYKEL VERKUYTEN is a Professor at the Faculty of Social and Behavioural Sciences, Utrecht University and Academic Director of the European Research Centre on Migration and Ethnic relations (ERCOMER) at Utrecht University. He has research interests in racism, discrimination, and ethnic relations. His latest book is on *The Social Psychology of Ethnic Identity*, Hove: Psychology Press, 2005.

Black Immigrants in Portugal: Luso–Tropicalism and Prejudice

Jorge Vala[*]
University of Lisbon

Diniz Lopes
ISCTE, Lisbon

Marcus Lima
Federal University of Sergipe

This article analyzes the relationship between the luso–tropicalist representation of the history of Portuguese colonization and overt as well as covert expressions of anti-immigrant prejudice. The luso–tropicalist representation emphasizes the uniqueness of the Portuguese colonial relations based on Portuguese empathy and capacity to deal with people from different cultures. This representation was created during Salazar's dictatorial regime and is still assumed to be a dimension of Portuguese national identity. The empirical findings presented in this article show that this luso–tropicalist representation may explain the salience of the norm against prejudice in Portugal and may contribute to weaken the traditional association between national identity and overt prejudice. A second dimension of the association between luso–tropicalism and integration of Black immigrants in Portuguese society was examined, that is, the impact of luso–tropicalism on the attribution and covert evaluation of cultural differences between White Portuguese and Black immigrants. Results show that despite the luso–tropicalist representation, White Portuguese individuals express a covert negative evaluation of cultural differences attributed to Black immigrants. This means that the luso–tropicalist representation can protect against the expression of overt prejudice but not against its covert dimensions.

---

[*]Correspondence concerning this article should be addressed to Jorge Vala, Instituto de Ciências Sociais da Universidade de Lisboa, Av. Prof. Aníbal de Bettencourt, 9, 1600-189 Lisboa [e-mail: jorge.vala@ics.ul.pt].

For many years, Portugal was a country of emigrants. In the last decades, and especially in the last 10 years, Portugal became a country of immigration receiving immigrants from the former Portuguese colonies in Africa, from Brazil, and from Eastern Europe. Official statistics show that 5% of the people living in Portugal are legal immigrants, most of them coming from the Portuguese ex-colonies. In this context, how does the Portuguese society react to immigration, specifically to immigrants who have an African origin?

This issue of the *Journal of Social Issues* is dedicated to the analysis of prejudice in Europe. Hence, we analyze the psychological dynamics of racial and anti-immigrant prejudice in Portugal within the context of a specific representation of the history of Portuguese colonial relations: the *luso–tropicalist* representation. Luso–tropicalism as a social representation emphasizes the uniqueness of Portuguese colonial relations based on the Portuguese capacity to deal with people from different cultures.

Luso–tropicalism is a theory proposed by the anthropologist Gilberto Freyre in 1933 to explain the construction of Brazilian identity. It was selectively appropriated by Salazar's dictatorial regime (1926–1974) in order to legitimize Portuguese colonialism, accentuating the absence of racism in the Portuguese colonies as well as Portuguese empathy toward other people, specifically Black people (Castelo, 1999; Freyre, 1933; Valentim, 2003). Today, luso–tropicalism is still considered a part of Portuguese national identity. This article is framed within the general hypothesis that representations of a nation concerning its history and its colonial past may contribute to understanding today's reactions toward immigrants and immigration in Portugal.

In a study of racism in Portugal, Vala, Brito, and Lopes (1999) showed that anti-Black prejudice could be described using Pettigrew and Meerten's (1995) distinction between blatant and subtle prejudice—a distinction found using Eurobarometer-30/1988 data-samples from the United Kingdom, Belgium, France, Holland, and Germany. In Vala et al.'s (1999) study, it was also shown that anti-Black prejudice in Portugal had the same predictors as those found by Pettigrew and Meertens. Nevertheless, there was a critical exception in the Portuguese sample: anti-Black prejudice was not predicted by national identity, as it was the case in the countries studied by Pettigrew and Meertens. How can this result be explained?

In an exploratory way, we propose that the absence of an association between national identity and prejudice, and the salience of an antiprejudice norm in Portugal can be explained within the framework of the luso–tropicalist representation. In the second part of this article we show that the luso–tropicalist representation does not affect covert forms of prejudice based on the attribution of cultural differences, as much as it affects open expression of blatant prejudice.

Luso–Tropicalism, Prejudice, and National Identification

Luso–tropicalism is based on the hypothetical existence of a specific Portuguese cultural trait: the natural capacity and ability of Portuguese to relate to people that are seen as different—a trait that would explain the unique character of colonial relationships and that would, nowadays, have a positive impact on the relationships between Portuguese and immigrants.

This hypothetical dimension of the Portuguese "national character" was created and spread by the anthropologist Gilberto Freyre in his famous book *Casa Grande e Senzala* (*Masters and Slaves*, 1933), a book in which he proposed the concept of luso–tropicalism[1] to explain the apparent success of relations between different cultures in Brazil, as well as the cultural and biological *mestiçagem*[2] that occurred in this same country. This anthropological theory was subjected to a selective interpretation by the ideology of Salazar's dictatorial regime (Alexandre, 1999) and was transformed into a social representation (Moscovici, 1984).

Shielded by this representation, the Portuguese colonization is seen as more humane than the Spanish or English colonization. English colonial systems were characterized by a social distance between the colonizers and the colonized; Spanish colonization practices included the extermination of the colonized, well described by De Las Casas (1552/1996). These characteristics find no equivalent in the Portuguese colonization process according to the luso–tropicalist representation. In G. Freyre's words, a Portuguese "would be Spanish without the war flame or the dramatic orthodoxy; and would be English without the puritan rules. He would be the 'non-conflictual' type—not with absolute ideas, nor inflexible prejudices" (Freyre, 1933, p. 191). In the past, these Portuguese characteristics would have generated harmonious relations between colonizers and colonized in Brazil. In the present these same characteristics may have generated "the Brazilian racial democracy" (for a discussion see Alexandre, 1999; Castelo, 1999; Valentim, 2003), and in Portugal a more positive attitude toward immigrants, namely Black immigrants, as compared to other European countries. A study carried out with Portuguese university students concerning the support of three of the main components of the luso–tropicalist representation showed that participants actually believe that the Portuguese colonization process was more benevolent, that

---

[1] The word *luso* comes from the Latin word *lusus* to designate the Portuguese. *Luso–tropicalism* generally refers to the relationship between the Portuguese and natives of "tropical countries."

[2] *Mestiçagem*, as in *miscegenation*, refers to a process of crossing "races" or individuals of different "races," specifically White Portuguese and Black Africans. According to Gilberto Freyre, in Brazil the process of *mestiçagem* was based, among other reasons, on the fact that Portugal was itself a product of a process of *mestiçagem*: "Portugal is a good example of a European country of 'transitory blonds' or of "half-blonds." In the regions where there is greater dissemination of Nordic blood, children are born blond and with "pink" skin, like a Flemish baby Jesus, and become dark skinned and dark haired when they reach adulthood... these 'double-colored hair mestizos' generated, in our view, the majority of the Portuguese colonizers of Brazil" (p. 204).

it originated more *mestiçagem*, and that, nowadays, racism is expressed less frequently in Portugal than in other European countries (Valentim, 2003).

From an objective point of view, it is hard to believe that the relations between Portuguese and colonized people were cordial. It will suffice to remember that De Las Casas wrote not only about the extermination of Indians by Spanish colonizers, but also about the extermination of Black people by the Portuguese (De Las Casas, 1552/1996). It should also be noted that between 3 million and 18 million Africans were made slaves and transported to Brazil, and that the Portuguese colonization in this last country led to the death of 5 million native Indians (Munanga, 1996; Schwarcz, 1996).

Luso–Tropicalism and the Antiprejudice Norm

Despite this somber history, luso–tropicalism functions as a representation of the uniqueness and kindness of the Portuguese colonization, and of the relations between Portuguese and other people. And it helps to explain the prevalence of an antiprejudice norm in Portugal. In fact, Vala et al. (1999), using Pettigrew and Meertens's scales, showed that the expression of anti-Black subtle prejudice is much higher than the expression of blatant prejudice: while 44.7% of the respondents express subtle prejudice, only 16% of the participants answered in a way that violated the norm of antiblatant prejudice against Black people. Nevertheless, it should be noted that when the target of prejudice is represented by people categorized as Angolans, Mozambicans, or Cape-Verdians (people from the former Portuguese African colonies), and not by "Black" people, the expression of blatant prejudice rises, showing that the antiprejudice norm only positively affects the specific target "Black people" (Cabecinhas, 2002).

The European Social Survey (ESS-1/2002) measured explicit traditional racism using two items: "Thinking about people who have come to live in Portugal from another country and who are of a different race or ethnic group from most of Portuguese people—how much would you mind or not mind if someone like this...(a) was appointed as your boss?; (b) married a close relative of yours ($0 = $ *not mind at all*; $10 = $ *mind a lot*). An analysis of these ESS data showed that Portugal manifests a lower expression of explicit traditional racism when compared to the remaining 14 countries of the European Community (EC; before the admission of the new EC members), $F(1, 29,692) = 10.96, p < .001$ ($M_{Portugal} = 2.89, M_{EUCountries} = 3.25$).

Also based on this survey's data, we calculated an index of ethnic orientation toward immigrants by subtracting the degree of rejection of immigrants of a "different ethnic group" from the degree of rejection of immigrants of the same "ethnic group." We compared the obtained results from Portugal ($n = 1,511$) with those of France ($n = 1,503$), the United Kingdom ($n = 2,052$), and Germany ($n = 2,919$). In the four samples there is a greater acceptance of immigrants of the same ethnic group than of a different ethnic group; but the ethnic orientation in

Portugal is, nevertheless, smaller than in the remaining countries, F (3, 16,323) = 47.13, $p < .001$ ($M_{Portugal} = .12$, $M_{France} = .18$, $M_{Germany} = .19$, $M_{UK} = .25$, post hoc Duncan $ps < .001$). Briefly, these results show that the antiprejudice norm is salient in Portugal, a result that might be attributed, at least partially, to the pervasiveness of the luso–tropicalist representation in the Portuguese society.

Portuguese National Identity as a Predictor of Prejudice

While the pervasiveness of the luso–tropicalist representation helps to explain the salience of the antiprejudice norm in Portuguese society, its pervasiveness may also explain the absence of a correlation between national identification and anti-Black prejudice in Portugal.

The data collected in five European countries reported in Pettigrew and Meertens' (1995) paper (see also Esses, Dovidio, Jackson, & Armstrong, 2001) show that national identification and prejudice toward minorities are strongly and positively related. But this association may be moderated in the way people represent their nation and its history (Brewer & Miller, 1996; Citrin, Wong, & Duff, 2001; Kelman, 2001); by the representation of patriotism versus nationalism (Kosterman & Feshbach, 1989; Mummendey, Klink, & Brown, 2001; Staub, 1997); and by the representation of a nation as an unique entity, or as an aggregate of entities (for the Belgium case, see Billiet, Maddens, & Beerten, 2003; for the Spanish case, see Ros, Huici, & Gómez, 2000).

What can be said about the influence of luso–tropicalism regarding the association between the identification with the nation and the orientation toward prejudice? We propose that luso–tropicalism weakens the association between ingroup identification and orientation toward explicit discrimination of minorities.[3]

In 1997, Vala, Brito, and Lopes ran a survey study about racism in Portugal using a probability sample of White Portuguese respondents, aged 18–64 years, living in the Lisbon urban area ($N = 600$). Using a regression model that included traditional prejudice predictors (such as relative deprivation; see Pettigrew et al., 2008), Vala et al. (1999) showed that white racial identification predicts blatant prejudice, while the same is not true for identification with Portugal (Table 1). However, using a similar model of predictors, Pettigrew and Meertens (1995) found

---

[3] As Gilberto Freyre refers, "the idea that Portuguese are not xenophobic might be attributed to the fact that Portuguese law never prohibited the existence of ethnical minorities within its reign—for instance, Moorish and Jews—nor of their traditions, recognizing, on the contrary, their possibility of having their own laws" (p. 198). Moreover, in Freire's interpretation, which forgets, for instance, the expulsion of Jews in 1496, "besides" not being xenophobe, the Portuguese colonizer was a real cosmopolitan, "a cosmopolitanism favored mainly by the geographical position of the reign: a country largely maritime, varying in human contacts since remote times" (p. 198). Anyway, Freyre invites us to recognize that "only the latifundium slavery colonization would be capable of resisting the enormous obstacles that were raised to the civilization of Brazil by the Europeans" (p. 240). Gilberto Freyre bases his assumption on Portuguese intellectuals who in the 1930s were concerned with the definition of national identity.

Table 1. Predictors of Blatant and Subtle Prejudice in Portugal (Stepwise Multiple Regression Analysis)

Predictors	Blatant Prejudice Beta Values
Sociodemographic variables	
Age	ns
Socioprofessional group+	ns
Educational level	−.12**
Intergroup/competition for resources variables	
Perception of interdependence+	.30*
Intergroup relative deprivation	.15*
Intergroup identity/self-categorization variables	
Racial identity	.19*
National identity	ns
Psychological individual differences variables	
Ethnocentrism	ns
Incongruence	.11**
Ideological individual differences variables	
Moral conservatism	.17*
Political conservatism+	ns
Political positioning (left-right)	ns
Social justice distributive norms+	ns
Interpersonal (contact) variables	
Black friend+	−.11**
Black neighbor (equal status)+	ns
Adj. R^2	.50

+Dummy variables; *$p < .001$; **$p < .01$.
Note. This table was adapted from "Expressões dos racismos em Portugal" by J. Vala, R. Brito, and D. Lopes with kind permission of Imprensa de Ciências Sociais, Lisboa, Portugal.

significant effects of national identification on prejudice in different European countries.

These results were replicated using data from the ESS-2/2004. This survey includes questions concerning opposition to immigrants from poor, non-European countries and to those who are perceived to belong to other "races" or different "ethnic origins." The Portuguese version of this same survey ($N = 2,052$; females $= 58.4\%$; mean age $= 46.4$) also included a measure of national identification. National identification was measured using an adaptation of Aron, Aron, and Smollan's (1992) Inclusion of Other in the Self Scale, and of Tropp and Wright's (2001) Ingroup in the Self Scale. This allowed testing our hypothesis with a new dependent variable and a new set of predictors. The results reveal that identification with Portugal is not a significant predictor of opposition to immigration. Regrettably, in this study, as well as in the previous one, it was not possible to draw direct comparisons between the results obtained in Portugal and the results obtained in other countries.

This limitation was surmounted in yet another study (Vala, Lima, & Lopes, 2004) comparing the predictive power of national identity in Portugal and in the remaining 14 European countries (before the admission of new members to the EU). Data from the 1999 European Values Study were used. The index of prejudice

Table 2. Predictors of Perception of Threat in European Countries (Stepwise Multiple Regression Analysis)

	8 European Countries[a]						Portugal[b]					
	Symbolic Threat		Safety Threat		Economical Threat		Symbolic Threat		Safety Threat		Economical Threat	
Predictors	Beta	p	Beta	p	Beta	p	Beta	p	Beta	p	Beta	p
Education	−.210	.000	−.182	.000	−.345	.000	−.116	.000	−.132	.000	−.270	.000
Age	.058	.000	.144	.000	.061	.000	.013	.628	.015	.571	−.102	.001
N. identity	.096	.000	.102	.000	.104	.000	.014	.608	.009	.728	.033	.201
Adj. R^2	.068		.083		.152		.013		.017		.051	

[a]$N = 11,300$; [b]$N = 1,600$.

used in this study is quite broad. As shown by the authors, national identification predicts prejudice in European countries as a whole but not in Portugal.

This pattern of results was replicated using data from the International Social Survey Program 2003/2004 (databases available in April 2005: Ireland, United Kingdom, Portugal, Sweden, Finland, France, Germany, Denmark, and Spain). A summary of these results is presented in Table 2. Using the perception of threat associated to immigration as the dependent variable, the findings showed, once again, that national identity predicts perception of symbolic threat (cultural threat) and realistic threat (economical threat and threat to security) in the eight national samples that were analyzed. However, this same pattern of associations was not found in Portugal. Separate analyses were also conducted for each country. While controlling for age and educational level, national pride and perception of threat show a positive and significant correlation in Denmark ($\beta = .22, p < .001$), Spain ($\beta = .23, p < .001$), Finland ($\beta = .14, p < .001$), France ($\beta = .13, p < .001$), Germany ($\beta = .13, p < .001$), and Sweden ($\beta = .14, p < .001$). In the United Kingdom and in Ireland this result was not obtained.

In short, even though luso–tropicalism targets are essentially Black individuals, these new results show that luso–tropicalism effects can spread to a more general category of "immigrants," independently of their country of origin or the color of their skin.

In summary, and within the more general framework of the representation of the nation as a moderator of the relationship between national identification and prejudice, we propose that the representation of the Portuguese "national character" created by luso–tropicalism might explain the absence of a correlation between national identity and ethnic prejudice observed in different surveys. This hypothesis seems highly plausible, despite the fact that we do not possess direct measures of the moderating role of luso–tropicalism.

Heteroethnicization, Luso–Tropicalism, and Prejudice

Does luso–tropicalism also constitute a buffer for subtle forms of prejudice? Consider the covert negative evaluation of attributed cultural differences. In fact, luso–tropicalism, as a social representation, assumes that the Portuguese have a special tolerance toward traditions, customs, and values of populations with whom they had contact in the past, during the period of colonization, and in the present, with immigrants—specifically Black immigrants.[4] Thus, contrary to the findings of the literature that hold that perceived cultural differences relate positively with prejudice toward out-groups (Leach, Peng, & Volkens, 2000; Pettigrew & Meertens, 1995; Rokeach, Smith, & Evans, 1960; Sears & Henry, 2003), according to luso–tropicalism, the Portuguese would not express the same negative attitudes. In order to analyze this new hypothesis, we will first present our prediction concerning the heteroethnicization process.

In the context of the construction of the representations of differences between human groups, we define *heteroethnicization* as the process through which a different and inferior culture is implicitly attributed to minority outgroups (Vala, Lopes, Lima, & Brito, 2002). This process should be understood in the context of the transformation of the expression of racism in democratic societies. In fact, these societies abandoned the explanations based on racial differences and replaced them by cultural differences, meaning that cultural inferiorization substituted for racial inferiorization. However, we put forward the hypothesis that nowadays cultural inferiorization is also no longer socially acceptable.

In this vein, we propose that, today, the expression of cultural inferiority of the "other" is not voiced in an overt way, but rather in a covert way. This covert expression of cultural inferiority might nowadays be manifested through the accentuation of cultural differences between minority and majority groups, a process that hides an implicit negative evaluation of the minority cultures. We are not proposing that traditional racism has vanished. Neither do we hold that the relation between biological racism and discrimination is mediated by perceived differences as proposed, but not empirically demonstrated, by Leach et al. (2000). We argue that today's racism can be expressed in a way that is not perceived as antinormative, for example, through the attribution and implicit negative evaluation of cultural differences. This hypothesis received indirect support in Pettigrew and Meertens' (1995) study. In fact, the cultural differences subscale is part of their Subtle Racism Scale, which in turn correlates with the Blatant Racism Scale.

Empirical Evidence with a Sample of "White" Portuguese Respondents

Can it be that in Portuguese society, contrary to other European societies, people do not endorse covert inferiorization of immigrants' culture, or immigrants'

---

[4] As we already emphasized in the previous note, this idea is central in the representation of Portuguese colonization as described by Gilberto Freyre. According to this author, "[The Portuguese] was the European colonizer that came closer to the so-called inferior races. The less cruel in the relation with slaves (...), oriented to race crossing and to *mestiçagem*, a tendency that stems from the higher social plasticity found in Portuguese people than in other types of European colonizers" (p. 191).

heteroethnicization? And is the process of heteroethnicization a functional equivalent of the process of heteroracialization? In order to answer these questions, we used a measure of overt racial inferiorization of Black people (items adapted from Pettigrew and Meertens' (1995) Intimacy Scale: "I would refuse to have sexual relationships with a Black person"; "I would mind if a Black person who had a similar economical background as me joined my close family by marriage"; "Black people come from less able races and this explains why they are not as well off as most Portuguese people"; "I would be bothered if a child of mine married a 'Black' person and that my grandchildren were 'mestizos'"—all response scales varying from *strongly agree* to *strongly disagree*). And we also used a measure of heteroethnicization that taps the perceived differences between White Portuguese and Black people in terms of family, religion, and sexual values (items adapted from Pettigrew and Meertens' (1995), subscale of accentuation of cultural differences: "How different or similar do you think Black people living here are to other Portuguese people like yourself...? (a) in the values that they teach to children; (b) in their religious beliefs and practices; (c) in their sexual values or sexual behaviors; (d) in their concern with their families' welfare; (e) in the education they give to children)." Note that the heteroethnicization measure does not involve an explicit evaluation of perceived differences or of the customs and values of the outgroup.

Using the data of Vala et al.'s (1999) correlational study presented above, we tested two models: a model that analyzes the nonassociation between the cultural differentiation (i.e., heteroethnicization) factor and the racial inferiorization (i.e., heteroracialization) factor, and another model that tests those two factors as being correlated. This last model corresponds to our hypothesis.

The fit indices obtained in the analyses show that the two correlated factors model fits the data better than the model that does not predict the association between the two factors. Indeed, the two factors correlated model presents better absolute and comparative fits, $\chi^2(26) = 78.06, p < .001$, Goodness of Fit (GFI) = .95, Comparative Fit Index (CFI) = .92, root mean square error of approximation (RMSEA) = .077, when compared to the two uncorrelated factors model, $\chi^2(27) = 103.49, p < .001$; GFI = .94; CFI = .89; RMSEA = .091. Moreover, when compared with the two uncorrelated factors model, the two correlated factors model shows a significant decrease in the chi-square model fit measure, $\Delta\chi^2(1) = 25.43, p < .001$. The confirmatory factor analysis supports our hypothesis of two distinct but correlated factors, suggesting that the accentuation of cultural differences is a process of inferiorization similar to that of the perception of racial differences.

However, to test our hypothesis fully, we must analyze the relations between the two-factors model and variables measuring discrimination and the negative evaluation of Black people (discrimination measure: participants were asked if it were a good idea or a bad idea to make the naturalization process easier for "Black" people. Participants were also asked how they would distribute 5,000 among the

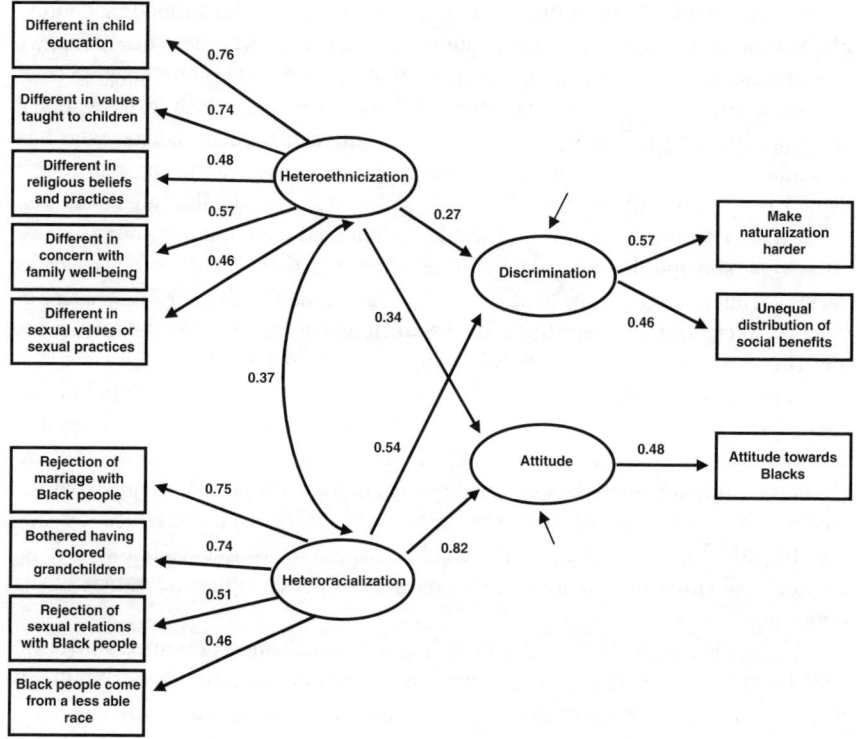

Note. Standardized solution; all coefficients significant at $p < .01$; $N = 338$; $\chi^2 (50) = 148.12$, $p < .001$; GFI = .94; CFI = .90; RMSEA = .076; Confidence Interval (CI) = .062–.091.

Fig. 1. Relation between heteroethnicization and heteroracialization, attitude toward "Black" people, and discrimination.

50 poorest "Black" people and by the 50 poorest "White" people of a poor Lisbon neighborhood—scale ranging from 0 to 5,000. And they were also asked to evaluate "Black" people using a scale that ranged from *not at all favorable* to *very much favorable*). The next structural equation model presented in Figure 1 tests the relationships between heteroethnicization and heteroracialization and attitudes and degree of discrimination of White Portuguese toward Blacks.

This model shows good absolute and relative fit indices. Both heteroethnicization and heteroracialization have a strong association with attitudes toward Blacks; thus, the greater the heteroethnicization or heteroracialization of Black Africans, the more negative the attitudes of White Portuguese toward them (respectively, $\gamma = .34$ and $\gamma = .82$). Also, these same two factors appear associated to a latent variable of discrimination. Note that the greater the heteroethnicization or heteroracialization, the more White Portuguese support the idea that the process of naturalization of Black immigrants should not be made easier, and the less they are willing to distribute social benefits to Blacks ($\gamma = .27$ and $\gamma = .54$, respectively).

These results are supported by different theoretical perspectives (Brewer & Campbell, 1976; Rokeach, 1960), and they answer the questions we raised previously. That is, the perception of cultural differences hides a process of inferiorization, as it correlates with racialization, discrimination, and negative evaluations of Black people. Moreover, these results also show that the luso–tropicalist representation does not protect the White Portuguese against covert cultural inferiorization of out-group minorities. Indirect empirical evidence for our assumptions is also offered in the study of Pettigrew and Meertens (1995) carried out in four different Western European countries. Indeed, these authors also found a positive correlation between the attribution of cultural differences and blatant racism.

Nevertheless, these results are inconsistent with the theories that hold that it is not the difference between values and other group features that leads to discrimination, but, on the contrary, it is the similarity between groups that leads to differentiation and, in some situations, to discrimination (Tajfel & Turner, 1979). Our findings also contradict the contentions of Coenders, Scheepers, Sniderman, and Verberk (2001). Partially reanalyzing the data used by Pettigrew and Meertens (1995, 2001), Coenders et al. (2001) maintained that general prejudice (explicit cultural inferiorization and explicit racial inferiorization) is independent of the "perception of cultural differences." In fact, Coenders, Lubbers, Scheepers, and Verkuyten (2008) assumed that the "perception of cultural difference items in Pettigrew and Meertens' scale (...) reflect not so much evaluative prejudices, but rather cognitive perceptions" (p. 295). They also argue that when, for instance, Dutch respondents say that a Turk is "very different" in religion, they are simply "acknowledging a social reality" (p. 298), and not necessarily expressing an evaluation. As plausible as the argument might seem at first, our results do not support it.

Empirical Evidence with a Sample of Young Black Respondents

Responding to this theoretical debate, we run another empirical test of our hypothesis, this time using a quota sample of Black respondents aged 15–29 years who live in the Lisbon urban area ($N = 400$; females $= 50\%$). The aim of this study was to analyze the psychological effects of Black people's perception of being seen as different, inasmuch as feeling discriminated. If the results of this study show that the perception of being seen as different is associated with discrimination, then we have new evidence from the targets themselves that the attribution of differences might not be a simple process of group description but a process of implicit group inferiorization.

In this study, we asked participants about the percentage of White Portuguese that would, in their opinion, agree with the items that, in the previous research, measured racialization and ethnicization.[5] As in the preceding analyses with the White Portuguese sample, we again ran a confirmatory factor analysis and tested two factorial models: an uncorrelated two-factors model and a correlated two-factors model.

The two correlated factors model produces once more the best absolute and comparative fit indices, $\chi^2(26) = 103.05, p < .001$, GFI $= .94$, CFI $= .93$, RMSEA $= .09$, over and above the uncorrelated two-factors model, $\chi^2(27) = 154.75, p < .001$, GFI $= .91$, CFI $= .88$, RMSEA $= .11$. Moreover, when compared with the two uncorrelated factors model, the two correlated factors model presents a better fit, $\Delta\chi^2(1) = 51.7, p < .001$.

A structural model testing the association between the perception by young Black people of heteroethnicization, perception of heteroracialization and procedural relative deprivation[6] is presented in Figure 2.

As shown in Figure 2, the model reveals good fit indices. Heteroethnicization evidences a strong association with discrimination ($\gamma = .43$), as is the case for heteroracialization ($\gamma = .72$). This means that the more young Blacks perceive that they are ethnicized or racialized, the more they believe that they are treated unjustly by Portuguese institutions. Although the effects of perceived racialization are stronger than those of perceived ethnicization, the latter remain significant. The psychological meaning that we can derive from these results is that young Blacks perceive that White Portuguese perceive them to be culturally different, and that this metaperception corresponds to a sentiment of stigmatization.

Discussion and Conclusions

This article argues that the relations between receiving societies and immigrants is influenced by the representations that receiving societies build regarding their own history, namely their colonial past. Specifically, this article analyzed

---

[5] Specifically, the questions we asked participants concerning heteroracialization were: "In your opinion, what percentage of 'White' Portuguese answered 'yes' to the following questions:" "Yes, I would be bothered if a child of mine married a 'Black' person and my grandchildren were 'mestizos'"; "Yes, I exclude having sexual relationships with a Black person"; "Yes, I consider that Black people belong to a less able race"; "Yes, I would mind if a Black person who had a similar economical background as me joined my close family by marriage." Concerning heteroethnicization, we asked for the percentage of "White" Portuguese that said that Black people were different in terms of (a) the values that they teach to children, (b) their religious beliefs and practices, (c) their sexual values or sexual behaviors, (d) the concern with their families' welfare, and (e) the education they give to children.

[6] The procedural relative deprivation (Tyler & Lind, 2001) index was created through the calculation of a difference score of two items: "How do you evaluate the way 'Black' people are treated in Portugal by public services and by offices of central administration (Health services, Schools, Court Houses, Foreign offices, etc). "How do you evaluate the way Portuguese are treated in Portugal by the public services and by the offices of central administration (Health services, Schools, Court Houses, Foreign offices, etc)? Both items were measured in a 5-point scale (1 $=$ *they are not treated with consideration and respect*, 5 $=$ *they are treated with consideration and respect*). The same analysis was repeated with other discrimination measures and we obtained similar results.

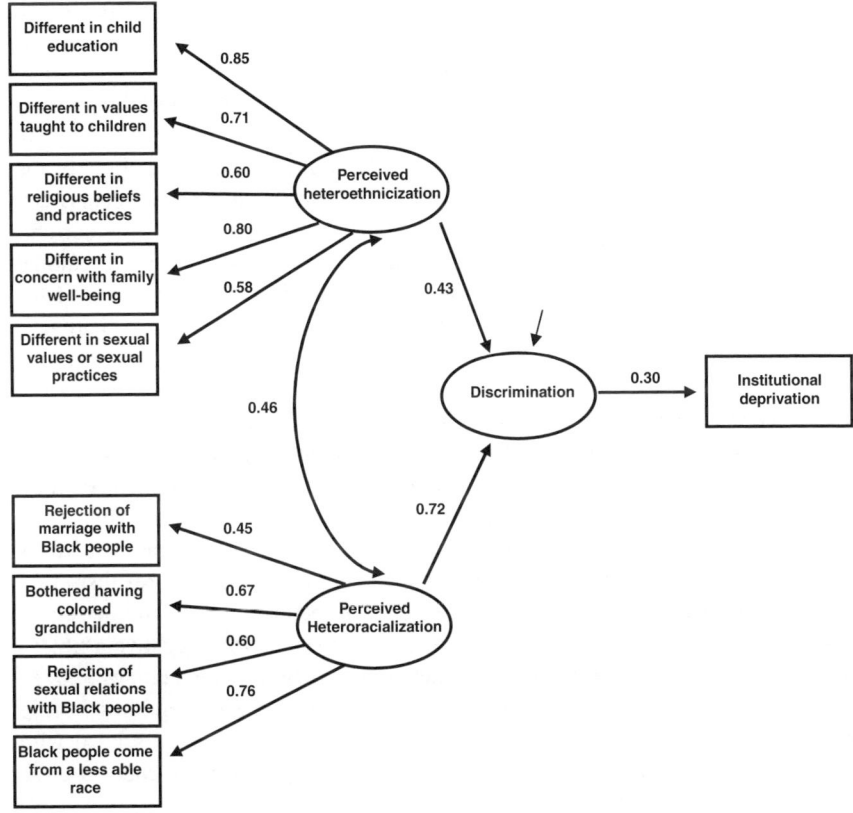

Note. Standardized solution. All coefficients significant at $p < .05$; $N = 362$; χ^2 (33) $= 123.17$, $p < .001$; GFI $= .93$; CFI $= .92$; RMSEA $= .087$ CI $= .071-.104$.

Fig. 2. Relation between perceived heteroethnicization and perceived heteroracialization and discrimination.

in an exploratory way an association between the luso–tropicalist representation of the Portuguese colonial past and the type of social relations White Portuguese presently maintain with Black immigrants originating from the former Portuguese African colonies.

Data from different probability and quota samples were analyzed in order to illustrate the impact of luso–tropicalism on the salience of the antiprejudice norm, and on the absence of the usual association between national identification and prejudice in Portugal. Results suggest that the luso–tropicalist representation can contribute to the explanation of the prevalence of the antiprejudice norm, and that it can also suppress the impact of national identification on prejudice. This last finding is particularly relevant because a positive association between prejudice and national identity has been generally found in most European countries, as shown by Pettigrew and Meertens (1995, 2001), and by Jackson, Brown, Brown, and Marks (2001).

We propose that the representations on the relations between colonizers and colonized people can exert today an impact on the relations between host societies and immigrants. In the Portuguese case, the luso–tropicalist representation, stressing the "plasticity," "non-conflictual," "flexibility," and "cordiality" of the Portuguese "national character," might contribute to the weak association between national identity and prejudice in Portugal. This perspective extends previous empirical and theoretical arguments arguing that the association between national identity and prejudice can be moderated by lay people's representations of the nation (e.g., Billiet et al., 2003; Ros et al., 2000), by the meaning of nationalism (Kosterman & Feshbach, 1989), and by the types of comparisons it raises (Mummendey et al., 2001).

A second dimension of the association between luso–tropicalist representation and integration of immigrants in the Portuguese society was also examined—the impact of luso–tropicalism on the attribution and covert evaluation of cultural differences. This problem was analyzed within the framework of the concept of heteroethnicization, a concept that refers to the attribution of cultural differences to minorities, resulting in their cultural inferiorization. In fact, our results reveal a correlation between heteroracialization and heteroethnicization, and these two forms of outgroup inferiorization are, in turn, correlated with negative attitudes toward Black African immigrants and intentions to discriminate them. Moreover, in the study of young Black Africans, we showed that the perception of being seen as different, or the perception of heteroethnicization, was correlated with the perception of being heteroracialized, and both perceptions were understood as forms of group stigmatization.

As a whole, results show that the luso–tropicalist representation about colonial relations may protect Portuguese against the public expression of overt prejudice, but does not protect them from new and hidden forms of prejudice, such as covert cultural inferiorization. However, the Portuguese myth about the uniqueness of Portuguese colonial relations was not measured directly in the studies we presented. Instead, we used a bottom-up strategy of argumentation associating the consistent differences of results found in Portugal and in other European countries, namely those relating national identity and prejudice, with the luso–tropicalist representation. Future research should directly measure the relationship between the luso–tropicalist representation and prejudice against immigrants.

References

Alexandre, V. (1999). O império e a ideia de raça (séculos XIX e XX) [The empire and the idea or race (XIX and XX centuries)]. In J. Vala (Ed.), *Novos racismos: Perspectivas comparativas* (pp. 133–144). Lisboa, Portugal: Celta Editora.

Aron, A., Aron, E. N., & Smollan, D. (1992). Inclusion of other in the self scale and the structure of interpersonal closeness. *Journal of Personality and Social Psychology, 63*, 596–612.

Billiet, J., Maddens, B., & Beerten, R. (2003). National identity and attitude towards foreigners in a multinational state: A replication. *Political Psychology, 24,* 241–257.
Brewer, M. B., & Campbell, D. T. (1976). *Ethnocentrism and intergroup attitudes: East African evidence.* New York: Halsted-Press.
Brewer, M. B., & Miller, N. (1996). *Intergroup relations.* Buckingham, UK: Open University Press Books/Cole.
Cabecinhas, R. (2002). *Racismo e etnicidade em Portugal: Uma análise psicossociológica da homogenei zação das minorias.* [Racism and ethnicity in Portugal: A psycho-sociological analysis of minorities' homogenization]. Unpublished doctoral dissertation. Universidade do Minho, Braga, Portugal.
Castelo, C. (1999). *O modo português de estar no mundo: O luso-tropicalismo e a ideologia colonial portuguesa—1933–1961* [The Portuguese way of relating to the world: *Luso-tropicalism* and the Portuguese colonial ideology]. Porto, Portugal: Afrontamento.
Citrin, J., Wong, C., & Duff, B. (2001). The meaning of American national identity: Patterns of ethnic conflict and consensus. In R. D. Ashmore & L. Jussim (Eds.), *Social identity, intergroup conflict, and conflict reduction* (pp. 71–100). London: Oxford University Press.
Coenders, M., Lubbers, L., Scheepers, P., & Verkuyten, M. (2008). More than two decades of changing ethnic attitudes in the Netherlands. *Journal of Social Issues, 64*(2), 269–285.
Coenders, M., Scheepers, P., Sniderman, P., & Verberk, G. (2001). Blatant and subtle prejudice: Different dimensions, different determinants, different consequences? Some comments on Pettigrew and Meertens. *European Journal of Social Psychology, 31,* 281–297.
De Las Casas, B. (1996). *Brevíssima relação da destruição de África* [A short report on the destruction of Africa]. Lisboa, Portugal: Antígona (Original work published 1552).
Esses, V. M., Dovidio, J. F., Jackson, L. M., & Armstrong, T. L. (2001). The immigration dilemma: The role of perceived group competition, ethnic prejudice, and national identity. *Journal of Social Issues, 57,* 389–412.
Freyre, G. (1933). *Casa grande e senzala* [Masters and slaves]. Lisboa, Portugal: Livros do Brasil.
Jackson, J. S., Brown, K. T., Brown, T. N., & Marks, B. (2001). Contemporary immigration policy orientation among dominant-group members in Western Europe. *Journal of Social Issues, 57,* 431–456.
Kelman, H. C. (2001). The role of national identity in conflict resolution: Experiences from Israeli-Palestinian problem-solving workshops. In R. D. Ashmore, L. Jussim, & D. Wilder (Eds.), *Social identity, intergroup conflict, and conflict reduction* (pp. 187–212). New York: Oxford University Press.
Kosterman, R., & Feshbach, S. (1989). Toward a measure of patriotic and nationalistic attitudes. *Political Psychology, 10,* 257–274.
Leach, C. W., Peng, T. R., & Volkens, J. (2000). Is racism dead? Comparing (expressive) means and (structural equation) models. *British Journal of Social Psychology, 39,* 449–465.
Moscovici, S. (1984). The phenomenon of social representations. In R. M. Farr & S. Moscovici (Eds.), *Social representations* (pp. 3–69). Cambridge: Cambridge University Press.
Mummendey, A., Klink, A., & Brown, R. (2001). Nationalism and patriotism: National identification and outgroup rejection. *British Journal of Social Psychology, 40,* 159–172.
Munanga, K. (1996). *Mestiçagem* e experiências interculturais no Brasil [*Mestiçagem* and intercultural experiences in Brasil]. In L. M. Schwartz & L. V. S. Reis (Eds.), *Negras imagens* (pp. 179–193). São Paulo, Brazil: Editora da Universidade de S. Paulo.
Pettigrew, T. F., Christ, O., Wagner, U., Meertens, R. W., van Dick, R., & Zick, A. (2008). Relative deprivation and intergroup prejudice. *Journal of Social Issues, 64*(2), 385–401.
Pettigrew, T. F., & Meertens, R. W. (1995). Subtle and blatant prejudice in Western Europe. *European Journal of Social Psychology, 25,* 57–75.
Pettigrew, T. F., & Meertens, R. W. (2001). In defense of the subtle prejudice concept: A retort. *European Journal of Social Psychology, 31,* 299–309.
Rokeach, M. (1960). *The open and closed mind.* New York: Basic Books.
Rokeach, M., Smith, P., & Evans, R. (1960). Two kinds of prejudice or one? In M. Rokeach (Ed.), *The open and closed mind* (pp. 132–168). New York: Basic Books.
Ros, M., Huici, C., & Gómez, A. (2000). Comparative identity, category salience and intergroup relations. In R. Brown & D. Capozza (Eds.), *Identity processes: Trends in theory and research* (pp. 81–95). London: Sage.

Schwarcz, L. M. (1996). Questão racial no Brasil [The racial issue in Brasil]. In L. M. Schwartz & L. V. S. Reis (Eds.), *Negras imagens* (pp. 153–177). São Paulo, Brazil: Editora da Universidade de S. Paulo.

Sears, D. O., & Henry, P. J. (2003). The origins of symbolic racism. *Journal of Personality and Social Psychology, 85*, 259–275.

Staub, E. (1997). Blind versus constructive patriotism: Moving from embededness in the group to critical loyalty and action. In D. Bar-Tal & E. Staub (Eds.), *Patriotism: In the lives of individual and nations* (pp. 213–228). Chicago: Nelson-Hall.

Tajfel, H., & Turner, J. C. (1979). An integrative theory of intergroup conflict. In S. Worchel & W. G. Austin (Eds.), *The social psychology of intergroup relations* (pp. 33–47). Monterey, CA: Brooks/Cole.

Tyler, T. R., & Lind, E. A. (2001). Understanding the nature of fraternalistic deprivation: Does group-based deprivation involve fair outcome or fair treatment? In I. Walker & H. J. Smith (Eds.), *Relative deprivation: Specification, development, and integration* (pp. 44–65). New York: Cambridge University Press.

Tropp, L. R., & Wright, S. C. (2001). Ingroup identification as the inclusion of ingroup in the self. *Personality and Social Psychology Bulletin, 27*, 585–600.

Vala, J., Brito, R., & Lopes, D. (1999). *Expressões dos racismos em Portugal* [Expressions of racisms in Portugal]. Lisboa, Portugal: Imprensa de Ciências Sociais.

Vala, J., Lima, M., & Lopes, D. (2004). Social values, prejudice and solidarity in the European Union. In W. Arts & L. Halman (Eds.), *European values at the end of the millennium* (pp. 139–161). Leiden, the Netherlands: Brill Academic Publishers.

Vala, J., Lopes, D., Lima, M., & Brito, R. (2002). Cultural differences and hetero-ethnicization in Portugal: The perceptions of White and Black people. *Portuguese Journal of Social Sciences, 1*, 111–128.

Valentim, J. P. (2003). *Identidade e lusofonia nas representações sociais de portugueses e de africanos* [Identity and *lusofonia* in the social representations of Portuguese and Africans]. Unpublished doctoral dissertation. Universidade de Coimbra, Coimbra, Portugal.

JORGE VALA was Full Professor at the Department of Social and Organizational Psychology, ISCTE, Lisbon. Currently, he is a Researcher at the Instituto de Ciências Sociais, University of Lisbon. He has published papers on social representations and intergroup relations, namely in organizational and political domains and in the field of immigration issues. His current research focuses on racist beliefs, social norms, and social justice, and on processes of social validation of everyday knowledge.

DINIZ LOPES obtained his PhD from the Department of Social and Organizational Psychology, ISCTE, Lisbon, where he is an Assistant Professor. His research interests cover not only intergroup relations and conflicts but also the mechanisms used by people to validate their everyday knowledge and how these mechanisms interplay with other social psychological phenomena, such as social influence, information processing, and persuasion.

MARCUS LIMA studied at the Federal University of João Pessoa and obtained his PhD in Psychology at ISCTE, Lisbon. Currently, he is an Associate Professor at the Federal University of Sergipe, Brazil. He has authored papers on stereotypes, prejudice, and discrimination. He currently develops research on social norms and racist prejudice against Black people and Indians in Brazil.

Postconflict Reconciliation: Intergroup Forgiveness and Implicit Biases in Northern Ireland

Tania Tam[*]
Legal Services Research Centre

Miles Hewstone
University of Oxford

Jared B. Kenworthy
University of Texas at Arlington

Ed Cairns
University of Ulster

Claudia Marinetti, Leo Geddes, and Brian Parkinson
University of Oxford

Even after a conflict has formally ended, there is still a need for postconflict reconciliation and the building of mutual forgiveness and trust between communities. This article addresses psychological processes crucial to moving beyond a history of violent sectarian conflict in Northern Ireland. We investigated the predictors of intergroup forgiveness, in terms of intergroup emotions, infrahumanization, empathy, and intergroup contact. Intergroup trust and measures of implicit intergroup bias were also explored in this area of real intergroup conflict. The results are discussed in terms of their implications for postconflict reconciliation in Northern Ireland and other conflict areas.

---

[*]Correspondence concerning this article should be addressed to Dr. Tania Tam, Legal Services Research Centre, 85 Grays Inn Road, London WC1X 8TX [e-mail: tania.tam@legalservices.gov.uk].

We wish to acknowledge the Templeton Foundation, the Russell Sage Foundation, the Community Relations Unit in Northern Ireland, and the Economic and Social Research Council for their research support.

Distinctly psychological components, such as strong group identities and perceptions of dehumanized enemies, are prevalent in sectarian conflicts such as the one in Northern Ireland. These psychological aspects of conflict perpetuate the sectarian violence—even long after the initial, more objective causes of conflict have been resolved. After the violence itself has ceased, there is still a need for postconflict reconciliation and the building of mutual forgiveness and trust between communities.

Although the Northern Irish peace process has recently met with great success—militant sectarian groups have disarmed, and democratic self-government has been reestablished in the region—still, the conflict's impact on the psychology of individuals persists. Segregation between Catholics and Protestants remains embedded in society—residentially as well as in friendships and marriages, and in the educational system: Over 90% of children in Northern Ireland attend either a Catholic or a Protestant school (Integrated Education Fund Research, 2007). Effective means of dealing with these less-visible consequences of violent conflict must be developed. Correspondingly, research must not only focus solely on mitigating detrimental intergroup relations, but also on developing reconciliation and building positive intergroup relations after the formal conflict ends. Violent aspects of conflict may capture attention; however, developing strategies to sustain the peace after the end of a conflict are also necessary.

Political analysts, policymakers, and official documents such as the Belfast, or "Good Friday," Agreement often make assumptions about psychological processes—for instance, when they talk about group behaviors, intentions, or feelings of fear and anger toward the other group. Such assumptions can be critically assessed with empirical psychological analyses (Kelman, 1997). For example, one of the aims of the Belfast Agreement was to create an "inclusive society," in which people would "firmly dedicate [themselves] to the achievement of reconciliation, tolerance, and mutual trust" (The Belfast, or "Good Friday," Agreement, 1998). This article addresses psychological processes underpinning these variables. An understanding of the sectarian history of the Northern Irish conflict, and strong sense of segregation between Catholics and Protestants, provides a basis for examining these psychological processes.

Since 1969, over 3,700 people have been killed and over 35,000 injured as a direct result of sectarian violence in Northern Ireland (Smyth & Hamilton, 2003). This is a considerable number, considering that the total population of Northern Ireland is only 1.7 million living in just 32,000 square miles (Northern Ireland Statistics and Research Agency, 2005). About 44% of the Northern Irish population is Catholic, and many believe the North of Ireland should leave the United Kingdom and become part of the Republic of Ireland. About 53% is Protestant, and most want to remain a part of the United Kingdom (Northern Ireland Statistics and Research Agency, 2005). More than half the Northern Irish population knows someone who was injured or killed in "the Troubles" (Smyth & Hamilton, 2003).

Religious polarization continues to be so strong that vital aspects of life (e.g., areas of residence, schools, shops, political parties, sports, cultural activities, places of worship, first and last names) can be identified as either being Catholic or Protestant (Hargie & Dickinson, 2003). Despite resolution of a range of economic and social issues (such as differential employment, education, and housing for Catholics and Protestants), division is still highly symbolic and psychologically real, and the conflict pervades the everyday lives of people in the area.

Moving beyond a history of violent sectarianism is crucial for postconflict reconciliation in Northern Ireland. We investigate the psychological processes involved in (a) forgiving the other community for past wrongdoing, and (b) coming to trust the other side in Northern Ireland, and we examine (c) the implicit intergroup biases that may persist long after a conflict has been formally resolved. In this article, we pay particular attention to positive human mechanisms such as empathy and emotions that allow people to overcome automatic negative biases in favor of own group members and against out-group members. Positive emotions elicited in human interactions can play a powerful role in intergroup relations (e.g., curiosity and respect), although they have received far less attention in intergroup research than negative emotions (e.g., fear and hate; Tam et al., 2008). We will examine both sorts of emotions in this article.

Intergroup Forgiveness

Intergroup forgiveness has been demonstrated in world affairs in the form of public apologies (e.g., Bill Clinton's apology for America's failure to act during the Rwandan genocide in 1998) and truth commissions (e.g., the Truth and Reconciliation Commission in South Africa). Forgiveness may indeed be necessary for reconciliation (Staub, 2001). However, as intergroup bias is a pervasive phenomenon, present at public and private, implicit and explicit levels (see Hewstone, Rubin, & Willis, 2002), we should not be surprised to find evidence that "we" are reluctant to forgive "them." One interesting question for psychology is to understand how or why certain individuals are able to forgive past wrongs and break the cycles of revenge that typically escalate intergroup conflict.

McLernon, Cairns, and Hewstone (2002) conducted a series of focus groups with people from organizations devoted to reducing conflicts, ex-paramilitary group members, and victims themselves, to elucidate the concept of *intergroup forgiveness* in Northern Ireland. Most agreed that it was easier to forgive an individual than a group because it was easier to trust an individual than each member of the other community. Victims were hostile to the idea of forgiveness and viewed it as justifying the wrongs done to them. Ex-members of paramilitary groups were similarly hostile; they felt their acts were justified at the time and that they did not need to ask for, or offer, forgiveness. All groups stressed that attempting to impose intergroup forgiveness was likely to be counterproductive, but that an act of remembrance such as building a monument might give people the opportunity to share the loss and make forgiving easier.

Survey research (using students and representative samples) and experimental studies (using student participants) showed that while religiosity was a weak predictor of forgiveness, identification with one's religious group and attitudes toward the other community were strong predictors of forgiveness (Cairns, Hewstone, Niens, & Tam, 2005). Intergroup forgiveness is therefore linked to lower levels of prejudice, whereas its ties to measures of religiosity are quite weak. In Northern Ireland the conflict is not about theology; rather, as Belfrage (1987) puts it, "religion is more a badge of identification to distinguish between two traditions, two tribal identities, two perspectives on the past, two views of cultural superiority, two mindsets about the border dividing Ireland, and two kinds of fear" (p. ix).

Our recent research further investigates psychological processes that lead to feelings of forgiveness toward the out-group, and ultimately to reconciliation. From the focus groups conducted by McLernon et al. (2002), we constructed a scale of intergroup forgiveness (including items such as "Only when the two communities of Northern Ireland learn to forgive each other can we be free of political violence"; "Northern Ireland will never move from the past to the future until the two communities learn to forget about the past"; Cronbach's alpha = .69; for full scale see Hewstone et al., 2004; Hewstone, Cairns, Voci, Hamberger, & Niens, 2006). We then examined intergroup forgiveness in a sample of Northern Irish students, and its relationship to empathy and a range of intergroup emotions—both positive and negative (Tam et al., 2007). We also assessed the links between intergroup forgiveness and infrahumanization, which involves seeing out-group members as less human than in-group members.

Intergroup Emotions

Relations between groups often involve a mix of emotions. An understanding of these emotions is important because it allows us to predict people's specific behavioral tendencies toward out-groups (Mackie, Devos, & Smith, 2000). Although fear and anger are both negative emotions, they are empirically distinct and provoke different intergroup behaviors: fear predicts avoidant behavioral tendencies, while anger predicts aggressive behavioral tendencies against the out-group (Devos, Silver, Mackie, & Smith, 2002). In our exploration of psychological processes involved in postconflict reconciliation, we examine the value of intergroup emotions for predicting intergroup forgiveness. Our recent studies have shown that positive and negative intergroup emotions make independent contributions to the explanation of variance in behavioral tendencies in Northern Ireland, and they are both significant mediators of the effects of intergroup contact on behavioral tendencies (Tam et al., 2008). That is, contact works, in part, because it increases positive intergroup emotions as well as reduces negative emotions. We assessed the impact of a range of positive emotions as well as negative ones, in our investigation of intergroup forgiveness.

Forgiveness is considered an emotional process that involves ceasing to feel angry or resentful over the transgression (Baumeister, Exline, & Sommers, 1998; Harber & Wenberg, 2005). In a study of a forgiveness intervention, the confrontation of anger, which involves releasing and not harboring the anger, leads to cognitive insights and forms the bases for forgiving a previous abuser. According to Baumeister et al. (1998) "to forgive someone means to cease feeling angry or resentful over the transgression" (p. 85). Confronting hostile emotions, in fact, precedes subsequent cognitive shifts that solidify forgiveness (Freedman & Enright, 1996). Thus, we expected a strong negative relation between anger and intergroup forgiveness.

To investigate the predictors of intergroup forgiveness, we surveyed 61 Catholic and 36 Protestant students in Northern Ireland, and asked them how they felt when they thought about members of the other community. Students are an especially interesting group of respondents to look at in Northern Ireland because for many of them attending a desegregated university after a vast majority of them had attended schools with either no members of the other religion or a massive in-group majority is their first experience of mixing with members of the other group. Participants rated (on a scale of 1–7) how much they felt positive intergroup emotions (e.g., cheerful, pleasant) and negative emotions such as anger (e.g., angry, furious) and fear (e.g., nervous, anxious), and we examined these emotions as potential predictors of forgiveness.

A factor analysis confirmed that anger, fear, and positive emotions were distinctly separate intergroup emotions. Moreover, anger, fear, and positive emotions differentially predicted forgiveness of the out-group for past wrongdoing. Preliminary correlational analyses (see Table 1) revealed that anger was negatively correlated with forgiveness, $r = -.40, p < .001$. However, neither feelings of fear nor positive emotion correlated with forgiveness, $r = -.16$ and $r = .15$, both ns. In other words, it is neither necessary for people to feel good about the other community in order to forgive them, nor does fearing them necessarily imply a lack of forgiveness. But people who feel angry do not forgive.

Infrahumanization

Intergroup forgiveness may also be related to a tendency automatically to see out-group members as less human than in-group members—infrahumanization (Leyens et al., 2001). Research has shown that people tend to ascribe an inherent "essence" (whether it be biological, cultural, religious, etc.) to social groups to explain their differences. In-groups, endowed with the human essence, are seen as superior, while out-groups are perceived as "infrahumans" (Leyens et al., 2001). Leyens and his colleagues suggest that this form of bias leads to

Table 1. Correlation Matrix of Infrahumanization, Intergroup Emotions, Empathy, and Forgiveness

	Contact	Infrahumanization (Differential Attribution of Secondary) Emotions	Differential Attribution of Primary Emotions	Anger	Fear	Positive Emotions	Empathy	Forgiveness
Contact	—	−.20*	−.10	−.26*	−.20*	.32**	.22*	.12
Infrahumanization		—	−.29**	.12	−.08	−.18	−.20*	−.22*
(differential attribution of secondary emotions)								
Differential attribution of primary emotions			—	.15	.15	.04	−.02	−.08
Anger				—	.72***	−.17	−.42***	−.40***
Fear					—	−.13	−.18	−.16
Positive emotions						—	.22*	.15
Empathy							—	.44***

Note. $^*p < .05$; $^{**}p < .01$; $^{***}p < .001$.

"moral exclusion" (Opotow, 1990), such as the Nazis regarding Jews as subhuman "beasts."

Infrahumanization has been demonstrated in multiple groups with a history of mild conflict (e.g., Flemish-speaking vs. French-speaking Belgians; Leyens et al., 2001). Leyens and his collaborators have shown that people perceive what emotion researchers (e.g., Ekman, 1992) call secondary emotions (e.g., nostalgia, guilt) as more unique to humans than primary emotions (e.g., anger, pleasure), which may also be attributed to animals. Our study of intergroup emotions and forgiveness also examined the differential attribution of secondary and primary emotions in Northern Ireland, and our results provided evidence of Leyens et al.'s concept of infrahumanization in this area with a history of extreme conflict.

We assessed infrahumanization with two checklists of 42 emotions pretested and established in previous research (Demoulin et al., 2004; Leyens et al., 2001). We asked participants to mark (a) the words that they believed to be typical of the other community (out-group) in one list, and (b) the words that they believed to be typical of their own community (in-group) in the other list. Composite scores for the number of primary and secondary emotions attributed to the in-group and out-group were computed for each participant by combining the number of selected emotions. To control for the number of emotions selected in general, proportion scores were calculated such that each composite score was divided by the total number of emotions selected. We also controlled for valence of emotions.

Results showed that participants attributed significantly more secondary (uniquely human) emotions (e.g., nostalgia, guilt) to the in-group than to the out-group, $t(96) = 3.87, p < .001$, establishing infrahumanization as a feature of sectarianism. Moreover, infrahumanization was strongly negatively related to forgiveness ($r = -.22, N = 97, p < .05$). A measure of the differential attribution of primary emotions (less uniquely human emotions that may also be attributed to animals: e.g., anger, pleasure) showed that it was the differential attribution of secondary and not primary emotions, or the valence of emotions, that was driving intergroup bias in our sample. Unlike infrahumanization, the differential attribution of primary emotions was unrelated to intergroup forgiveness and empathy (see Table 1).

Empathy

Empathizing with a member of an out-group has been shown to lead to reductions in bias against the group as a whole (Batson, Polycarpou, Harmon-Jones, & Imhoff, 1997) and also encourages people to behave in a more supportive way toward others, independent of how much they like them (Batson & Shaw, 1991). Our recent studies have revealed empathy to be a crucial mediator of the influence of cross-community contact on behavioral tendencies toward the out-group in Northern Ireland (Tam et al., 2008). That is, contact is associated with more positive behavioral tendencies toward members of the other community because it enhances empathy with them. The literature on interpersonal relationships has also documented the powerful effects of empathy on forgiveness (McCullough, Worthington, & Rachal, 1997); coming to empathize with a past transgressor is, in fact, a crucial part of forgiveness interventions (Worthington, 1998).

In our survey, we examined empathy as another variable that may promote outgroup forgiveness. We adapted items from Davis' (1994) scale to provide a measure of empathy toward the out-group in Northern Ireland, and asked participants to rate two items, "I often feel very sorry for people from the other community when they are having problems" and "When I see someone from the other community being treated unfairly, I sometimes don't feel very much pity for them" (reverse coded), on a scale of 1–4 (1 = *never*, 4 = *often*; Cronbach's alpha = .69). As predicted, empathy was strongly positively correlated with forgiveness ($r = .44$, $p < .001$) (see Table 1).

What Can be Done to Promote Intergroup Forgiveness in Northern Ireland?

For postconflict societies such as Northern Ireland, an understanding of the factors that promote intergroup harmony—in addition to diminishing conflict and intergroup violence—is imperative. One of the keys for positive intergroup relations is positive, cooperative intergroup contact. Researchers have found that positive interaction between members of different groups can reduce intergroup prejudice and hostility (Allport, 1954; Pettigrew, 1998), and these findings have been claimed as social science's major contribution to reducing intergroup bias and conflict (Gaertner, Dovidio, & Bachman, 1996). Although the Northern Irish peace progress was set in motion with the Belfast Agreement, Northern Irish society remains heavily segregated (see Cairns & Hewstone, 2002; Gallagher, 2003).

We propose intergroup contact as a possible means of lessening anger toward the out-group, seeing them as more human, and promoting empathy toward them— the variables we have shown are associated with intergroup forgiveness. In our survey, we asked Northern Irish citizens how much contact they had with the other community, and how pleasant they found that contact, to assess both quantity and quality of their contact experiences. To create an index of frequent, positive contact, we multiplied quantity and quality of contact.

A path model summarized our findings (see Figure 1). The tested model fit the data well. $\chi^2 (3, N = 97) = 2.76, p = .43$; root mean square error of approximation (RMSEA) = .00; standardized root mean square residual (SRMR) = .048; Comparative Fit Index (CFI) = 1.00. A good fit is indicated by a nonsignificant chi-square test, an RMSEA of less than .06, an SRMR of less than .08, and a CFI value greater than .95 (Hu & Bentler, 1999). Contact predicted the three variables we identified in the promotion of forgiveness: decreased anger and infrahumanization, and increased empathy. Anger felt toward the other community and the denial of human emotions to the other community (infrahumanization) impede

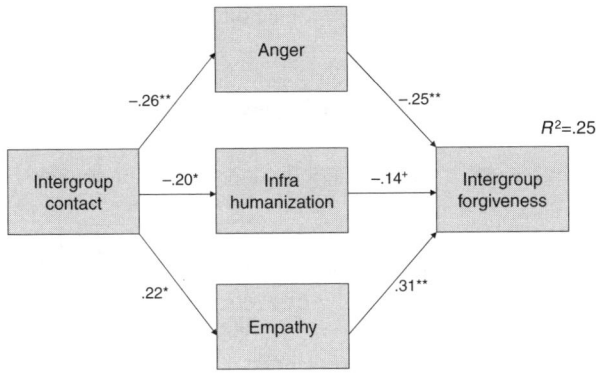

Additional correlation: Anger – Empathy: −.39.
*$p < .05$; **$p < .01$; $^+p = .11$

Fig. 1. Path model of the predictors of intergroup forgiveness.

forgiveness. In contrast, empathy felt toward the other community promotes forgiveness. These findings suggest that contact is a means of influencing all three variables, decreasing anger and infra-humanization while increasing empathy. Reduced anger and increased empathy, in turn, predict intergroup forgiveness.[1] Together these variables explained 25% of the variance in forgiveness. Given the limitations of a cross-sectional study with a small sample size, the results from this survey suggest a demonstration rather than a conclusive test of the validity of this model. However, alternative models and prior research (e.g., Batson et al., 1997; Mackie et al., 2000; Vaes, Paladino, Castelli, Leyens, & Giovanazzi, 2003) suggest the directions of causality depicted in the model. Our recent research also shows that even when respondents have positive attitudes toward the other community, anger and infrahumanization still determine whether or not they forgive the other community (Tam, et al., 2007).

Building trust between communities is another vital component of postconflict reconciliation in conflict societies. Trust can be defined as a psychological means to overcome uncertain social interactions by making benign assumptions about other people's behavior (Kollock, 1994), and it is a prosocial facilitator when conflict exists between groups. A central component of intergroup conflict is distrust. But who exactly are the recipients of forgiveness or distrust in an intergroup setting? Our focus groups' findings suggest that, not surprisingly, extremist sectarian groups from the other community come to mind when people consider forgiving the out-group for the hurt they have caused the in-group, or similarly distrusting

---

[1] Although infrahumanization was correlated with intergroup forgiveness ($r = .22, p < .05$), controlling for the other variables in the model, infrahumanization was no longer a significant predictor of the forgiveness ($\beta = .14, p = .11$).

them (McLernon et al., 2002). We investigate intergroup forgiveness, distrust, and implicit biases in a separate study.

Implicit Biases

We examined Northern Irish Catholic and Protestant students' implicit associations not only with the group labels *Catholics* and *Protestants*, but also with Catholic and Protestant militant sectarian groups (e.g., IRA, UVF, UFF). We expected, first of all, that these implicit associations would differ according to whether the students were Catholic or Protestant themselves—that is, rating perceived in-group or out-group targets. Second, we investigated how these two forms of implicit biases related to forgiveness, distrust, and behavioral tendencies toward out-group members. We examined these concepts in a study of 59 students (35 Catholics and 24 Protestants) in a large Northern Irish university. We used a similar measure of intergroup forgiveness to the one used in our first study (Cronbach's alpha = .61), and we assessed intergroup distrust with a four-item scale (e.g., "I can't trust politicians from the other community to act fairly in the interests of everyone," "I can't trust them because they want revenge for things we have done to them"; Cronbach's alpha = .79).

Implicit measures differ from self-report measures in that they reflect thoughts and feelings that operate outside of conscious awareness (Greenwald, McGhee, & Schwartz, 1998). They reveal unintentional bias, of which those who consider themselves unprejudiced may be largely unaware (Dovidio, Kawakami, & Gaertner, 2002). Implicit measures of attitudes have been shown to predict spontaneous nonverbal behaviors, while explicit measures of attitude predict more deliberative and controlled behaviors toward out-groups (Chen & Bargh, 1997; Dovidio et al., 2002). Both are therefore important for investigation in Northern Ireland. Moreover, even though explicit conscious attitudes may be positive toward outgroup members, implicit attitudes may not be—especially in areas with residual tensions from the conflict.

We employed the Implicit Association Test (IAT) (Greenwald et al., 1998), a widely used assessment tool, to measure the degree to which people automatically associated images of Catholic and Protestant extremist sectarian groups (e.g., IRA, UVF, UFF; images obtained from the CAIN website, www.cain.ulster.ac.uk) with positive and negative words (e.g., rainbow or ugly). Participants' response times, recorded by a computer, provided the measure of implicit group evaluation. We compared the Extremist Sectarian IAT scores with results of a standard Catholic-Protestant IAT, which measured the degree to which people associated Catholic names (e.g., Patrick, Maire) and Protestant names (e.g., Robert, Jane) with positive and negative words (e.g., rainbow, ugly).

To assess explicit prejudice, we employed a standard feeling thermometer (Haddock, Zanna, & Esses, 1993): Northern Irish citizens were asked to rate the degree to which they felt "cold" or "warm" on a scale of 0° to 100° for Catholics,

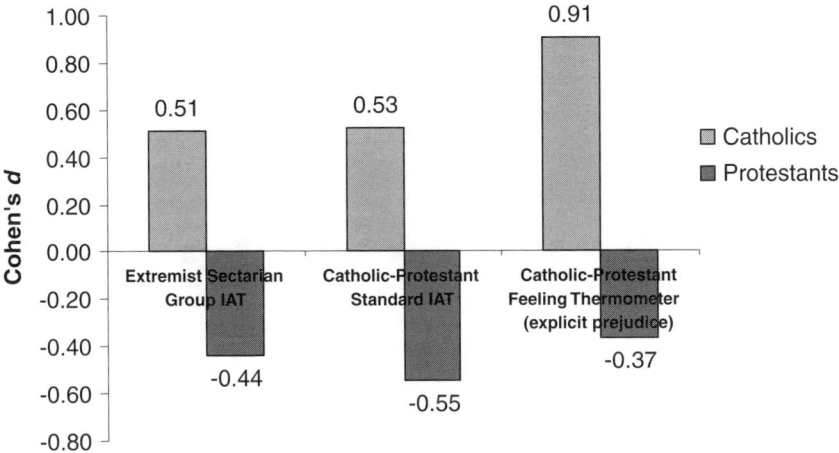

Note: Positive Cohen's *d*s indicate more positive associations with Catholic sides, and negative Cohen's *d*s indicate more positive associations with Protestant sides.

Fig. 2. Results of implicit (IAT) and explicit (feeling thermometer) measures of prejudice.

and for Protestants, on separate counterbalanced scales. Figure 2 shows the results of the implicit and explicit measures; Catholics and Protestants clearly displayed relative in-group–out-group bias on both implicit and explicit levels. Catholics and Protestants showed similar levels of implicit bias toward their own communities; however, Catholics showed higher levels of implicit bias in favor of Catholic extremist sectarian groups (and against Protestant ones) as well as higher levels of explicit bias than Protestants did.

Brewer (1999) pointed out that a positive attitude toward the in-group does not necessarily imply a negative one toward the out-group. In-group favoritism and out-group derogation are orthogonal concepts. However, because the IAT does not allow for separation of these concepts (Catholic-Good is always linked to Protestant-Bad in the IAT), we used the go-no-go-association-task (GNAT) and had the same respondents complete this additional implicit measure to investigate separately implicit in-group favoritism (Catholic-Good vs. Protestant-Good) and out-group derogation (Catholic-Bad vs. Protestant-Bad) separately. For the GNAT, participants were instructed to respond quickly to items that fall into one of the categories (e.g., "Catholic name" or "Good") by pressing the space bar but to ignore any item that did not fit either category. The GNAT determines statistical performance using signal detection theory's estimate of sensitivity, d' (Green & Swets, 1966), and results showed that Catholics and Protestants displayed both in-group favoritism and out-group derogation on the implicit level (see Figure 3).

Further analyses revealed that implicit associations with extremist sectarian groups in particular (as opposed to the out-group in general) were related to

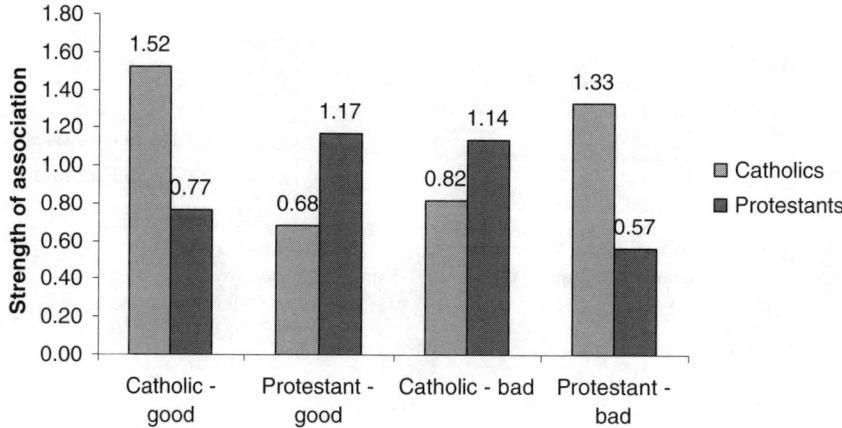

Fig. 3. Catholic and Protestant in-group favoritism and out-group derogation as shown by the GNAT measure.

Table 2. Correlation Matrix for Implicit and Explicit Measure

	Forgiveness	Distrust	Aggressive Behavioral Tendencies	Avoidant Behavioral Tendencies	Explicit Prejudice
IAT scores: negative associations with out-group extremist groups	−.24[++]	.33*	.42**	.22[+]	.24[++]
IAT scores: negative associations with out-group in general	−.06	.17	.08	.04	.16
GNAT scores: in-group favoritism	.05	−.15	.04	−.06	−.19
GNAT scores: out-group derogation	.12	−.11	.24	.15	.06

Note. * $p < .05$; ** $p < .01$; [+]$p = .10$; [++]$p = .08$; [+++]$p = .07$.

intergroup outcomes, in terms of trust, forgiveness, and behavioral tendencies (see Table 2). The extremist group IAT predicted several intergroup measures that the Catholic–Protestant IAT did not: Negative associations with the out-group extremists were associated with decreased forgiveness toward the other community ($r = -.24, N = 56, p = .07$) and increased distrust toward them ($r = .33, p < .02$). Interestingly, while negative associations with out-group extremists were strongly related to aggressive behavioral tendencies toward the other community ($r = .42$.

$p = .001$) (e.g., argue with them, confront them), they were only marginally related to avoidant behavioral tendencies ($r = .22, p = .10$) (e.g., avoid them, keep them at a distance). Negative associations with the out-group in general (measured by the IAT) were not associated with these three variables ($r = -.17, r = -.04, r = .08$, all ns), or were the GNAT measures of in-group favoritism and out-group derogation toward the out-group in general. We therefore concluded that implicit associations with the extremist groups from the other community were distinct markers of intergroup distrust, aggressive behavioral tendencies, and a lack of forgiveness.

Little research has examined the relationships between extremist groups and intergroup relations in general, although there is a clear link between the two, especially in relation to intergroup forgiveness, distrust, and aggression. A closer examination of these relationships is warranted.

Conclusion

Forgiveness may play a key role in helping groups in conflict put the atrocities of the past behind them and is an integral part of the achievements of organizations such as the Northern Ireland Victims Commission (see Bloomfield, 1998). In this article, we have explored the concept of *intergroup forgiveness* and identified some of its key correlates. Results from the first study reveal that distinct intergroup emotions predict forgiveness. The specific emotion of *anger* (but not fear or positive emotions) was highly correlated with a lack of forgiveness. Infrahumanization (the denial of human emotions to the out-group) and empathy moreover explained further variance in forgiveness, in the predicted directions. More important, our data revealed one key to lessening anger and infrahumanization while simultaneously enhancing empathy—intergroup contact. These results add to the weight of studies that demonstrate the vital role contact plays in the amelioration of conflict in this segregated society (see Hewstone et al., 2004, for a review).

Psychological theories of intergroup relations have moved from examinations of blatant prejudice and discrimination to more differentiated assessments of intergroup bias. Our research revealed that negative implicit associations with out-group extremist groups are particularly powerful in predicting decreased intergroup forgiveness, distrust, and aggressive behavioral tendencies against the out-group in general. This raises theoretical questions about the nature of intergroup relations and cross-community conflict and suggests that postconflict reconciliation involves specific fears and associations with extremist groups rather than with the out-group in general. Interventions to build more positive intergroup relations need to take these particular concerns into account. We suggest that future studies examine not only in-group–out-group bias but also thoughts and impressions of in-group–out-group extremist groups, on the explicit as well as the implicit level.

The work presented here represents initial efforts to examine psychological processes involved in postconflict reconciliation and as such is subject to limitations. One limitation is the cross-sectional nature of our studies, which makes it impossible to determine the direction of causality in our model. A second limitation is the relatively small sample sizes utilized (however, we have obtained comparable results in other research using larger samples of students and even representative samples; see, e.g., Hewstone et al., 2006; Paolini, Hewstone, Cairns, & Voci, 2004). Future research may use the underlying theory and these empirical findings as a springboard to further explore the links among forgiveness, trust, intergroup emotions, behavioral intentions, and implicit biases.

Although outsiders to the conflict may view intergroup forgiveness and trust as the way forward for the rebuilding of a postconflict society, focus groups have shown that those most personally involved in the conflict (e.g., paramilitary group members and victims of the conflict) may not necessarily agree (McLernon et al., 2002). Indeed, any attempts to impose forgiveness or trust on groups may be ineffective and may even backfire. It is therefore important to examine the predictors of forgiveness, trust, and behavioral tendencies toward the out-group to illuminate the psychological processes that may improve intergroup relations without direct impositions. Having contact with members of the other community helps to achieve this without forcing positive relations.

We have presented a range of measures of prejudice in Northern Ireland beyond the assessment of simple intergroup attitudes—from intergroup forgiveness to differentiated intergroup emotions, infrahumanization, and empathy, to distrust and implicit associations. Such measures are crucial for understanding the conflict. Attitudes are changing in Northern Ireland. Politicians who some years ago would not even speak to each other or even sit in the same room now cooperate and share power in government. The examination of simple attitudes cannot account for such differentiated intergroup behaviors—therefore, an array of measures of sectarian bias is necessary to provide a more differentiated and nuanced understanding of intergroup relations.

In this article, we have revealed an array of such measures, which not only apply to Northern Ireland but also to intergroup conflicts in other areas. The same principles may pertain to a wide variety of intergroup conflicts between Catholics and Protestants in Northern Ireland, ethnic or racial groups, or nations. We hope that this research can serve as a base for further theory-driven empirical work in the amelioration not only of intergroup conflict, but also of postconflict animosity, and aid efforts in reconciliation.

References

Allport, G. W. (1954). *The nature of prejudice*. Oxford, UK: Addison-Wesley.
Batson, C., & Shaw, L. L. (1991). Evidence for altruism: Toward a pluralism of prosocial motives. *Psychological Inquiry, 2*, 107–122.

Batson, C., Polycarpou, M. P., Harmon-Jones, E., & Imhoff, H. J. (1997). Empathy and attitudes: Can feeling for a member of a stigmatized group improve feelings toward the group? *Journal of Personality and Social Psychology, 72*, 105–118.

Baumeister, R., Exline, J. J., & Sommer, K. L. (1998). The victim role, grudge theory, and two dimensions of forgiveness. In E. L. Worthington (Ed.), *Dimensions of forgiveness: Psychology research and theoretical perspectives* (pp. 79–104). Philadelphia: Templeton Foundation Press.

Belfrage, S. (1987). *Living with war: A Belfast year*. London: Penguin Books.

Bloomfield, K. (1998). *"We will remember them: Report of the Northern Ireland Victims Commissioner, Sir Kenneth Bloomfield, KCB (April 1998)"*. Belfast, Ireland: The Stationery Office Northern Ireland.

Brewer, M. B. (1999). The psychology of prejudice: Ingroup love or outgroup hate? *Journal of Social Issues, 55*, 429–444.

Cairns, E., & Hewstone, M. (2002). Northern Ireland: The impact of peacemaking in Northern Ireland on intergroup behavior. In B. Neov & G. Salomon (Eds.), *Peace education: The concept, principles and practices around the world* (pp. 217–228). Hilldale, NJ: Lawrence Erlbaum Associates.

Cairns, E., Hewstone, M., Niens, U., & Tam, T. (2005). Intergroup forgiveness and intergroup conflict: Northern Ireland, a case study. In E. L. Worthington (Ed.), *Handbook of forgiveness* (pp. 461–476). New York: Brunner-Routledge.

Chen, M., & Bargh, J. A. (1997). Nonconscious behavioral confirmation processes: The self-fulfilling consequences of automatic stereotype activation. *Journal of Experimental Social Psychology, 33*, 541–560.

Davis, M. H. (1994). *Empathy: A social psychological approach*. Boulder, CO: Westview Press.

Demoulin, S., Leyens, J. P., Paladino, M. P., Rodriguez, R. T., Rodriguez, A. P., & Dovidio, J. F. (2004). Dimensions of "uniquely" and "non-uniquely" human emotions. *Cognition and Emotion, 18*, 71–96.

Devos, T., Silver, L. A., Mackie, D. M., & Smith, E. R. (2002). Experiencing intergroup emotions. In D. M. Mackie & E. R. Smith (Eds.), *From prejudice to intergroup emotions* (pp. 111–134). New York: Taylor & Francis.

Dovidio, J. F., Kawakami, K., & Gaertner, S. L. (2002). Implicit and explicit prejudice and interracial interaction. *Journal of Personality and Social Psychology, 82*, 62–68.

Ekman, P. (1992). Are there basic emotions? *Psychological Review, 99*, 550–553.

Freedman, S. R., & Enright, R. D. (1996). Forgiveness as an intervention goal with incest survivors. *Journal of Consulting and Clinical Psychology, 64*, 983–992.

Gaertner, S. L., Dovidio, J. F., & Bachman, B. A. (1996). Revisiting the contact hypothesis: The induction of a common ingroup identity. *International Journal of Intercultural Relations, 20*, 271–290.

Gallagher, T. (2003). Education and equality in Northern Ireland. In O. Hargie & D. Dickson (Eds.), *Researching the troubles: Social science perspectives on the Northern Ireland conflict* (pp. 59–84). Edinburgh: Mainstream Publishing.

Green, D. M., & Swets, J. A. (1966). *Signal detection theory and psychophysics*. Oxford, UK: Wiley.

Greenwald, A. G., McGhee, D. E., & Schwartz, J. L. K. (1998). Measuring individual differences in implicit cognition: The implicit association test. *Journal of Personality and Social Psychology, 74*, 1464–1480.

Haddock, G., Zanna, M. P., & Esses, V. M. (1993). Assessing the structure of prejudicial attitudes: The case of attitudes towards homosexuals. *Journal of Personality and Social Psychology, 65*, 1105–1118.

Harber, K.D., & Wenberg, K. (2005). Disclosure and closeness towards offenders. *Personality and Social Psychology Bulletin, 31*, 734–746.

Hargie, O., & Dickson, D. (2003). *Researching the troubles: Social science perspectives on the Northern Ireland conflict*. Edinburgh: Mainstream Publishing.

Hewstone, M., Rubin, M., & Willis, H. E. (2002). Intergroup bias. *Annual Review of Psychology, 53*, 575–604.

Hewstone, M., Cairns, E., Voci, A., McLernon, F., Niens, U., & Noor, M. (2004). Intergroup forgiveness and guilt in Northern Ireland: Social psychological dimensions of "The Troubles". In N. R. Branscombe & B. Doosje (Eds.), *Collective guilt: International perspectives* (pp. 193–215). New York: Cambridge University Press.

Hewstone, M., Cairns, E., Voci, A., Crisp, R. J., Niens, U., & Craig, J. (2004). Intergroup contact in a divided society: Challenging segregation in Northern Ireland. In D. Abrams, J. M. Marques, & M. A. Hogg (Eds.), *The social psychology of inclusion and exclusion.* (pp. 265–291). New York: Psychology Press.

Hewstone, M., Cairns, E., Voci, A., Hamberger, J., & Niens, U. (2006). Intergroup contact, forgiveness, and experience of 'The Troubles' in Northern Ireland. *Journal of Social Issues, 62*, 99–120.

Hu, L., & Bentler, P. M. (1999). Cut-off criteria for fit indexes in covariance structure analysis: Conventional criteria versus new alternatives. *Structural Equation Modeling, 6*, 1–55.

Integrated Education Fund Research. (2007). http://www.ief.org.uk.

Kelman, H. C. (1997). Social-psychological dimensions of international conflict. In I. W. Zartman & J. L. Rasmussen (Eds.), *Peacemaking in international conflicts: Methods and techniques* (pp. 191–233). Herndon, VA: USIP Press.

Kollock, P. (1994). The emergence of exchange structures: An experimental study of uncertainty, commitment, and trust. *American Journal of Sociology, 100*, 313–345.

Leyens, J. P., Rodriguez-Perez, A., Rodriguez-Torres, R., Gaunt, R., Paladino, M. P., Vaes, J., & Demoulin, S. (2001). Psychological essentialism and the differential attribution of uniquely human emotions to ingroups and outgroups. *European Journal of Social Psychology, 31*, 395–411.

Mackie, D. M., Devos, T., & Smith, E. R. (2000). Intergroup emotions: Explaining offensive behavioral tendencies in an intergroup context. *Journal of Personality and Social Psychology, 79*, 602–616.

McCullough, M. E., Worthington, E. L., Jr., & Rachal, K. C. (1997). Interpersonal forgiving in close relationships. *Journal of Personality and Social Psychology, 73*, 321–336.

McLernon, F., Cairns, E., & Hewstone, M. (2002). Views on forgiveness in Northern Ireland. *Peace Review, 14*, 285–290.

Northern Ireland Statistics and Research Agency. (2005). *Government statistics website.* Retrieved September 1, 2005, from http://www.nisra.gov.uk/.

Opotow, S. (1990). Moral exclusion and injustice: An introduction. *Journal of Social Issues, 46*, 1–20.

Paolini, S., Hewstone, M., Cairns, E., & Voci, A. (2004). Effects of direct and indirect cross-group friendships on judgments of Catholics and Protestants in Northern Ireland: The mediating role of an anxiety-reduction mechanism. *Personality and Social Psychology Bulletin, 30*, 770–786.

Pettigrew, T. F. (1998). Intergroup contact theory. *Annual Review of Psychology, 49*, 65–85.

Smyth, M., & Hamilton, J. (2003). The human costs of the Troubles. In O. Hargie & D. Dickson (Eds.), *Researching the Troubles: Social science perspectives on the Northern Ireland conflict* (pp. 15–36). Edinburgh: Mainstream Publishing.

Staub, E. (2001). Individual and group identities in genocide and mass killing. In R. D. Ashmore, L. Jussim, & D. Wilder (Eds.), *Rutgers series on self and social identity: Vol. 3. Social identity, intergroup conflict, and conflict reduction* (pp. 159–184). New York: Oxford University Press.

Tam, T., Hewstone, M., Cairns, E., Tausch, N., Maio, G., & Kenworthy, J. (2007). The impact of intergroup emotions on forgiveness. *Group Processes and Intergroup Relations, 10*, 119–136.

Tam, T., Hewstone, M., Kenworthy, J., Voci, A., Cairns, E., & Van Dick, R. (2008). *Positive emotions in intergroup conflict? The mediational role of intergroup emotions and empathy in contact between Catholics and Protestants in Northern Ireland.* Unpublished manuscript.

Vaes, J., Paladino, M. P., Castelli, L., Leyens, J. P., & Giovanazzi, A. (2003). On the behavioral consequences of infra-humanization: The implicit role of uniquely human emotions in intergroup relations. *Journal of Personality and Social Psychology, 85*, 1016–1034.

Worthington, E. L., Jr. (1998). The pyramid model of forgiveness: Some interdisciplinary speculations about unforgiveness and the promotion of forgiveness. In J. E. L. Worthington (Ed.), *Dimensions of forgiveness: Psychology research and theoretical perspectives* (pp. 107–137). Philadelphia: Templeton.

TANIA TAM received her D Phil from the University of Oxford in 2005. Her research examined the role of emotions in intergroup interactions and explored more positive aspects of intergroup relations—hope, respect, admiration for outgroup members and approach behaviors toward them. She now conducts social exclusion and diversity, Internet, and memory research—among a number of other diverse projects—at the Legal Services Research Centre.

MILES HEWSTONE is Professor of Social Psychology and Fellow of New College at the University of Oxford. His current work centers on the reduction of intergroup conflict, via intergroup contact, stereotype change, and crossed categorization. He is a past recipient of the Presidents' Award for Distinguished Contributions to Psychological Knowledge (British Psychological Society, 2001), the Gordon Allport Intergroup Relations Prize (Society for the Psychological Study of Social Issues, 2005), and the Kurt Lewin Award for Distinguished Research Achievement (European Association for Experimental Social Psychology, 2005).

JARED KENWORTHY is an Assistant Professor of Psychology at the University of Texas at Arlington and is an expert in the psychological effect of conflict and threat, intergroup bias, intergroup contact, consensus estimation, and social projection. His latest publication is "Moderators and Mediators of Intergroup Contact", (with M. Hewstone, R. Turner, and A. Voci, in J. Dovidio, P. Glick, and L. Rudman (Eds.), *Reflecting on the Nature of Prejudice*. Blackwell, 2005).

ED CAIRNS is Professor of Psychology at the University of Ulster and has spent the last 30 years studying the psychological aspects of political violence in relation to the conflict in Northern Ireland. During this time he has been a visiting scholar at the Universities of Florida, Cape Town, and Melbourne. He is a Fellow of the British Psychological Society and of the American Psychological Association (APA) and Past President of the Division of Peace Psychology of the APA. He has published some 100 plus works including three books, the most recent of which was *The Role of Memory in Ethnic Conflict* (with Michael Roe, Palgrave Macmillan: London, New York, 2003).

CLAUDIA MARINETTI is a D Phil candidate at the Experimental Psychology Department of the University of Oxford. She has been working on the role of emotions in intergroup conflict since 2003, including projects on infrahumanization, intergroup contact, and group emotions. Her research is now focused on expression and experience of emotions in interpersonal contexts.

LEO GEDDES received an MSc in Research Methods in Psychology from the University of Oxford in 2004. He has since joined the British Foreign Office where he has worked in the Conflict Issues Group, focusing on Iraq. He is currently preparing for a posting to China.

BRIAN PARKINSON completed his undergraduate and postgraduate degrees at Manchester University, UK. Since then, his research has focused on the social and communicative aspects of emotion. His books include *Ideas and Realities of*

Emotion (1995), *Changing Moods* (with Totterdell, Briner, & Reynolds, 1996) and *Emotion in Social Relations* (with Fischer & Manstead, 2005). He is currently chief editor of the *British Journal of Social Psychology* and lectures in social psychology at Oxford University, UK.

Types of Identification and Intergroup Differentiation in the Russian Federation

Anca Minescu,* Louk Hagendoorn, and Edwin Poppe
Utrecht University

The fall of the Soviet Union affected the established identity patterns and intergroup relations in the Russian Federation. A survey investigates the effect of Russians' and titulars' identifications with their ethnic group, their republic, and the Russian Federation on intergroup stereotypes. We hypothesized that identification at various inclusiveness levels is differently reflected in the positive/negative stereotypes about in-group and out-groups. While in-group stereotypes would be positively affected by all types of identification, out-group stereotypes would turn more negative by ethnic identification and more positive by republican and federal identification. Further, we expected that republican identification would improve titulars' in-group stereotypes and Russians' out-group stereotypes, while federal identification would enhance Russians' in-group stereotypes and titular's out-group stereotypes. Russians favored their in-group mostly in positive terms. Titular minorities favored their in-group mostly on negative stereotypes. A model of intergroup differentiation is proposed that takes into account social identification at different inclusiveness levels. This model makes clear the potential threat posed by republican identifications to the stability of intergroup relations in Russia.

The disintegration of the Soviet Union in 1991 resulted in the independence of 14 borderland Union Republics from the Russian Federation (Hagendoorn, Linssen, & Tumanov, 2001). The complex administrative structure of the former Soviet state was designed to govern a mosaic of some 128 national, ethnic, and cultural groups (Tishkov, 1997). However, it did not eventually prevent the emergence of the nationalistic aspirations that contributed to its own demise. The same complex administrative system characterizes the remaining Russian Federation since 1991 (Brubaker, 1996; Hagendoorn et al., 2001; Laitin, 1998; Tishkov, 1997). This study focuses on the intergroup relations between the two main ethnic groups in

---

*Correspondence concerning this article should be addressed to Anca Minescu, ERCOMER, Department of Sociology, Faculty of Social Sciences, Utrecht University, PO Box 80140, 3508 TC Utrecht, The Netherlands [e-mail: A.Minescu@uu.nl].

autonomous republics of the Russian Federation, the Russians, and the so-called titulars, that is, the ethnic group after which the republic is named (e.g., Tatars in Tatarstan, Karelians in Karelia). The question is whether there is a lot of tension between the Russians and titulars and which factors affect the intergroup relations. First, we will discuss previous research on the intergroup situation in some former Soviet Union republics and then present new findings on the emerging identifications and intergroup differentiations of Russians and titulars in the Russian Federation.

Intergroup Polarization in Former Soviet Republics

The breakdown of the Soviet regime resulted in a reversal of the intergroup position of Russians and titulars in the newly independent republics bordering Russia. From a favored high-status dominant majority, Russians became the less powerful minority, while titulars, incited by nationalistic independence movements, fought themselves in higher-status positions (Laitin, 1998).

In previous research we focused on the intergroup relations in former Soviet republics by examining Russians' and titulars' national–ethnic identifications, their mutual stereotypes, and their negative intergroup stereotypes and attitudes (Hagendoorn, 1993; Hagendoorn, Drogendijk, Tumanov, & Hraba, 1998; Hagendoorn et al., 2001; Poppe & Hagendoorn, 2001; Poppe & Hagendoorn, 2003). Hagendoorn et al. (2001) used the term *intergroup polarization*, in a study among Russians and titulars in five former Soviet republics, to describe "the pattern of associations between the attachment to the national ingroup and the negative evaluations of national outgroups." One of the strongest negative correlations was found between national identification and an ethnic definition of citizenship by which out-groups are excluded. This shows one of the important factors leading to out-group exclusion: the denial of civic citizenship. National identification was also related to negative stereotypes of the out-group and positive stereotypes of the in-group. In addition, negative stereotypes appeared to be affected by perceived competition and relative deprivation, whereas positive in-group stereotypes were affected by speaking the in-group language and ethnic homogeneity of the family. These associations were further strengthened by perceived threats, such as the fear of an economic crisis, the possible disloyalty of the Russians, and the threat of Russian intervention (Hagendoorn et al., 2001). Hence, national identifications as well as perceived realistic causes of conflict and language and family composition affected the intergroup evaluations. At the aggregate level, the group attachments of one group appeared to affect those of the other group. For example, titulars seemed to have stronger feelings of national superiority if Russians identified stronger with the republic and felt more attached to it (republican patriotism). Similarly, Russians' feelings of national superiority were stronger in republics in which titulars had positive stereotypes of Russians. In other words, across republics, positive views of out-groups covaried with the feelings of superiority among these out-groups.

A further analysis showed that (national) identification is a multidimensional phenomenon, both Russians and titulars did not identify with just one group, but with several groups to different degrees. Besides ethnic and national identification, people simultaneously identified with their republic of residence and with the Russian Federation. This made clear that there are different patterns of identifications, reflecting ethnic segregation at the one extreme and civic integration at the other extreme (Poppe & Hagendoorn, 2001). Specific individual-level factors as well as aggregate factors relate to specific patterns of identification. If the Russians are better integrated in the republic, then their identification as Russians and as republican citizens were more strongly connected, and this was also true if the titulars were more accepting and less derogative of Russians. However, most of the aggregate-level effects on national identification could be explained by a differential distribution of individual-level factors, which shows that the aggregate-level effects are actually composition effects. For example, a larger Russian minority and a poor economic situation in the republics affected Russians' national identification through the effects they had on perceived ethnic competition (Poppe & Hagendoorn, 2003).

To sum up, it appears that there is a complex circular relationship between national identification, and the positive and negative stereotypes of the respective out-groups, stimulated by perceived intergroup competition and threat. This outcome is in certain respects counterintuitive. It would be expected that positive stereotypes about out-groups would always lead to better intergroup relations, but they seem to fuel the superiority feelings of the members of the out-groups. In return, feelings of national superiority fired negative intergroup reactions, especially if the identification with the superior in-group was strong and the competition from the out-group was feared.

In this article we will extend the analysis of how different types of identification are connected. We will do this on the basis of new data gathered in the Russian Federation in 1999 and 2000. We focus on the question of how intergroup polarization varies with respect to different types of identification. Additionally, given the crucial role played by intergroup competition as indicated above, we control for this factor in order to better identify the predictive power of identification types.

From the Republics of the Former Soviet Union to the Russian Federation

For the political elite of the Russian Federation, it is vital to prevent ethnic conflict and keep all the ethnic and national groups together in the federation. The republics of the Russian Federation have a multiethnic composition. The titular populations are an important demographic force in various parts of the Russian Federation; they are a demographic majority in 15 out of the 21 autonomous republics (Tishkov, 1997). Politically, this raises the question of defining "what is a Russian?" and "who is a Russian?" The answers differ from a titular, a Russian, and a federal nationalistic perspective (Tishkov, 1997). Russian national identity is an issue on which individuals as well as political administrators struggle. From this perspective it is obvious that a proper understanding of the intergroup differentiation in the Russian Federation has to start with an analysis of the relevant dimensions of the identifications of Russians and titulars.

The multinational Russian Federation has no tradition of civic principles and citizenship. In the Soviet era the common identity was the Soviet identity. Soviet people were perceived as united by the Russian language, a common ideology, and an interdependent economic and social infrastructure. The dissolution of the Soviet Union transferred the Soviet institutions to the new political elite of the Russian Federation, but the Russian Federation was the only one unit in the Soviet Union that lacked internal cohesion. Hence, the Russian Federation as a true federal state, based on civic rather than ethnic principles of national belonging, had to be built up from the beginning. It was a political entity that did not incite strong feelings of identity. By the same token, as a multiethnic system, the Russian Federation will only be able to survive if a federal identity overarches and includes the full variety of the different and potential conflicting ethnic identifications and thus prevents the resurgence of new national aspirations. Our analysis will focus on the potential of civic identifications that have to fulfill this role, that is, to improve the stereotypes of out-groups as well as of the in-group. To put it differently, the question is whether or not identifications at a higher level of inclusiveness (i.e., civic in contrast to ethnic, federal in contrast to republican) have the potential to reduce the intergroup polarization.

A Social–Psychological Approach to Intergroup Differentiation

We approach the question of the associations between different types of identifications and intergroup differentiation from the perspective of social identity theory (SIT) (Tajfel & Turner, 1986). Social identity theory poses that intergroup differentiation results not only from conflicts of interests, but also from the psychological need to positively distinguish one's group from others. In this view intergroup differentiation is dependent on the manner in which group members comparatively define their place (identity) in society in relation to other groups (Hogg & Abrams, 1990). Individuals' desire for positive self-evaluations may result in opinions, attitudes, and behaviors that will favor the in-group to the detriment of out-groups (Bourhis, Turner, & Gagnon, 1997). Within this frame of reference we pose the question: What are the consequences of social identifications at different levels of inclusiveness?

National identification is one of the most prevalent forms of social identity in contemporary societies (Billig, 1994). While national states usually hold the monopoly of violence and protection, national identification defines where individuals belong and which are the others that do not belong. After the collapse of the Soviet Union, the newly independent states including the remaining Russian Federation became contested domains. This implied that the solidarity and self-esteem found through belonging to social group shifted from higher to lower levels of inclusiveness, eventually locating the primordial feelings of identity in ethnic and national belonging (Hagendoorn et al., 2001). However, the identifications of the previous period did not immediately wither away and thus a system of "multiple, multi-layered, overlapping or embedded national, ethnic, civic or supra-national categories" remained of which the ultimate balance was yet unknown (Poppe & Hagendoorn, 2001, p. 59).

Types of Identification in the Context of the Russian Federation

In the Russian Federation, at least three types of politically significant social identifications are relevant for Russians and titulars: ethnic, republican, and federal identification. Along the inclusiveness dimension, the republican and the federal identifications are superordinate to the ethnic identification, whereas the republican identification is subordinate to the federal identification. The concept of *concentric loyalties* (Brewer, 1999) suitably captures Russians' and titulars' simultaneous membership in an ethnic group, within an autonomous republic, within the Russian Federation.

Ethnic identifications are at the forefront of public preoccupations in the Russian Federation because ethnonationalism is a threat to the unity of the federation and an important tool of political mobilization (Tishkov, 1997). In the autonomous republics, the numerical differences between the Russians and the titulars make republican identification an important political factor. The identification with the Russian Federation is the most encompassing type of identification, and this makes it an important tool for keeping the federation together. The Russians hold the demographic majority position within the Russian Federation while the autonomous republics are the strongholds of the non-Russian populations that bear their name. This intergroup situation implies that the titulars have a special affinity with the (superordinate) republican identification and that the Russians have a special affinity with the (superordinate) federal identification. These affinities and the implied claims of legitimacy may lead to a projection of norms onto the superordinate categories in which the in-group offers the typical standard for conduct, which may lead to explicit negativity toward the other groups (Waldzus, Mummendey, & Wenzel, 2005; Wenzel, Mummendey, Weber, & Waldzus, 2003; Waldzus, Mummendey, Wenzel, & Weber, 2003). Now we can further specify our initial question: Which type of (inclusiveness of) identification is most likely to promote a positive intergroup relation for Russians as well as for titulars? If the two superordinate identifications have a different inclusive potential for Russians and titulars, do they cancel out each other's effects? Does identification at higher levels of inclusiveness reduce the intergroup differentiation equally for Russians and titulars?

Intergroup Differentiation: Hypotheses on In-Group and Out-Group Stereotypes

We are interested in the associations between identification at different inclusiveness levels and intergroup differentiation as reflected in in-group and out-group stereotypes. In our view identification comes first and stereotypes are the expression of the evolving evaluation of relative group positions. Motivated by the search for a positive social identity, people represent intergroup differences along various hierarchies. Research into ethnic hierarchies shows that stereotypes express people's tendencies to positively value those perceived as closer to the in-group and negatively devalue those who are to be excluded from the in-group (Hagendoorn, 1993). The pattern of evaluative biases reflected in such stereotypes does reflect the actual intergroup dynamics, albeit in a static "one-moment-in-time" picture (Spears, Oakes, Ellemers, & Haslam, 1997). The positive–negative stereotypes of the out-group (as compared to the in-group) can be seen as a step in the direction of intergroup tension (Brewer, 2001).

The empirical question is whether superordinate identifications will lead to the increased acceptance (positive stereotypes) of other ethnic groups, and whether this pattern is opposite to the effects of ethnic identifications, which should lead to more rejection (negative out-group stereotypes). However, if we take into account that intergroup discrimination is considered illegitimate and objectionable in most societies, then it should be expected that intergroup evaluations generally will be less discriminative in terms of negative than in terms of positive criteria. This effect is known as the positive–negative asymmetry effect (Mummendey & Otten, 1998). Various studies have shown that the positive–negative asymmetry effect is less present under specific circumstances, for instance when the out-group has low social status (Mullen, Brown, & Smith, 1992; Mummendey & Otten, 1998; Sachdev & Bourhis, 1991). Therefore, we expect that Russians in the Russian Federation, where titular populations have a subordinate position, show a stronger positive–negative asymmetry effect than the titulars (Hypothesis 1).

Inclusive versus Exclusive Identifications and Intergroup Differentiation

The consequences of different levels of inclusiveness of group categorization for people's behaviors are recognized by self-categorization theory (Turner, Hogg, Oakes, Reicher, & Wetherell, 1987). *Category inclusiveness* is defined as the extent to which a categorization subsumes other social categories in the immediate intergroup context (Crisp, Ensari, Hewstone, & Miller, 2002). In the context of our research, the political administrative structure of the Russian Federation determines the various levels of inclusiveness: the federal, republican, and the ethnic level.

In order to derive hypotheses about the effect of identifications at different levels of inclusiveness on intergroup differentiation, we briefly have to consider which theoretical positions are relevant. The first is optimal distinctiveness theory and the second is the common in-group identity model. Brewer (2001) developed the optimal distinctiveness model of social identity, arguing that an optimal social identity is achieved when one's distinctiveness and inclusiveness needs are simultaneously satisfied. In this view, the expanding boundaries of superordinate identifications reduce distinctiveness, and higher levels of inclusiveness therefore lead to more intergroup discrimination (Brewer, 2001; Hornsey & Hogg, 2000). The common in-group identity model, however, leads to the expectation that the opposite effect will occur (Gaertner, Dovidio, Anastasio, Bachman, & Rust, 1993). Recategorization at a superordinate level will decrease the discrimination between the previous subgroups, because they now share common in-group boundaries. Thereby, the processes of in-group favoritism are shifted away from the level of subgroups to the level of the superordinate identification.

A third model, the mutual intergroup differentiation model, tries to integrate these conflicting predictions (Hewstone & Brown, 1986; Hornsey & Hogg, 2000). The reasoning is that the extension of group boundaries does not lead to a loss of distinctiveness if the lower-level in-group boundaries remain intact in parallel with a superordinate (re-) categorization. The maintenance of a dual identity ("different groups on the same team") leads to decreased discrimination, and to the generalization of positivity (Gaertner et al., 1993; Gonzalez & Brown, 2003; Hewstone & Brown, 1986).

Consequently, what is required is a test of the simultaneous additive effects of social identifications (Gaertner et al., 1993; Reicher, Hopkins, & Condor, 1997; Van Knippenberg & Ellemers, 1990). On the basis of the mutual intergroup differentiation model we expect that the positive effects of superordinate identifications are manifest (also) in the presence of subgroup identifications.

In-Group and Out-Group Stereotypes

To study the impact of various types of identifications on intergroup differentiation, we analyze in-group and out-group stereotypes. By examining in-group stereotypes separately from out-group stereotypes, the two sides of intergroup differentiation: "in-group focused" (what factors affect in-group evaluations) and "out-group focused" (what influences out-group evaluations) can be investigated (Brewer, 2001; Verkuyten, 2005). We expect that the identification types have a positive effect on in-group stereotypes but do not necessarily have a negative effect on out-group stereotypes. The effects of different levels of identification are expected to follow the assumption that the smallest group (most clearly and exclusively defined) provides more positive images of the in-group than the higher-order ones (Brewer & Schneider, 1990). Ethnic groups, rather than more inclusive civic types of groups, should contribute more to the creation of a secure ("optimal") sense of self. Therefore, ethnic identification should have stronger positive effects on the in-group stereotypes than the republican and federal identifications (Hypothesis 2a).

Out-group stereotypes should be affected differently. Dichotomous categorizations in terms of "us–them," usually along primary identities like ethnicity or religion, have an inherent dimension of intergroup comparison. They are built through opposition against the "other" (negative interdependence), being more likely to lead to intergroup differentiation and conflicts than other types of identification (Brewer, 2001; Simon, Kulla, & Zobel, 1995). Identification at lower inclusive levels (such as ethnic vs. civic, or republican vs. federal) will result in more negative out-group evaluations than higher superordinate identifications. Based on the mutual differentiation model, we expect that (in the presence of ethnic identification) republican and federal identifications will strengthen the positive stereotypes of the ethnic out-group (Hypothesis 2b).

Effects of the Superordinate Identifications on In-Group and Out-Group Stereotypes

A last set of hypotheses considers the differences in the effects that the superordinate identifications have on the in-group–out-group evaluations of Russians compared to titulars. In the context of the Russian Federation, the two superordinate identifications, republican and federal, have a different meaning for Russians than for titulars. The autonomous republics were named after the titular populations, which gives them a claim of ownership to the superordinate republican identification. At the federal level, Russians are a majority group, which allows them to claim the natural ownership of the federal identification.

According to the in-group projection model (Mummendey & Wenzel, 1999), a superordinate category that is typically claimed by one of the subgroups will lead to the exclusion of the other subgroups (more negative evaluations of the out-groups). Therefore, we assume that the republican and federal identification will have differential effects for Russians and titulars. Republican identification will have more inclusive effects for the Russians than for the titulars. A Russian who identifies with the republic is expected to have more positive stereotypes of the titulars than a (similarly identified) titular will have of Russians. The opposite should be true for the federal identification: a titular who identifies with the Russian Federation will have more positive stereotypes of the Russians than a Russian who does the same will have of titulars (Hypothesis 3a). Similar effects should be found for in-group stereotypes: a republican identification contributes more to positive in-group stereotypes for titulars than it does for Russians and a federal identification contributes more to positive in-group stereotypes for Russians than it does for titulars (Hypothesis 3b).

The hypotheses will be tested by controlling for the effects of perceived intergroup competition. We may expect that sharing group membership at a higher level of inclusiveness will reduce competition. Gaertner et al. (1993) illustrated how intergroup co-operation reduced intergroup differentiation by inducing members to conceive of themselves as one superordinate group, instead of two groups. In order to isolate the independent contribution of identification types to in-group and out-group evaluations, besides and in addition to the effects of intergroup competition, we control for the centered competition variable (Aiken & West, 1991). No specific predictions are formulated with respect to this variable, as the focus of this research is on the differential impact of identification types, rather than the well-documented impact of intergroup competition on intergroup attitudes (see e.g., Hagendoorn et al., 2001).

Survey Study

This study is based on two data sets of comparative samples of Russians and titulars in 10 autonomous republics of the Russian Federation in 1999 and 2000: Karelia, Adigey, Udmurtia, Komi, Yakutia, Tatarstan, Tuva, Bashkortostan, Kabardino–Balkaria, and Daghestan.[1] The surveys were carried out in urban areas with a minimum of 10% Russians. All republic capital cities were included, other cities being chosen at random.[2] Respondents were selected using random procedures: Within the cities, an alpha-numerical pool randomly identified street names, house numbers were randomly picked, and if older than 15 years, respondents were randomly chosen if their birthday was closest to the day of the interview.

Participants

Nationality was asked before the start of the interview, and only respondents who considered themselves Russian or titular were selected. Participation was on a voluntary basis, and nonresponse was less than 3%. Approximately 500 respondents of each ethnic group in each republic, and about 600 of each group in

---

[1] The survey data were collected by the OPINIO Centre for Sociological Studies, based in Moscow State University, the Russian Federation, during two joint projects with the European Research Centre of Migration and Ethnic Relations (ERCOMER) from Utrecht University, funded by the Dutch National Science Foundation (NWO).

[2] The cities were Maykop, Ufa, Beloreck, Neftekamsk, Sterlitamak, Salavat, Meleuz, Machatchkala, Kielyar, Naltchik, Naptkala, Trnauz, Prochladni, Maickii, Bakcan, Petrozavodsk, Pitkjaranta, Olonec, Suojarvi, Sictvkar, Uchta, Petchora, Emva, Yakutsk, Njurba, Pokrovsk, Kazan, Naberechne Tchelni, Almetebsk, Elabuga, Mendeleevsk, Zainsk, Kyzyl, Shagonar, Turan, Ishevsk, Votkinsk, Glazov, and Moshga.

Tatarstan were interviewed. In total, 5,182 titulars and 5,233 Russians participated, 44.4% were males and 55.6% females. Respondents were aged between 16 and 98 years, with a mean of 40.56.

Dependent and Independent Variables

The dependent variables were constructed from survey questions on attributions of positive and negative traits to the in-group and the out-group. The questions were formulated in terms of percentages of target group characterized by the respective trait: "How many Russians/titulars, in your opinion, have the following characteristic...?" with a continuous answering scale from 0% to 100%. The traits were *honest, smart, peaceable, lazy, hostile, showing initiative, rude*, and *deceitful*. The selection of these traits was based on previous research that illustrated the potential of these stereotypical traits in differentiating between groups in Eastern European and former Soviet Union contexts (Hagendoorn et al., 2001; Poppe & Linssen, 1999). Simultaneous component analysis (SCA) was performed on these questions, for the 20 groups (Russians and titular groups in 10 republics), on in-group stereotypes and out-group stereotypes. SCA identifies principal components that optimally account for the variance in all 20 groups simultaneously, making them comparable across populations. Both in-group stereotypes and out-group stereotypes appeared to have two components (explained variance of 52.59%, and 53.30%, respectively), that is, a positive (*honest, smart, peaceable, showing initiative*) and a negative one (*lazy, hostile, rude*, and *deceitful*). Across groups, for in-group stereotypes, Cronbach's alpha of the positive component ranged between .40 and .67, and for the negative component: between .58 and .83; for out-group stereotypes, they ranged between .31 and .78, and between .55 and .80, respectively. Although the reliability coefficient is rather low among a few of the 20 groups, it is adequate across groups and the dimensions are optimal for group comparison according to SCA. Therefore, we computed four variables as the mean scores of the respective traits: in-group positive, in-group negative, out-group positive, and out-group negative stereotypes.

Identification variables were constructed on the mean score of two questions in which the participants indicated on a 5-point scale the degree of agreement with respect to the importance and pride of group membership (see Appendix A). Cronbach's alphas are for ethnic identification 0.84 for Russians and 0.91 for titulars, 0.71 for republican identification and .86 for identification with the Russian Federation. The variable *perceived intergroup competition* was computed as a mean score of three questions on jobs, economic interest, and political competition (see Appendix); Cronbach's alpha is .73.

All the independent variables were centered (Aiken & West, 1991). In this way, the effects of the superordinate identifications are interpreted when ethnic identification and intergroup competition are at average values (rather than at the value of zero).

Analysis and Results

Preliminary Analyses

Table 1 presents the degree of identification of Russians and titulars on the various identification types. As expected, the titulars have a stronger republican identification, and the Russians have a stronger federal identification.

The different patterns of identification of the Russians and the titulars are also reflected in the higher correlations between the ethnic and republican identification among titulars, and the higher correlation between ethnic and federal identification among Russians (Table 2). The significance of these correlation differences was estimated using the Fisher's Z' transformation that converts Pearson rs to the normally distributed variable Z'. For the difference between the correlations between the ethnic and republican identifications (titulars: $r_t = .532, N = 5,182$; and Russians: $r_r = .037, N = 5,067; r_t - r_r = .495$), a 95% confidence interval with the lower limit of, .47 and upper limit of .52. was identified. Similarly, for the difference in correlations between ethnic and federal identifications (titulars: $r_t = .110$ and Russians: $r_r = .373; r_t - r_r = -.263$), the interval was between $-.22$ and $-.30$. It seems therefore, that the differences between the correlations of titulars and Russians between the specific identification types are significant at the accepted levels.

Hypothesis 1: Intergroup Differentiation in the Russian Federation

In order to test the patterns of intergroup differentiation, repeated measurements multivariate analysis of variance (MANOVA) was performed on the four dependent variables, across the ethnic groups (Russians and titulars); two within-subject factors were generated: target group (in-group and out-group) and valence of trait (positive and negative).

The interaction effect between the within-subject factors predicted by Hypothesis 1 was significant, $F(1, 7,366) = 1,303.33, p < .001, B = 6.56 (SE = .18)$: In-group evaluations and out-group evaluations varied as a function of the valence of traits. Across the two ethnic groups the differentiation in favor of the in-group was almost 3 times higher on the positive items, $F(1, 7,366) = 1,471.73, p < .001, B = -11.09 (SE = .19)$, than on the negative items, $F(1, 7,366) = 533.39, p < .001, B = 3.79 (SE = .19)$.[3] The positive–negative asymmetry effect was confirmed (see Table 3 for the means on each stereotype component).

Additionally, we found a significant three-way interaction with ethnic groups, $F(1, 7,366) = 12.23, p < .001, B = .63 (SE = .18)$, indicating differences between

---

[3] The square root of the ANOVA F statistics is the t statistic as would be calculated in a regression analysis. A comparison of the F values is possible and valid as long as they are estimated within the same model. Similar to the t statistics of the regression models, F values indicate the strength of an effect.

Table 1. Identification Types and Differences Between Ethnic Groups

	Ethnic Identification	Republican Identification	Federal Identification
Titulars	4.18 (1.17)	4.36 (.91)	3.54 (1.28)
Russians	3.90 (1.26)	3.81 (1.19)	4.10 (1.13)
Univariate analysis results	.136 (.012)	.273 (.010)	−.280 (.012)
	$F = 127.93^{***}$	$F = 678.72^{***}$	$F = 551.51^{***}$

Note. These are results of a multivariate analysis of variance on the three identification variables, with the Multivariate Pillais $F(3,5,121) = 585.48, p < .001$, reflecting the overall significant differences between Russians and Titulars.

The values in the upper level of the table represent mean score on the identification variables, on a scale from 1 to 5; with standard errors between parentheses. The values in the lower level of the table are unstandardized regression coefficients (standard errors between parentheses) of the univariate MANOVA analysis concerning differences between Russians and titulars, $F(1,10,247)$ with significance levels: *** $p < .001$.

Table 2. Correlations Between Identification Types

		Republican Identification	Federal Identification	Intergroup Competition
Ethnic identification	Russians	.037**	.373***	.135***
	Titulars	.532***	.110***	.074***
	Overall	.263***	.202***	.080***
Republican identification	Russians		.237***	−.205***
	Titulars		.274***	.001
	Overall		.180***	−.165***
Federal identification	Russians			.049***
	Titulars			.056***
	Overall			.042***

**$p < .01$; ***$p < .001$.

Russians and titulars in the positive–negative asymmetry effect. Simple main effect analyses revealed that for Russians the differentiation between in-group and out-group stereotypes on positive traits was more than 8 times larger than on negative traits, $F(1, 7,366) = 871.64, p < .001, B = -6.01$ ($SE = .20$), and $F(1, 7,366) = 103.66, p < .001, B = 2.37$ ($SE = .23$), respectively. Similarly, for titulars, differentiation was higher on positive stereotypes, $F(1, 7,366) = 610.42, p < .001, B = -4.98$ ($SE = .20$) than on negative stereotypes, $F(1, 7,366) = 508.18, p < .001, B = 5.20$ ($SE = .23$), but of a much lower magnitude. Hypothesis 1 was fully confirmed. While both groups clearly favored their in-group over the out-group in allocating positive and negative traits, they are less extreme on the negative items. Titulars seem to negatively differentiate almost 5 times stronger than Russians between their in-group and the out-group; while Russians manifest the strongest effect in their differentiation on positive traits. The positive–negative

Table 3. Positive and Negative Stereotypes about In-Group and Out-Group

	Stereotypes			
	In-Group Positive	Out-Group Positive	In-Group Negative	Out-Group Negative
Titulars	61.20 (14.23)	54.16 (15.25)	29.56 (15.78)	36.92 (17.32)
Russians	59.63 (13.48)	51.13 (16.81)	33.65 (15.79)	37.00 (19.07)
Univariate analysis results	.79 (.16) $F = 23.73^{***}$	1.52 (.19) $F = 65.77^{***}$	−2.04 (.18) $F = 123.33^{***}$	−.04 (.21) $F = .04$

Note. These are results of a multivariate analysis of variance on the four stereotype variables, with the Multivariate Pillais $F(4, 3,680) = 55.56$, $p < .001$, reflecting the overall significant differences between Russians and titulars.

The values in the upper level of the table represent mean score on the stereotype dimensions, on a scale from 0 to 100; with standard errors between parentheses. The values in the lower level of the table are unstandardized regression coefficients (standard errors between parentheses) of the univariate ANOVA analysis concerning differences between Russians and titulars, $F(1, 7,366)$ with significance levels: $^{***}p < .001$.

asymmetry effect is most salient for the high-status Russian group, and much lower for the low-status groups of titulars, as predicted.

Hypothesis 2: Effects of Identification Types on Intergroup Differentiation

The main test concerned the effects of identification types on in-group and out-group stereotypes while controlling for perceived intergroup competition. The model included the ethnic groups as a factor (Russians and titulars), the two-way interactions between the factor and each identification type, and perceived competition. We employed multivariate analysis of covariance (MANCOVA), which allowed for the valid test of correlated dependent variables; the default regression approach was used, allowing for the correction of the individual effects for every other variable in the model (Aiken & West, 1991). MANCOVA also allowed for the test of the additive contributions of the identification types on intergroup stereotypes; this way the effect of each identification type on in-group–out-group evaluations could be identified while keeping constant (at average values) the identification with the other types as well as the perception of intergroup competition.

For the test of Hypothesis 2, we look at the main effects of the identification types. Hypothesis 2a predicts that, given its optimal distinctiveness, ethnic identification more than republican or federal identification would reinforce in-group stereotypes. This prediction was not confirmed: the effects of republican identification were twice as strong on both positive and negative in-group stereotypes, as the effects of ethnic identification, while the effects of federal identification were the weakest (see Table 4). It turns out that the republican superordinate identification contributes the most to people's self-evaluations when people identify on average at the ethnic and federal level. The main effects of the superordinate identifications

Table 4. Effects of Identification Types, Intergroup Competition, and Their Interactions with Ethnic Groups

Predictors	Multivariate Pillais $F(4, 3,647)$	Stereotypes			
		In-Group Positive	In-Group Negative	Out-Group Positive	Out-Group Negative
Ethnic identification	30.73***	.99 (.15) $F = 43.45***$	−.57 (.17) $F = 10.87**$	−.98 (.17) $F = 34.52***$	.10 (.19) $F = .27$
× ethnic groups	1.83, ns	−.22 (.15) $F = 2.23$	.40 (.17) $F = 5.40*$	−.18 (.17) $F = 1.15$	.03 (.19) $F = .02$
Republican identification	50.74***	1.70 (.18) $F = 90.43***$	−.97 (.21) $F = 22.21***$	2.37 (.20) $F = 142.21***$	−1.69 (.23) $F = 56.11***$
× ethnic groups	36.81***	.95 (.18) $F = 27.95***$	−.87 (.21) $F = 17.99***$	−1.50 (.20) $F = 56.61***$	1.17 (.23) $F = 26.96***$
Federal identification	4.98***	.43 (.14) $F = 9.05**$	−.12 (.17) $F = .51$	.64 (.16) $F = 15.91***$	.01 (.18) $F = .00$
× ethnic groups	19.64***	−.44 (.14) $F = 9.37**$	.38 (.17) $F = 5.14*$	1.06 (.16) $F = 43.70***$	−.51 (.18) $F = 7.67**$
Intergroup competition	177.33***	−.32 (.14) $F = 4.78*$	1.21 (.17) $F = 52.41***$	−2.84 (.16) $F = 312.38***$	4.31 (.18) $F = 557.22***$
× ethnic groups	13.38***	−.64 (.14) $F = 19.41***$	.17 (.17) $F = 1.04$	.23 (.16) $F = 2.08$	−.91 (.18) $F = 24.84***$
Ethnic groups	43.41***	.30 (.18) $F = 2.78$	−1.47 (.20) $F = 51.43***$	.37 (.20) $F = 3.44$	1.59 (.22) $F = 50.00***$

Note. All the effects presented in this table were estimated in one model, with the four dependent variables, as well as the factor "Ethnic groups," covariates, and the two-way interactions between the factor and the covariates.

The values represent unstandardized regression coefficients (with standard errors between parentheses) of the univariate ANCOVA analysis $F(1, 7,299)$ with significance levels: $*p < .05$; $**p < .01$; $***p < .001$.

on in-group stereotypes were qualified by significant interaction terms that will be discussed under Hypothesis 3b.

Hypothesis 2b predicts negative effects of ethnic identification and positive effects of the superordinate identifications on *out-group stereotypes*. Table 4 shows that the predictions on positive stereotypes were confirmed, with the effect of republican identification almost 4 times stronger than the effects of ethnic identification. Federal identification has the weakest effects. Neither the ethnic nor the federal identifications had a significant effect on the negative stereotypes, but the effect of republican identification was significant and in the predicted direction: those who identify stronger with the republic have more positive stereotypes of the out-group. The main effects of the superordinate identifications on out-group stereotypes were also further qualified by significant interactions with ethnic groups, which will be discussed under Hypothesis 3a.

In summary, the results show different effects of identification at different inclusiveness levels. The republican identification should have an intermediate inclusiveness effect, in between the more exclusive ethnic identification and the higher-order federal identification. However, republican identification contributes the most to improving the evaluations of the in-group as well as the out-group. By the same token, ethnic identification is the identification that is the most exclusive of out-groups (Brewer, 2001). Identification at the superordinate level of the Russian Federation has a much weaker impact: It has a significant effect only on the positive in-group and out-group stereotypes, while it did not affect the negative stereotypes.

Hypothesis 3: Differential Effects of the Superordinate Identifications for Russians and Titulars

Hypothesis 3a predicts that the superordinate identifications will have different effects on *out-group stereotypes* of Russians and titulars. The last two rows of Table 5 show the results of simple slope analyses that confirm the hypothesis. For Russians, republican identification improves positive and decreases negative stereotypes of titulars. For titulars, these effects are not significant for negative stereotypes and very weak for positive stereotypes. Similarly, federal identification improves positive and decreases negative stereotypes titulars have of Russians but has no significant effects among Russians.

Table 5. Superordinate Identifications and Ethnic Groups: Results of Simple Slope Analyses

Ethnic Groups	Republican Identification		Federal Identification	
	Russians	Titulars	Russians	Titulars
Multivariate Pillais $F(4, 3,647)$	89.36***	22.63***	7.00***	20.45***
Univariate results				
In-group positive stereotypes	.76 (.14)	2.65 (.30)	.88 (.22)	−.00 (.18)
	$F = 14.07$***	$F = 80.11$***	$F = 15.22$***	$F = .00$
In-group negative stereotypes	−.10 (.23)	−1.84 (.34)	−.50 (.26)	.26 (.20)
	$F = .18$	$F = 29.34$***	$F = 3.67$	$F = 1.53$
Out-group positive stereotypes	3.87 (.22)	.87 (.33)	−.42 (.25)	1.70 (.20)
	$F = 298.43$***	$F = 7.09$**	$F = 2.84$	$F = 71.17$***
Out-group negative stereotypes	−2.86 (.25)	−.52 (.37)	.51 (.28)	−.50 (.23)
	$F = 126.91$***	$F = 1.93$	$F = 3.24$	$F = 4.75$*

Note. These are the results of the simple slope main effect analysis of two interaction terms: the interaction between ethnic groups and republican identification (Multivariate Pillais' test: $F(4, 3,647) = 36.81, p < .001$) and the interaction between ethnic groups and Russian Federation identification. $F(4, 3,647) = 19.64, p < .001$).
The values represent unstandardized regression coefficients (with standard errors between parentheses) of the univariate ANCOVA analysis $F(1, 7,299)$ with the respective significance levels: *$p < .05$; **$p < .01$; ***$p < .001$.

Hypothesis 3b refers to the analysis of the interaction effects between superordinate identifications and ethnic groups on *in-group stereotypes*. The first two rows of Table 5 summarizing the effects on in-group stereotypes confirm our expectations almost entirely. Republican identification (more typical for titulars) strongly contributes to improving in-group stereotypes for titulars, but it is much weaker in its effects for Russians, that is, the effect on positive stereotypes is 6 times weaker, and it is insignificant on negative stereotypes. Similarly, federal identification (more typical for Russians) has no effect on in-group stereotypes of titulars, while it does contribute to the positive stereotypes of Russians.

In conclusion, identification at more inclusive levels does not always reflect improving intergroup relations; its effect seems to depend on the typicality of the superordinate identification. Those subgroups who are not supposed to claim ownership of the superordinate category, but who do identify at the superordinate level are more positive about the other subgroup than those who are supposed to claim ownership. Russians' republican identification, for instance, results in improved stereotypes of titulars. On the other hand, those subgroups who are supposed to raise claims on being the typical representatives of the superordinate category seem to feel justified not to include other subgroups if they identify with the superordinate category: titulars' republican identification as well as Russians' federal identification less strongly or not significantly improve positive out-group stereotypes or weaken negative out-group stereotypes.

Finally, we present the effects of intergroup competition. Intergroup competition had a very strong effect on out-group stereotypes in particular (almost 4 times stronger than the maximum effect of republican identification), and more on negative than on positive stereotypes. These effects are in the expected direction: more perceived competition leads to more negative and less positive out-group stereotypes. However, perceiving higher intergroup competition also slightly lowers one's positive in-group stereotypes and increases the negative in-group stereotypes. This latter effect is surprisingly strong. The simple slope analysis of the interaction with the ethnic groups, as shown in Table 5, indicates that the perception of intergroup competition strengthens Russians' negative stereotypes of titulars (the effect is twice as strong as for titulars and for positive out-group stereotypes). This result is consistent with what could be expected from threat and the relative group positions theories: the dominant group (Russians) is more likely to feel threatened by a subordinate group (titulars) than vice versa.[4] This implies that perceived intergroup competition may undermine the benign (inclusive) effects of the republican identification among Russians (republican identification highly improved Russians' stereotypes of titulars). Further studies should focus on the

---

[4] The mean scores on perceived intergroup competition were as follows: Russians: 2.66 ($SD = 1.17$), titulars: 2.19 ($SD = 1.09$). They are significantly different, with F (1, 10,413) = 461.91, $p < .001$). Russians perceive more intergroup competition between themselves and the respective titulars living in the same autonomous republic, than the titular groups do.

Table 6. The Effects of Intergroup Competition for Each Ethnic Group: Results of Simple Slope Analyses

Ethnic Groups	Intergroup Competition	
	Russians	Titulars
Multivariate Pillais $F(4, 3,647)$	130.93***	60.75***
Univariate results		
In-group positive stereotypes	.32 (.20)	−.95 (.21)
	$F = 2.53$	$F = 21.13$***
In-group negative stereotypes	1.04 (.23)	1.38 (.24)
	$F = 19.91$***	$F = 33.17$***
Out-group positive stereotypes	−3.07 (.22)	−2.61 (.23)
	$F = 188.01$***	$F = 128.13$***
Out-group negative stereotypes	5.22 (.25)	3.40 (.26)
	$F = 420.49$***	$F = 168.64$***

Note. These are the results of the simple slope main effect analysis of the interaction term between ethnic groups and intergroup competition (Multivariate Pillais' test: $F(4, 3,647) = 13.38, p < .001$).

The values represent unstandardized regression coefficients (with standard errors between parentheses) of the univariate ANCOVA analysis $F(1, 7,299)$ with the respective significance levels: ***$p < .001$.

possible interactions between intergroup competition and identification types, to specifically test this assumption (see Table 6). These dynamics were beyond the scope of the current analysis.

General Discussion and Conclusions

In addition to their primary ethnic identities, people are attached to multiple overlapping identification categories (Poppe & Hagendoorn, 2001). The effects of multiple identifications on patterns of polarization between groups may be rather complex, in particular in the former Soviet Union where a hierarchically layered political structure was designed in order to prevent ethnic conflict. We investigated whether intergroup polarization between Russians and titulars in autonomous republics of the Russian Federation is moderated by superordinate civic identifications (i.e., republican and federal identification).

We found support for the claim that the civic superordinate identifications may ensure the desired regional stability. A higher identification with the republic relates to more positive stereotypes and less negative stereotypes of the out-group, whereas federal identification also relates to more positive outgroup stereotypes, but not affect negative stereotypes of the out-group.

The study shows that a simple dichotomy of in-group–out-group should be avoided. Ethnic identification was differentially connected to the republican and the federal identifications for the Russians and the titulars, and therefore it was obvious that the two superordinate identifications differed in their consequences for Russians' and titulars' negative evaluations of out-groups. For this reason the effect of the superordinate identifications did not completely conform to the mutual differentiation model. Instead, the effects were qualified by the meaning Russian and titulars attached to the superordinate categories and are therefore more in line with the predictions of the in-group projection model (Waldzus et al., 2003). In other words, the more attached a group is to the superordinate identification, the more it emphasized its own positive characteristics and the less it emphasized the positive attributes of the other subgroup subsumed under the shared higher-level category.

The meaning of the two superordinate categories (republic and federation) for Russians and titulars in our research is defined by the political reality of the intergroup relations in the current Russian Federation. This reality determines the optional identification choices for both ethnic groups. The social psychological consequences of their choices are as complex as the hierarchically embedded structure of autonomies of the Russian Federation. It is not the case that the higher-level units simply unify the lower-level units. The higher-level units rather emerge as a new field of struggle for dominance. The titulars generally seem to claim a special "right" on the republican level (which bears their ethnic name), and Russians claim to be the "true owners" at the federal level. Therefore, it appeared that the superordinate categories did their work as unifiers only halfway for Russians, the republican identification did indeed lead to more positive stereotypes of titulars, but the same was not true for the stereotypes by titulars of Russians. The same dynamic reappeared at the federal level: here the evaluations of Russians by titulars improved, but not those of titulars given by Russians. The two superordinate identifications, in addition, affected the in-group stereotypes in such a way that the polarization between the groups only increased. Hence, the effects of the superordinate categories on the in-group side of the intergroup differentiation were negative.

There was another important finding, namely that Russians were much more reluctant than titulars to be explicitly negative about the out-group. While titulars favored their in-group on both negative and positive evaluations, the dominant Russian group favored their in-group only on the positive stereotypes. Hence, also the positive–negative asymmetry manifested itself only halfway, namely for the dominant (Russian) group of the Russian Federation. This finding has to be qualified, Russians' discrimination (expressed by the reduction of their positive stereotypes of the titulars) exceeded the discrimination manifested by the titulars.

In addition to the literature on intergroup relations between Russians and titulars in the borderland republics of Russia (e.g., Hagendoorn et al., 2001), this study indicates the tensions present between Russians and titulars within the Russian Federation itself. Russians seem insecure about their position in the autonomous republics in the Russian Federation. They seem to hesitate between integration in the republic and acknowledging that large conflicts of interest with the titulars are possible. Although Russians perceive the republic in principle as an inclusive unit that grants them an equal position, titulars perceive their republic more as a platform that guarantees their dominance. This antagonistic dynamics is not fully counterbalanced by the inclusive effects of identifying with the federation. Meanwhile, it should not be denied that the superordinate republican identification is partially fulfilling its role for maintaining peaceful intergroup relations: it makes Russians feel included in the lower administrative levels of the federation, at the price of fueling feelings of pride and ethnic belonging of titulars.

The pattern of associations between identification types and intergroup polarization suggests that political entrepreneurs in Russia can easily destroy the beneficial effects of superordinate identifications by trying to mobilize groups: appealing to republican identity for titulars and federal identity for Russians.

Our findings show that identification at a superordinate level affects intergroup evaluations, rather than triggering the personalization of group members (Brewer & Schneider, 1990). Therefore, also superordinate identifications can be used for collective mobilization. This study shows this strategic potential of social identifications and thus complements the previous studies in which this role was assigned only to intergroup competition and threat (Hagendoorn et al., 2001; Poppe & Hagendoorn, 2001, 2003), and it raises new questions about the forms this political mobilization may take.

In any social context, different identity categories can be defined in more or less exclusive terms, reflecting asymmetric claims of entitlement to specific rights. Analyzing the implications that specific categories have on the intergroup relationship, as a function of the meanings attributed to these categories by the groups involved, could be a fruitful contribution of social psychology to understanding real-life power struggles (cf. Reicher et al., 1997). Currently, too little attention is paid to the constructed and disputed character of identity categories. While the strength of our findings lies in testing the consequences of the assumed meanings of the identification types for Russians and titulars, here lies also one limitation of this research: the lack of measurement of the perceived typicality of the superordinate categories, or individual understanding of the political reality. Future quantitative and qualitative studies should address the way people relate to the political reality of their intergroup context. Currently, we addressed the way identification at various levels reflect the administrative layers that confer differential power and legitimacy to entitlement claims to the groups of Russians and titulars. Future research could also focus on the impact of different ideologies, such as multiculturalism or assimilation, on defining the inclusiveness or typicality of certain identity categories (cf. Billig, 1994).

References

Abrams, D., & Hogg, M. A. (1990). *Social identity theory. Constructive and critical advances.* New York: Harvester Wheatsheaf.

Aiken, L. S., & West, S. G. (1991). *Multiple regression: Testing and interpreting interactions*. London: Sage Publications.
Billig, M. (1994). *Banal nationalism*. London: Sage Publications.
Brewer, M. B. (2001). Ingroup identification and intergroup conflict. When does ingroup love become outgroup hate? In R. D. Ashmore, L. Jussim, & D. Wilder (Eds.), *Rutgers series on self and social identity: Vol. 3. Social identity, intergroup conflict, and conflict reduction* (pp. 17–41). New York: Oxford University Press.
Brewer, M. B. (1999). The psychology of prejudice: Ingroup love or outgroup hate? *Journal of Social Issues, 55*(3), 429–444.
Brewer, M. B., & Schneider, S. K. (1990). Social identity and social dilemmas: a double-edged sword. In D. Abrams & M. A. Hogg (Eds.), *Social identity theory. Constructive and critical advances* (pp. 169–184). New York: Harvester Wheatsheaf.
Bourhis, R. Y., Turner, J. C., & Gagnon, A. (1997). Interdependence, social identity and discrimination. In R. Spears, P. J. Oakes, N. Ellemers, & S. A. Haslam (Eds.) *The social psychology of stereotyping and group Life* (pp. 273–296). Cambridge, MA: Blackwell.
Brubaker, R. (1996). *Nationalism reframed: Nationhood and the national question in the new Europe*. Cambridge, MA: Cambridge University Press.
Crisp, R. J., Ensari, N., Hewstone, M., & Miller, N. (2002). A dual-route model of crossed categorization effects. *European Review of Social Psychology, 13*, 35–73.
Gaertner, S. L., Dovidio, J. F., Anastasio, P. A., Bachman, B. A., & Rust, M. C. (1993). The common ingroup identity model: Recategorization and the reduction of intergroup bias. In W. Stroebe & M. Hewstone (Eds.), *European review of social psychology*, Vol. 4 (pp. 1–26). Chichester, UK: Wiley.
Gonzalez, R., & Brown, R. (2003). Generalization of positive attitude as a function of subgroup superordinate group identifications in intergroup contact. *European Journal of Social Psychology, 33*, 195–214.
Hagendoorn, L. (1993). Ethnic categorization and outgroup exclusion: Cultural values and social stereotypes in the construction of ethnic hierarchies. *Ethnic and Racial Studies, 16*, 226–251.
Hagendoorn, L., Drogendijk, R., Tumanov, S., & Hraba, J. (1998). Inter-ethnic preferences and ethnic hierarchies in the former Soviet Union. *International Journal of Intercultural Relations, 22*, 483–503.
Hagendoorn, L., Linssen, H., & Tumanov, S. (2001). *Inter-group relations in states of the former Soviet Union: The perception of Russians*. Hove, UK: Psychology Press.
Hewstone, N., & Brown, R. J. (1986). Contact is not enough: An intergroup perspective on the contact hypothesis. In M. Hewstone & R. J. Brown (Eds.), *Contact and conflict in intergroup encounters* (pp. 1–44). New York: Blackwell.
Hornsey, M. J., & Hogg, M. A. (2000). Subgroup relations: A comparison of mutual intergroup differentiation and common ingroup identity models of prejudice reduction. *Personality and Social Psychological Bulletin, 26*, 242–256.
Laitin, D. (1998). *Identity in formation, The Russian-speaking populations in the Near Abroad*. New York: Cornell University Press.
Mullen, B., Brown, R., & Smith, J. (1992). Ingroup bias as function of salience, relevance, and status: An integration. *European Journal of Social Psychology, 22*, 103–122.
Mummendey, A., & Otten, S. (1998). Positive-negative asymmetry in social discrimination. In W. Stroebe & M. Hewstone (Eds.), *European review of social psychology*, Vol. 9 (pp. 107–143). Chichester, UK: Wiley.
Mummendey, A., & Wenzel, M. (1999). Social discrimination and tolerance in intergroup relations: Reactions to intergroup difference. *Personality and Social Psychology Review, 3*, 158–174.
Poppe, E., & Hagendoorn, L. (2001). Types of identification among Russians in the near abroad. *Europe-Asia Studies, 53*, 57–71.
Poppe, E., & Hagendoorn, L. (2003). Titular identification of Russians in former soviet republics. *Europe-Asia Studies, 55*, 771–787.
Poppe, E., & Linssen, H. (1999). Ingroup favoritism and the reflection of realistic dimensions of difference between national states in Central and Eastern European nationality stereotypes. *British Journal of Social Psychology, 38*, 85–102.

Reicher, S., Hopkins, N., & Condor, S. (1997). Stereotype construction as a strategy of influence. In R. Spears, P. J. Oakes, N. Ellemers, & S. A. Haslam (Eds.), *The social psychology of stereotyping and group life* (pp. 94–118). Oxford, UK: Basil Blackwell.

Sachdev, I., & Bourhis, R. Y. (1991). Power and status differentials in minority and majority group relations. *European Journal of Social Psychology, 21*, 1–24.

Simon, B., Kulla, C., & Zobel, M. (1995). On being more than just a part of the whole: Regional identity and social distinctiveness. *European Journal of Social Psychology, 25*, 325–340.

Spears, R., Oakes, P. J., Ellemers, N., & Haslam, S. A. (1997). *The social psychology of stereotyping and group life*. Oxford: Blackwell Publishers.

Tajfel, H., & Turner, J. C. (1986). The social identity theory of intergroup behavior. In S. Worchel & W. G. Austin (Eds.), *Psychology of intergroup relations* (pp. 7–24). Chicago: Nelson-Hall.

Tishkov, V. (1997). *Ethnicity, nationalism and conflict in and after the Soviet Union*. London: Sage Publications.

Turner, J. C., Hogg, M. A., Oakes, P. J., Reicher, S. D., & Wetherell, M. S. (1987). *Rediscovering the social group: A self-categorization theory*. New York: Basil Blackwell.

Van Knippenberg, A., & Ellemers, N. (1990). Social identity and intergroup differentiation processes. In W. Stroebe & M. Hewstone (Eds.), *European review of social psychology*, Vol. 1 (pp. 137–169). Chichester, UK: Wiley.

Verkuyten, M. (2005). *The social psychology of ethnic identity*. Hove and New York: Psychology Press.

Waldzus, S., Mummendey, A., & Wenzel, M. (2005). When "different" means "worse": Ingroup prototypicality in changing intergroup contexts. *Journal of Experimental Social Psychology, 41*, 76–83.

Waldzus, S., Mummendey, A., Wenzel, M., & Weber, U. (2003). Towards tolerance: Representations of superordinate categories and perceived ingroup prototypicality. *Journal of Experimental Social Psychology, 39*, 31–47.

Wenzel, M., Mummendey, A., Weber, U., & Waldzus, S. (2003). Ingroup as pars pro toto: Projection from the ingroup onto the inclusive category as a precursor to social discrimination. *Personality and Social Psychology Bulletin, 29*, 461–473.

ANCA MINESCU is a University College Utrecht graduate, currently working on her PhD project at ERCOMER, within the ICS, at Utrecht University. She has a research master degree in Migration, Ethnic Relations, and Multiculturalism (2004). Her research interests lie at the intersection between social psychology, sociology, and political science. Her doctoral thesis is about the effects of relative group size on intergroup attitudes, varying from stereotypes, intergroup competition, minority rights, and political separatism. Specific conditions that catalyze or moderate the effects of group size as well as social psychological mediation of these interactions are analyzed. The aim is to develop and test a theory on the generalization of group size effects on intergroup attitudes.

LOUK HAGENDOORN is Professor of Social Sciences and Dean of the Graduate School of Social and Behavioural Sciences at Utrecht University in the Netherlands. He was the Academic Director and cofounder of the European Research Centre on Migration and Ethnic Relations (ERCOMER) in Utrecht. His research is focused on intergroup relations, prejudice, and political psychology. He did research in Western and Eastern Europe and published on ethnic relations, stereotypes, and nationalism in sociology, social psychology, and political science journals. Recent publication is *When ways of life collide. Multiculturalism in the Netherlands and its discontents* (with P. Sniderman), 2007.

EDWIN POPPE is Assistant Professor at the Department of Interdisciplinary Social Sciences and staff member of ERCOMER at Utrecht University. He conducted a survey study in six Central and Eastern European countries on national and ethnic stereotypes and was involved in various survey studies in the Russian Federation and other republics of the former Soviet Union. He has published on the content of stereotypes in social psychology journals and on the identification of Russians in journals focusing on the former Soviet Union. His lecturing activities include the topics of intergroup relations, migration, ethnic prejudice, and nationalism.

Appendix. Scale Items for the Predictors

Predictor	Scale Items
Ethnic identification	"It is of great importance for me to be a Russian/to be regarded as a fellow titular by the titular population"
	"I am proud to be a Russian/to be regarded as a titular person"
Republican identification	"I feel attached to the republic in which I live"
	"I am proud of the republic in which I live"
Federal identification	"It is of great importance for me to be a citizen of the Russian Federation"
	"I am proud to be a citizen of the Russian Federation"
Perceived intergroup competition	"The titular population/Russian people in our republic have better job opportunities than the Russians/titulars"
	"The economic interests of the titular population in the republic are in conflict with the Russians in this republic"
	"The political interests of the titular population in the republic are in conflict with the Russians in this republic"

Anti-Semitic Attitudes in Europe: A Comparative Perspective

Werner Bergmann[*]
Technical University Berlin

The article uses available survey data to depict the depth and spread of anti-Semitic attitudes across Europe. The main assumption is that European anti-Semitism, both currently and historically, is closely tied to issues and crises of national self-identification; for this reason, social identity theory is employed to study the varying configurations of anti-Semitic prejudice. In most European countries, Jews are a small and socially integrated minority. Attitudes toward them are determined less by concrete experiences of cultural differences, or conflicts over scarce resources, but rather by a perceived threat to the national self-image. This leads to an accentuation of the pertinent prejudices that blame Jews to be responsible for that threat. This perspective brings to light considerable differences between Eastern and Western Europe and the continuing influence of national traditions.

Surveys on anti-Semitism have been continually conducted in the United States since the end of World War II (Dinnerstein, 1994). In Europe, if at all, this is the case only for West Germany, Austria, and, with greater gaps, France. In the remaining countries, from 1945 until 1990, there are only a few occasional studies available at best, in many cases none at all (see Bergmann, 1996). It was not until the collapse of the Eastern bloc that opinion polls were conducted throughout Europe asking about the populations' attitude toward national minorities and in particular toward Jews. Since then, the American Jewish Committee (AJC) and the Anti-Defamation League (ADL) have commissioned a number of surveys based on comparable questions in several European countries.[1] These data allow at least

---

[*]Correspondence concerning this article should be addressed to Prof. Dr. Werner Bergmann, Zentrum für Antisemitismusforschung, Technische Universität Berlin, Ernst-Reuter-Platz 7, D-40587 Berlin, Germany [e-mail: berg0154@mailbox.tu-berlin.de].
Translated from German by Paul Bowman.

[1] The series of surveys commissioned by the American Jewish Committee based on a representative national sample in each country (between 1,100 and 2,000 respondents, accurate within ± three

a tentative comparative analysis. The rise in the number of anti-Semitic incidents in Europe over recent years has once more put the problem of anti-Semitism in the public spotlight, prompting surveys to be conducted in countries such as Sweden, Switzerland, France, Germany, Italy, Poland, and Hungary. However, there are no data available for many other European countries.

Given this patchy database, a valid comparative analysis of the scale and structure of anti-Semitism in European countries is a difficult task. The following analysis is based primarily upon the AJC and ADL sources and complements them with additional data taken from particular countries. However, the analysis can only furnish conclusions on the distribution of attitudes across the range of the whole population; the data do not allow a comparative analysis of the influence on attitudes toward Jews by age, education, religion, political orientation etc.

The theoretical perspective follows the social identity approach, not least because European anti-Semitism is closely connected to issues and crises of the national self-identification, both today and in the past.

Theoretical and Historical Considerations

In the social identity approach, cognitive categorization processes generate intergroup differences and similarities. In-group favoritism emerges, for categorization processes not only serve to structure the environment, but also possess emotional and motivational functions. Through identification with the in-group, group members partially gain a sense of their self—their social identity. Accordingly, they strive for an image of the in-group as positive as possible that is in part reached through a negative classification of out-groups. According to Tajfel and Turner (1986), the tendency to draw negative distinctions increases when (a) social identity is perceived as being under threat and (b) when there is a conflict of interests between groups or when a conflict of interest makes group membership more salient. In keeping with these theoretical assumptions, persons who are especially inclined to utilize prejudices as a means of stabilizing their social identity are those who

(a) identify very strongly with their in-group and therefore draw a large part of their individual identity from group membership,
(b) perceive a threat to their social identity, and

---

percentage points). The face-to-face interviews were conducted by experienced national survey institutes. The surveys commissioned by the Anti-Defamation League based on telephone interviews of about 500 people in each country (margin error is ±4 at 95% level of confidence). The fieldwork was done by Taylor Nelson Sofres (TNS).

(c) perceive a conflict between the in-group and out-group.

The available data on anti-Semitism do not allow an examination of the connection between attitudes and personality structures. More important for the current analysis are the social functions of prejudices: (a) they accentuate differences between groups (social distinctions); (b) they provide for justification for the social treatment and judgment of specific social groups (social legitimacy); and (c) they offer implicit explanations for social conditions and events (social causality; see Zick, 1997).

From this perspective, this article will examine

(a) how Jews are categorized in European countries (stereotypical ascriptions) and the differences this is supposed to accentuate;
(b) whether there are in fact any real conflicts of interest between Jews and non-Jews and in which areas these conflicts are perceived;
(c) to what extent Jews are felt to threaten the social identity of the majority; and
(d) for which social conditions or events anti-Jewish prejudices provide an "explanation" or "justification."

Do Jews Differ? Anti-Semitism and its Historical Impact

According to the results of a series of studies from different countries, anti-Semitism correlates closely with xenophobia, Islamophobia, homophobia, and the like (Ambrosewicz-Jacob, 2003; Bergmann & Erb, 2003; Heitmeyer, 2007; Kovács, 1999, 2005; Living History Forum & Swedish National Council for Crime Prevention, 2004). Nonetheless, the analysis starts with the hypothesis that the attitudes toward Jews in Europe differ from those toward immigrant minorities and national minorities whose ethnic background lies in neighboring nations. We advance this hypothesis because the categorization of Jews is based less on the current group position and social contact in the respective country but rather on their past situation. This means that the category *Jew* gains its salience primarily when the past is activated as a reference point. This category is therefore essentially symbolic. Available empirical studies show that in countries where anti-Semitism was not very widespread prior to 1945, such as in Scandinavia, the Netherlands, the United Kingdom, Italy, and the Czech Republic, the population today is less anti-Semitic than in those countries with a more deeply rooted tradition of anti-Semitism, such as Germany, Austria, Poland, Russia, Ukraine, Lithuania, Romania, and Slovakia. The role the country played in the Holocaust is decisive for the content of attitudes toward Jews, naturally above all, in Germany and Austria. But this factor also strongly influences attitudes in Latvia, Lithuania,

Romania, Slovakia, and Hungary (partially in Poland as well), and more recently, in Switzerland.

If this hypothesis is correct, then the negative classification of Jews does not primarily employ categories like religion, race, current economic status or competition, or any other terms covering social problems. Rather it refers to the specific social position that Jews held historically. The national anti-Semitism that evolved in the 19th century did not view Jews simply as "aliens," as immigrant members of another nation, but rather as a group that stood outside the national order of the world. Jews were both outside and inside at the same time, and therefore embodied the counterprinciple of a "national nonidentity" (Holz, 2001). This ambivalent position predestined the Jews to become perceived as the embodiment of supranational modern phenomena like international finance markets, Communism, and liberal values. Their rapid social advancement in most European societies and their continuing connection with the money economy were interpreted as a confirmation of these "myths about the Jews," the core of which is the insinuation that Jews secretly dominate the economic and political world. The founding of Israel has not changed this ambivalent position. The misconceptions that identify Jews with international financial power and world domination remain, because Israel (Zionism) is now included into this image as a kind of "Jewish agency."

From this specific position, the core of the anti-Semitic prejudice can be defined as follows:

Jews are seen not as individuals but as a collective, putting their own group before all other commitments. Jews remain essentially alien in the surrounding societies, and they bring disaster into their "host societies" or the whole world, and they are doing it secretly (Bering, 2002, p. 474).

In line with this structure of an envious prejudice, Jews are perceived as a powerful and threatening group that is not part of the national collective.

The damage Jews are alleged to inflict on their host societies covers a number of fields:

(a) They can undermine a society's religious and cultural cohesion, for example, through secularization or endangering the national culture through universal values and ideas;
(b) They can harm a society economically through financial exploitation or manipulating international financial markets;
(c) They can destabilize and threaten politically by acts of betrayal to ones country, by acting as a revolutionary force, or by controlling a country's political system; and
(d) They can damage a society morally by utilizing their role of victim in the Holocaust to portray a negative image of the country or to demand restitution payments (See b.)

Whether one views the Jews as a group that damages the nation in the present or has damaged it in the past depends greatly on the individual's identification with the in-group. A strong national identification forms the core of this attitude, and politically it is preeminent in the right-wing conservative spectrum. Bergmann and Erb (2003) showed with a multivariate analysis of anti-Semitic attitudes in Germany that the factors with the highest explanatory power are those on the level of ideology and value orientation (right-wing political orientation, conservative value orientation, and, above all, nationalistic pride and authoritarianism), whereas the fear of economic crisis expresses itself today only very weakly in the form of intolerance toward Jews. Studies in other countries confirm this connection (for Hungary, see Kovács, 2005; for Poland, see Krzemiński, 1996, p. 302).

Stereotypical Categorization

Jews as Targets of Envious Prejudice

According to the ethnic hierarchies model (Hagendoorn, 1993) and social dominance theory (Sidanius & Pratto, 1999), stereotypes and racist arguments serve to justify differences in group positions, an assumption first stated by Allport in 1954 (see Bobo & Hutchings' group-position model, 1996). Thus, immigrant minorities and Gypsies are classified at the bottom of the hierarchy. This perception is manifested in greater social distance toward them, resistance to their equal treatment, more negative judgments about them, and accusations that their behavior is normatively deficient. In contrast to these out-groups, Jews are placed far up the hierarchy, experiencing clearly less social distance (AJC, 2001, Table 10; AJC, 2002) and enjoying equal treatment before the law. This status, together with the fact that the Jewish minority is in most countries extremely small (see Table 4, below), means that conflicts about jobs, housing, and social security support are rare. It is their special skills and capabilities that are perceived as a threat to the in-group. Although the threat is perceived as real, it resides on a higher level of abstraction as a kind of ominous symbolic menace, replicating fears and prejudices especially widespread in Central and Eastern Europe prior to 1945 (e.g., Jews control the press, the economy, etc.).

On the one hand, Jews are socially integrated and perceived to be successful. But, on the other hand, they are also seen as an integral part of the respective national society, or rather perceived as a closely knit group that primarily looks after itself, less concerned with the welfare of the nation in which they live (see Table 1). If we follow the stereotype content model (SCM), which divides stereotyped out-groups into two clusters, Jews belong to the envied groups due to the high societal status ascribed to them. The SCM asserts that "out-groups often fall in two mixed clusters: paternalized groups liked as warm but disrespected as incompetent . . . and envied groups respected but disliked as lacking warmth." (Lin, Kwan, Cheung, & Fiske,

Table 1. Categorization of Jews as Lacking Sociability/Jewish Power in Business (% Agree)

Country	Items			
	Jews Are More Loyal to Israel Than to This Country	Jews Don't Care What Happens to Anyone but Their Own Kind	Jews Stick Together More than Others (Italians, Dutch ...).	Jews Have too much Power in the Business World
Austria	46	29	70	24
Belgium	46	20		33
Denmark	37	14		11
France	28	15		25
Germany	50	30		20
(Hungary)	(37)			(55)
Italy	57	24	73	33
Netherlands	44	15	37	18
(Poland)	(52)			(43)
Spain	48	23	47	45
Switzerland	46	30	64	26
United Kingdom	40	18		14

Source. ADL, 2004; figures in parentheses ( ), ADL, 2005, Table 1.

2005, p. 35) Groups admired for their competence (intelligence, industriousness, and discipline), embodied for example by Jews and Asian Americans, are described as lacking sociability with the dominant group and are therefore disliked. The presumed competence of the envied out-group engenders a sense of threat and competition among the in-group. Anti-Semitism can be seen as the ideological form of an envious prejudice, which is "a crucial mediator of scapegoating" (Glick, 2002, p. 114)

The accusation of a lack of sociability is exacerbated in the case of the Jewish out-group by history. For centuries Jewish communities, marginalized in Christian societies, were extensively self-administered up until the 19th century, giving rise to the widespread impression that the Jews formed a "state within the state." The "knowledge" about the Jewish claim to be the "chosen people" further encouraged the image of arrogant segregation. In international comparisons this dimension of prejudice is addressed with three items focusing on the question of double loyalty and in-group favoritism.

Table 1 shows that the Jews are placed in a close relationship with Israel by a large section of the population in European countries, and that they are viewed as forming a cohesive and separate group. This may not necessarily indicate a negative attitude, for it can instead be meant as a simple observation. The lower percentage approving the statement that "Jews don't care..." is an evidence of this; at the same time however, a section regards the close connection of the country's Jews with Israel negatively as an expression of clannishness. In the following paragraphs, several indicators that reveal the stereotyping of Jews are discussed. Further on, the special position ascribed to Jews compared to that of other minorities, who are targets of contemptuous prejudice (Glick, 2002), are demonstrated.

Religious Stereotyping

Religious difference, which into the early 20th century was a key dimension of disapproval of Jews, is hardly articulated in the surveys[2] (Cohen & Golub, 1991, Table 11). Yet about one-fifth of Europeans still agreed "strongly or somewhat" with the statement, "The Jews are responsible for the death of Christ" (ADL, 2005; Gudkov & Levinson, 1994). The fact that this religious prejudice is limited mostly to older, poorly educated people, living mainly in rural areas or small towns, as Krzemiński (1996) has observed for Poland, indicates that its significance will diminish in the future. Moreover, I think that we may interpret agreement with the aforementioned statements as an expression of common historical "knowledge," which is likely to be of little consequence for the respondents, rather than being a sign of religious hatred or scapegoating.

The Dominant Stereotype: International Jewish Power

The items typically selected in the surveys to measure attitudes toward Jews refer to the stereotypes "power or influence" (see Tables 1 and 3), "money and greed connected with dishonestly earned wealth," "slyness," and "clannishness" (for Russia: Brym, 1996; Krichevsky, 1999; for Hungary: Kovács, 1999, Tables 1 and 3; and for Slovakia: Bútorává & Bútora, 1995, pp. 5f). In its survey to gauge "anti-Semitism in Europe" (2002), the Anti-Defamation League (ADL) used an anti-Semitism index that contained the following four statements: (a) Jews do not care what happens to anyone but their own kind; (b) Jews are more willing to use shady practices to get what they want; (c) Jews are more loyal to Israel than to this country; and (d) Jews have too much power in the business world. These stereotypes indicate an asymmetrical group relationship, where the Jews are categorized as powerful, while the self-characterization is that of a weaker group threatened by the might of the other. The cause for this superior strength can be seen in part in the abilities of Jews, who are ascribed intelligence (frequently in the negative sense of cunningness) and an ethos of hard work. But they are also alleged to use unfair practices (deceit, preferential treatment for their own group). The "stereotype of the Jews" differs greatly from that associated with the lower strata of society and ascribed to immigrant minorities. Table 2 shows that a certain proportion of the population believes that Jews possess too much influence in the country. At the same time however, other social groups or organizations are far more frequently ascribed such influence.

These figures show that respondents in most Western European countries hardly perceive a continuing Jewish influence in their own country, while the

---

[2] In contrast to the United States (Glock & Stark, 1966), the influence of denomination, religious practice, and particularism have yet to be systematically investigated in Europe (cf. Konig, Scheepers, & Felling, 2001).

Table 2. Influence in Society "Do You Feel that the Following Groups Have Too Much, Too Little, or the Right Influence in Our Society?" (Too Much Influence,%)

Country	Groups							
	Jews	Journalists/ Media	Politicians/ Political Parties	Businessmen/ Entrepreneurs	Intellectuals	Workers/ Trade Unions	Civil Servants	Other Nations/ Groups
Austria (2001)	19	41	61 58	22*	18	3	38	26[a]
Belarus (1992)	15	42	28	63*	29	10	72	42[b]
Czech Republic (1999)	8	53	70	42	26	4	39	
Germany (2002)	20	70	42	68+	16	32[#]	—	51[a]
Great Britain (1993)	8	77	—	60+	—	26[#]	—	36[d]
Hungary (1991)	17		58		29	2	32	24[b]
Latvia (1992)	8	19	25	31*	12	3	36	12[b]
Lithuania (1992)	11	58	28	30*	38	25	39	22[b]
Poland (1995)	16	32		43		12[#]		27[a]
Russia (1996)	14	35	62 39	57*	10	4	75	43[c]
Slovakia (1999)	15	39	76	62	23	3	29	
Sweden (1999)	2	59	50	36+	13	21[#]		
Switzerland (2000)	17	53	39	31+	20			
Ukraine (1992)	9	33	35	33*	17	11	51	11[b]

Sources. Cohen & Golub, 1991, Golub & Cohen 1993, Table 16; AJC, 1996, Item 20; Gudkov & Levinson, 1994, Items 6–20; AJC, 1999, 2000a, 2000b, 2001, 2002.
Note. * entrepreneurs; + big business, business leaders, or foreign business men; # trade or labor unions; [a] = Americans; [b] = foreigners, [c] = Caucasians; [d] = Japanese.

proportion is slightly higher in a few Eastern European countries (Poland, Hungary, Slovakia, Russia, and Belarus). It reaches its peak in Germany and Austria traceable largely to coping with their national historical burdens. Respondents see the Jews as using this past as a lever to exert moral pressure publicly. There is no reference here to a general Jewish influence in business and politics. If, due to the small size of their group and because only the small minority perceives a disproportionate influence, the prejudice of "Jewish power" has no factual basis in the real situation of Jews in the respective country, so what does it link into?

Markovitz (2003) claimed that European anti-Semitism has changed to the extent that expressions of prejudice and hate against the "powerless" European Jews are still regarded as illegitimate, but that such expressions against the "powerful Jews" in Israel and the United States are permitted. Presumably, one might say, this type of anti-Semitic prejudice finds a kind of "environmental support" in the pro-Israeli policy of the United States, which is "explained" by the power of the Jewish lobby in the United States and Israel's influence on American policy. This fits well the basic structure of the anti-Semitic stereotype that Jews form an international, closely networked, powerful group, and we may expect that "Jewish power" is conceived in the form of a worldwide influence. This prejudice serves less the

Table 3. International Jewish Influence

"Now, as in the Past, Jews Exert Too Much Influence on World Events" (%)

Country	Strongly Agree	Somewhat Agree	Somewhat Disagree	Strongly Disagree	Don't know or No Answer
Austria (2001)	12	28	23	13	24
Czech Rep. (1999)	9	25	39	12	15
Germany (2002)	14	26	21	17	22
Latvia (1992)	12	19	21	7	41
Lithuania (1992)	12	22	22	7	36
Russia (1996)	8	24	31	8	28
Slovakia (1999)	23	30	20	4	23
Sweden (1999)	2	12	11	64	11
Switzerland (2000)	13	20	32	23	12
Ukraine (1992)	7	10	27	11	40

Sources. AJC, Austria, 2001, Table 12; Gudkov & Levinson, 1994, Item 72.

purpose of drawing social distinctions, but rather furnishes a pattern for implicit explanations of social conditions or events. Because Jewish influence is conceived as being exerted "behind the scenes" it is possible to project responsibility for any kind of threat, disaster, and negative phenomena onto the Jews.

Table 3 shows that, a good one third (and more) of the respondents are in agreement with the statement "Now, as in the past, Jews exert too much influence on world events." In some places, more than one half of the respondents agree with this. The only exception is Sweden, where only 14% agreed with the assumption. A familiar pattern is once more discernible in this distribution: respondents in Germany, Austria, and Slovakia agree most frequently, closely followed by Lithuania, Latvia, Switzerland, and the Czech Republic, while in the remaining Western European countries, like Sweden, respondents are again less inclined to subscribe to such a view. In the ADL survey of 2005 the question concerning international influence was reframed to concentrate on the "business world" because Jewish "world power" is allegedly often located in the economic realm (see Table 1).

Conflicts of Interest

The second of my core questions refers to the role of group competition as a possible explanation of anti-Semitism. Perceptions of threat can be related to the quantitative relationships between groups. Threat might thus, for example, emerge from minorities being very large or continually growing through immigration. After the Holocaust, however, most European countries are faced with "anti-Semitism without Jews"; Jews merely form a diminishing minority of a few thousand people (nowhere more than 1% of the population—see Table 4), with the only notable immigration country being Germany. Meanwhile, in Eastern European countries, the Jewish population is decreasing because of emigration. Table 4 shows

Table 4. Jewish Population and Anti-Jewish Prejudice

Country	Total Population (N)	Jewish Population (N)	Prefer not to Have Jews as Neighbors (%)	Jews Are Willing to Use Shady Practices to Get What They Want (%)
Russia	147,000,000	350–450,000	17	
France	60,000,000	600,000		15
United Kingdom	58,400,000	283,000	12	13
Germany	82,000,000	100,000	22	22
Hungary	10,300,000	60–140,000	17	
Belgium	10,300,000	35,000		14
Spain	40,000,000	20–40,000		24
Italy	56,300,000	30,000		10
Netherlands	16,000,000	30,000		8
Sweden	8,900,000	18,500	2	
Switzerland	7,100,000	18,000	8	21
Austria	8,000,000	8,000	18	23
Denmark	5,300,000	7,000		14
Czech Republic	10,400,000	5,000	17	
Poland	38,800,000	5,000	30	
Slovakia	5,000,000	3,000	16	

Sources. Anti-Semitism Worldwide 2000/2001; AJC, 2001, Table 10; ADL, 2004.

that a systematic connection between the numerical strength of the minority and anti-Semitic attitudes or social distance toward Jews is not discernible. In countries with a larger Jewish proportion of the population like the United Kingdom, anti-Semitic attitudes are less widespread than in countries with very small Jewish minorities such as Poland, Slovakia, and Austria.

One might presume that Jews arouse animosity and make enemies by showing hostile behavior. But the data do not confirm that anti-Semitic attitudes evolve from this cause. In response to the question, "Which of the following groups behave in a manner that provokes hostility in our country," Jews were specified as follows: 14% of the respondents in Austria named Jews, 4% in the Czech Republic, 6% in Germany, 8% in Great Britain, 6% in Hungary, 23% in Poland (for conflicts of the "victim rivalry" type, see below), 4% in Russia, 9% in Slovakia, and 3% in Sweden. Most accused of provoking hostility through their behavior are groups that are regarded as being embroiled in more or less real cultural, economic, or political conflicts. In Russia for instance, this kind of reproach is directed above all against Chechens (71%) and members of those former Soviet Republics where independence was accompanied by conflict (nationalities of the Baltic States 16%, Armenians 25%, and Azerbaijanis 31%); in Western Europe, it is the larger Muslim minorities, of whom the working immigrants or asylum-seekers especially are accused of hostile behavior. One exception from this explanation are the "Gypsies"—they are rejected all over Europe.

Today, other characteristics of historical animosity toward Jews than the racist dimension, or professional competition, are rare in Europe. We still find anti-Semitic sentiments among the extreme-right population or in circles strongly influenced by folk religious ideas and practices. Meanwhile, during the last few years, the conflict in the Middle East has become a key reference point for anti-Semitism. This new context currently serves—on the international level at least—as the main focus for hatred of Jews. It is more pronounced in Western, Northern, and Southern Europe than in Eastern European countries. For Russia and the Ukraine (Gidwitz, 2003) and also for Bulgaria, Croatia, etc., "the Middle East conflict is certainly not producing anti-Jewish sentiment" (AJC, 2005). Old anti-Semitic accusations of "biblical revenge" are now attributed to Israel. By accusing Israel of perpetrating the worst crimes of the National Socialists—apartheid, ethnic cleansing, or genocide—an opposition to Nazism and racism goes along with opposition to Israel and the Jews and backing of the Palestinian cause. While this mode of legitimacy is to be found predominantly among the extreme left and right in Europe, Israeli politics might be an important cause for anti-Jewish attitudes among other sections of the population as well. This connection between the perception of Israel and anti-Semitic attitudes has yet to be empirically researched in greater detail (it has only been investigated empirically in Germany, France, and Switzerland: Heyder, Iser, & Schmidt, 2004; Mayer, 2005; Schweizerische Gesellschaft für praktische Sozialforschung, 2007).

Jews as a Collective Threat to Social Identity

If the Jewish minorities represent no actual danger to either the religious or cultural identity or the political or economic system, then from where does the threat perceived by anti-Semites evolve? A threat to group identity emerges, on the one hand, in those countries that were in some way involved in the Holocaust, for the Holocaust attacks national "honor." And on the other hand, it emerges in those countries that consider themselves to be victims of National Socialism, for this generates a "rivalry for claiming victim status" with the Jews, which confuses the national self-image. This means that the Jewish minority in a country is at once a legacy and instance of remembrance. After the political transformations of 1989, there are signs on the European level that the Holocaust is increasingly entering into the construction of the respective national histories, as has been the case in Germany and Austria since 1945 and in many Western European countries in the last two decades. Eastern European states are beginning to face up to and study their own involvement in the Holocaust, after remembrance had been suppressed for a variety of reasons during Communist rule (Orla-Bukowska, 2004; Zuroff, 2005). With the political transitions marked by the year 1989, the question of restitution of Jewish property has become a topical issue in these countries because it is closely tied to issues of reprivatizing state-owned property, economic reforms, and

Table 5. Jews and the Holocaust "Jews Still Talk Too Much about What Happened to Them in the Holocaust" (% Yes)

Country	Year		
	2002	2004	2005
Austria	56	56	46
Belgium	38	40	41
Denmark	30	29	35
France	46	35	34
Germany	58	56	48
Hungary			46
Italy	43	43	49
Netherlands	35	35	34
Poland			52
Spain	57	57	46
Switzerland	52	52	48
United Kingdom	23	31	28

Source. ADL, 2002a, 2002b, 2004, 2005.

national identity. In Western European countries, too, restitution raises difficult and awkward questions about the role played by governments and companies in World War II in collaborating with the Nazi occupying power that touch on national self-image and material interests. This situation could become a source of real conflict.

One indication of how an emphasis on the Holocaust generates a negative defense reaction is the reproach that Jews exploit the Holocaust for their own purpose. In four surveys conducted by the ADL in 2002, 2004 and 2005, the question was posed in nine European Union countries and Switzerland whether "Jews still talk too much about the Holocaust." Although a positive response to this statement does not necessarily indicate an anti-Semitic attitude, it does appear that this issue represents a certain emotive potential out of which resentment could grow.

Table 5 summarizes the results. As expected, this statement finds especially high levels of approval in Germany and Austria, those countries where anti-Semitic attitudes are particularly motivated by issues of guilt and responsibility for the murdering of European Jews. And yet, in Spain (57%) and Switzerland (52%), countries not or only indirectly having been involved in the persecution, the majority of the population clearly shows its "annoyance." In other Western European states almost one-third of respondents agree with this statement.

Table 6 shows that anti-Semitic motivation is more clearly evident in the suspicion that the Jews would exploit the Holocaust for their own purposes. As was to be expected with this "harder" item, approval is far lower; only answers in Germany, Austria, and Poland are conspicuous. In these countries a large section of the population suspect other "Jewish interests" behind the demands for remembering the Holocaust. While strong agreement is very low in the listed countries, when

Table 6. Exploitation of the Holocaust "Jews are Exploiting the National Socialist Holocaust for Their Own Purposes" (% Yes)

Country	Strongly Agree	Somewhat Agree	Somewhat Disagree	Strongly Disagree	Don't Know or No Answer
Austria (2005)	12	30	29	22	7
Czech Republic (1999)	6	17	43	17	17
France (2005)	10	22	28	37	3
Germany (2005)	16	26	34	15	9
Great Britain (2005)	8	16	30	35	11
Poland (2005)	14	33	30	13	10
Slovakia (1999)	7	18	32	15	29
Sweden (2005)	4	30	28	30	8
Switzerland (2000)	9	30	27	20	13

Source. AJC, 2001, Table 9; AJC, 2005; in Hungary (1995) 26% agreed (Kovacs, 2005).

taken together with the category "somewhat agree," which tends to represent an evasive response to awkward questions, 16%–39% of the respondents reproach the Jews for exploiting the Holocaust. In Hungary, even 20% agreed completely and a further 25% partly to a similar statement: "Jews try to gain profit even from their persecution" (Erös & Fabian, 1995, p. 353). A similar question, which however does not refer directly to the Holocaust, was posed in 1992 in the Commonwealth of Independent States: "Jews greatly overstate their misfortunes, sufferings, and sacrifices." In Russia, 35% of respondents agreed with this statement, 39% in Ukraine, 54% in Belarus, and 24%–27% in the Baltic States, while only 16%–30% rejected this statement explicitly (Gudkov & Levinson, 1994).

Among the causes for the rise of anti-Semitic attitudes in Russia and other former Eastern bloc states, Gorvin (2003) named the attempts undertaken by Jewish organizations to reclaim the property of Jewish communities that had been expropriated during Nazi occupation or Communist rule. In this case, there would be a realistic group conflict over scarce resources. In the context of the Polish debate, Stola (2003, p. 217) pointed out that the restitution mainly entails returning property to Jews who today live overseas, a circumstance that creates xenophobic and anti-Semitic reactions against Jews and foreign pressure.

The Swiss population's reaction to the "Raubgold controversy" is a further illustration of this issue.[3] After all, 39% of the respondents (Table 6) accuse the Jews of exploiting the Holocaust, while at the same time a majority of the Swiss think that "Switzerland does not have to apologize for its behavior toward Jews during World War II" (agreed to by 45% of respondents, while 39% rejected it— Schweizerische Gesellschaft für praktische Sozialforschung [GfS], 2000). Thus, for the GfS study, the "controversy about Switzerland's behavior in World War II is

---

[3] During World War II, the Swiss National Bank accepted gold from the German Reichsbank as payment for exports. This gold was, however, confiscated from occupied countries or Holocaust victims by the Nazis.

the crucial issue for anti-Semitic thinking." In turn, this is primarily mobilized by currently prevailing "prejudices on Jewish world domination," about which 33% of the Swiss respondents are more or less convinced.

In Hungary, 47% did not share the opinion in 1995 that "Jews are right to ask for compensation from the Hungarian government for their persecution during the War," although 52% readily recognized the responsibility Hungary bore "for what happened to the Hungarian Jews during the War" (Kovács, 2005, p. 213). Kovács pointed out that the refusal to pay compensation is not necessarily motivated by anti-Semitism. In many European countries, the question of Jewish suffering gives rise to controversies about the relationship between Jewish victims and their own victims of persecution and war. As already evident in the attempts by Germans and Austrians to set off Jewish suffering against that of their own victims of bombing and expulsion, something like a victim rivalry is observable in many Eastern and Central European states since 1990. This phenomenon functions as an important defense motive against any specific emphasis granted to Jewish victims. There is a tendency to align cases of suffering of one's own nation to the Holocaust narrative, which, in turn, leads to a rivalry between these narratives of suffering ("competitive martyrology" of the Holocaust and the GULAG; Raportul Comisei, 2004). Orla-Bukowska (2004) feared that any preference given to the Jews as a victim group, when coupled with a simultaneous lack of attention to other victim groups, could lead to a rise in anti-Semitism. An additional problem in this context is recognizing the suffering inflicted on countries under the Stalinist regime, which are more present in the public awareness than the Holocaust (Orla-Bukowska, p. 340).

The AJC investigated this phenomenon in its surveys in Poland and Slovakia. Regarding the question, "In your eyes, who was the main victim of the Nazis during the Second World War," the answers of the Polish respondents were nearly equally distributed. In 1995, 26% of the Polish respondents viewed the Poles as main victims, 28% named the Jews, and 28% named both the Poles and the Jews (Golub & Cohen, 1995, Table 12). Asked to respond to a direct comparison ("Which group suffered more from Nazi persecution during the Second World War: the Poles or the Jews?"), 28% said Poles, 29% Jews, and 40% decided that both had suffered roughly the same. Asked if the Jews had suffered more than the rest of the population in World War II, 60% of the Slovakian respondents answered "yes" and 18% "no" (19% were insufficiently informed; Bútorová & Bútora, 1993). In Hungary, 67% agreed with the statement "Hungarians suffered just as much as Jews during the War" in 1995 (Kovacs, 2005, p. 126). In comparison with Poland, it becomes clear that victim rivalry is less pronounced in the populations of those states once allied to the Third Reich than among the prime victims of the war (Poland, Russia); on the other hand, however, large sections of the population lack a critical stance toward these war-time governments. In Slovakia only 37% affirmed joint responsibility of the Slovak population for the deportation of the Jews (AJC, 1999b), and in Romania nationalist politicians and historians attempt to scale down the numbers of Jewish victims during the "Romanian Holocaust." to exonerate political leaders like Antonescu and Codreanu and to present Romanians as victims of "Judeo-Communism" (Hausleitner, 2004, p.188). According to Braham, it is evident in Eastern Central Europe that, although there is only a fringe group of Holocaust deniers, there are "the history cleaners who denigrate and distort the Holocaust," and these are frequently "respectable" public figures (Braham, 2001, p. 198).

Anti-Semitic Prejudices as Explanations and Justifications

Similar to conspiracy theories, anti-Semitic arguments are used today to explain a variety of phenomena, ranging from the social problems caused by globalization and neoliberal capitalism, such as unemployment and economic downturns, to the Iraq war and terrorism. For example, 25% of German respondents regarded "Jewish influence" on American politics as one main reason for U.S. military action against Iraq (AJC, 2002). Jews were seen as actors and profiteers behind threatening structural and political developments for which no conclusive explanations can be given. Furthermore, phenomena such as Islamic terrorism are seen as a logical, almost unavoidable consequence of Israel's policies, which a majority of Europeans regard as a threat to world peace.[4] The Middle East conflict has also reinforced the traditional linkage between anti-Semitism and anti-Americanism, a strain of resentment that became particularly virulent with the portrayal of the United States as Israel's protector and servant, acting under the dual influence of an alleged Jewish/Zionist lobby.

These anti-Semitic prejudices not only provide "explanations" for recent problems, but are also projected "backwards" to justify behavior toward Jews in past conflicts. In this context, anti-Semitic arguments today frequently serve the purpose of rejecting guilt and responsibility for the persecution of the Jews. People holding anti-Semitic prejudices seek to document evidence of wrongdoing by Jews, whether accurate or not. This defensive mechanism takes two forms: either the Jews are ascribed a joint responsibility for what happened by insinuating that they had behaved in a hostile and damaging way in the past. That Jews were themselves responsible for their persecution was agreed to by 30% in Russia, 27% in the Ukraine, 35% in Belarus, 31% in Lithuania (Gudkov & Levinson, 1994), and 17% in Germany in 2004 (Heitmeyer, 2007, p. 24). Or they are turned into the "scapegoat" for the political developments in their country. Here the old anti-Jewish "Judas motif" of betrayal and collaboration with the enemy is exploited. In

---

[4] In a Eurobarometer survey, a list of countries was presented to participants, who were asked which of them presented a danger to world peace. On average, Israel was named most frequently with 59%. Multiple choices were possible. (Flash EB No. 151: "Iraq and Peace in the World" (08/10/2003–16/10/2003)–Report p. 78.).

this way, the Holocaust is connected with the crimes of Stalinism in some Eastern European countries. The most predominant stereotype activated in this legitimacy strategy is that of "Judeo-Communism." According to Gorvin (2003), anti-Semites in the Baltic States legitimate the Holocaust by claiming that the Jews acted as Soviet collaborators in 1940–1941 and were actively involved in deporting Balts to Siberia. This interpretive pattern of Jewish betrayal and collaboration with the Soviet occupying forces also emerged in the debate in Poland on the Jedwabne pogrom. Moreover, in Romania, high-ranking politicians and historians are endeavoring to legitimate the war against the Soviet Union as "just," namely as a defensive operation against the Communist threat, and to present "dangerous minorities," such as the Ukrainians, Russians, and Jews as Soviet collaborators. The figure of "Judeo-Communism" represents a classical example of the scapegoat motif of anti-Semitism that allows the national collective to acquit itself of responsibility and to shift the burden of guilt for Stalinist crimes and Communism onto the Jews. Because the argument of Stalinism as a kind of foreign rule does not fit for the Soviet Union, this attitude is not widespread in the Commonwealth of Independent States (Gudkov & Levinson, 1994, item 96).

Conclusions

The attitude toward Jews correlates strongly, on the one hand, with other expressions of group-focused enmity, while, on the other, it shows a different structure of prejudice than that directed against immigrant or national minorities. Far less social distance is shown toward Jews, the proportion of Jews in the overall population has no correlation with the extent of anti-Semitism, and Jews are neither accused of refusing to integrate culturally, nor of not adhering to the host society's normative values, or of provoking animosity by their behavior.

The role the Jewish minority plays in any particular country is obviously of less significance than the historically transmitted image of the Jews as an internationally interconnected group that is insinuatingly presumed to exert a far-reaching and corrosive influence on the world economy and politics. In this respect, Jews are regarded as not belonging to the national collective, although in most cases they have been citizens of a country for centuries. A second prejudice complex is tied to the persecution of the Jews in the Holocaust and the negative repercussions this has for the sense of national esteem and self-confidence today. Here, anti-Semitism is tightly interwoven with right-wing, nationalist attitudes. A third prejudice complex, yet to be thoroughly researched, emerges from the association between Jews and the state of Israel, in a way that opinions and sentiments about the Middle East conflict influence attitudes toward Jews. At the same time however, the reverse interconnection also applies: anti-Semitic patterns of thought determine perceptions of Israeli policy. This last aspect must be of special significance for the Muslim population in Europe—who here have been left out of our considerations.

In terms of European comparison, differences emerge in these three complexes between Eastern and Western European countries. Germany and Austria represent unique situations, however, with anti-Semitism motivated by a defense mechanism against the burden of historical responsibility being very pronounced. In Eastern Central Europe, hostility toward the Jewish minority was and continues to be more intensive and widespread than in Western Europe, simply because this minority was far larger and entangled in competition with the lower middle classes aspiring to climb the social ladder. This long tradition of prejudice has to be taken into account when analyzing these countries. Second, the Holocaust and the collaboration of certain sections of the nation during the Nazi persecution were initially suppressed from public consciousness after 1945 in Eastern European countries. These issues could be addressed and discussed only after the breakup of the Communist bloc in 1989, leading to confusion and irritation in national self-identification. In the Western European countries, in contrast, it is Israel's politics toward the Palestinians, which risks conflict and triggers a mobilization of anti-Semitic attitudes.

References

Allport, G. W. (1954). *The nature of prejudice*. Cambridge, MA: Addison-Wesley.
Ambrosewicz-Jacobs, J. (2003). *Me, us, them. Ethnic prejudice among youth and alternative methods of education. The case of Poland*. Cracow, Poland: Universitas.
American Jewish Committee. (1996). *Current Russian attitudes toward Jews and the Holocaust. A public-opinion survey*. New York: American Jewish Committee.
American Jewish Committee. (1999). *Knowledge and remembrance of the Holocaust in the Czech Republic*. Retrieved 9/28/2007, from http://www.ajc.org/site/c.ijITI2PHKoG/b.846741/k.8A33/ Publications_Surveys/apps/nl/newsletter3.asp.
American Jewish Committee. (1999b). *Knowledge and remembrance of the Holocaust in Slovakia*. Retrieved 9/28/2007, from http://www.ajc.org/site/c.ijITI2PHKoG/b.846741/k.8A33/ Publications_Surveys/apps/nl/newsletter3.asp.
American Jewish Committee. (2000a). *Knowledge and remembrance of the Holocaust in Sweden*. New York: American Jewish Committee.
American Jewish Committee. (2000b). *Swiss attitudes toward Jews and the Holocaust. A public-opinion survey*. New York: American Jewish Committee.
American Jewish Committee. (2001). *Attitudes toward Jews and the Holocaust in Austria*. New York: American Jewish Committee.
American Jewish Committee in Deutschland. (2002). *Die Einstellung der Deutschen zu Juden, dem Holocaust und den USA* [German attitudes toward Jews, the Holocaust and the U.S]. Berlin: American Jewish Committee.
American Jewish Committee. (2005). *Thinking about the Holocaust 60 years later. A multinational public-opinion survey*. New York: American Jewish Committee.
Anti-Defamation League. (2002a). *European attitudes toward Jews, Israel and the Palestinian-Israeli Conflict, June 27, 2002*. Retrieved 9/28/2007, from http://www.adl.org/Anti_semitism/European_Attitudes.pdf.
Anti-Defamation League. (2002b). *European attitudes toward Jews: A five country survey October 2002*. Retrieved 9/28/2007, from http://www.adl.org/Anti_semitism/EuropeanAttitudes Poll-10-02.pdf.
Anti-Defamation League. (2004). *Attitudes toward Jews, Israel and the Palestinian-Israeli conflict in ten European countries*. Retrieved 9/28/2007, from http://www.adl.org/Anti_semitism/ European_Attitudes_april_2004.pdf.

Anti-Defamation League. (2005). *Attitudes toward Jews in twelve European countries.* Retrieved 9/28/2007, from http://www.adl.org/Anti_semitism/European_Attitudes_May_2005.pdf.

Bergmann, W. (1996). Antisemitismus-Umfragen nach 1945 im internationalen Vergleich [International post-war surveys on Anti-Semitism in a comparative perspective]. *Jahrbuch für Antisemitismusforschung, 5*, 172–195.

Bergmann, W., & Erb, R. (2003). Anti-Semitism in the late nineties. In R. Alba, P. Schmidt, & M. Wasmer (Eds.), *Germans or foreigners? Attitudes toward ethnic minorities in post-unification Germany* (pp. 163–186). New York/Houndmills: Palgrave Macmillan.

Bering, D. (2002). Gutachten über den antisemitischen Charakter einer namenpolemischen Passage aus der Rede Jörg Haiders, 28.2.2001 [Expert opinion on the anti-Semitic content of a polemical speech of Jörg Haider, 28th of February 2001]. In A. Pelinka & R. Wodak (Eds.), *"Dreck am Stecken" – Politik der Ausgrenzung "Not being entirely innocent" – Politics of exclusion]* (pp. 173–186). Vienna: Czernin.

Bobo, L., & Hutchings, V. L. (1996). Perceptions of racial group competition: Extending Blumer's theory of group position to a multiracial social context. *American Sociological Review, 61*, 951–972.

Braham, R. L. (2001). Assault on historical memory: Hungarian nationalists and the Holocaust. In R. L. Braham (Ed.), *Studies on the Holocaust. Selected writings, Vol. 2* (pp. 197–224). New York: East European Monographs, DLXXV.

Brym, R J. (1996). Russian attitudes towards Jews: An update. *East European Jewish Affairs, 26*, 55–64.

Bútoravá, Z., & Bútora, M. (1993). Vigilance vis-a-vis the Jews as an expression of post-communist panic – Slovakia's case. In J. Hančil & M. Chase (Eds.), *Anti-Semitism in post-totalitarian Europe* (pp. 137–150). Prague: Franz Kafka Publisher.

Bútorová, Z., & Bútora, M. (1995). *Attitudes toward Jews and the Holocaust in independent Slovakia.* New York: American Jewish Committee.

Cohen, R., & Golub, J. L. (1991). *Attitudes toward Jews in Poland, Hungary, and Czechoslovakia. A comparative survey.* New York: American Jewish Committee.

Dinnerstein, L. (1994). *Anti-Semitism in America.* New York: Oxford University Press.

Erös, F., & Fábián, Z. (1995). Anti-Semitism in Hungary 1990–1994. *Jahrbuch für Antisemitismusforschung, 4*, 342–356.

Gidwitz, B. (2003). Anti-Semitism in the post-soviet states. *Post-Holocaust and anti-Semitism.* Jerusalem: Jerusalem Center for Public Affairs.

Glick, P. (2002). Sacrificial lambs dressed in wolves' clothing: Envious prejudice, ideology, and the scapegoating of Jews. In L. S. Newman & R. Erber (Eds.), *Understanding genocide: The social psychology of the Holocaust* (pp. 113–142). London: Oxford.

Glock, C. Y., & Stark, R. (1966). *Christian beliefs and anti-Semitism.* New York: Harper & Row.

Golub, J., & Cohen, R. (1993). *What do the British know about the Holocaust?* New York: American Jewish Committee.

Golub, J., & Cohen, R. (1995). *Knowledge and remembrance of the Holocaust in Poland.* New York: American Jewish Committee.

Gorvin, Y. (2003). Anti-Semitic trends in post-communist Eastern European states—An overview. *Jewish Political Studies Review, 15*, 3–4,

Gudkov, L., & Levinson, A. (1994). *Attitudes toward Jews in the Commonwealth of Independent States.* New York: American Jewish Committee.

Hagendoorn, L. (1993). Ethnic categorization and outgroup exclusion: Cultural values and social stereotypes in the construction of ethnic hierarchies. *Ethnic and Racial Studies, 16*, 26–51.

Hausleitner, M. (2004). Der rumänische Holocaust und die Holocaust-Kontroverse in Rumänien [The Romanian holocaust and the holocaust-controversy in Romania]. In C. von Braun & E.-M. Ziege (Eds.), *Das "bewegliche Vorurteil". Aspekte des internationalen Antisemitismus* (pp. 175–192). Würzburg, Germany: Königstein und Neumann.

Heitmeyer, W. (Ed.) (2007). *Deutsche Zustände. Folge 5* [The German situation. Part 5]. Frankfurt, Germany: Suhrkamp.

Heyder, A., Iser, J., & Schmidt, P. (2004). Israelkritik oder Antisemitismus? Meinungsbildung zwischen Öffentlichkeit, Medien und Tabus [Criticism of Israel or Anti-Semitism? Forming an opinion under the influence of the public, the media and taboos]. In W. Heitmeyer (Ed.), *Deutsche Zustände. Folge 3*. (pp. 144–165). Frankfurt, Germany: Suhrkamp.

Holz, K. (2001). *Nationaler Antisemitismus. Wissenssoziologie einer Weltanschauung*[National Anti-Semitism. A sociological analysis of an ideology]. Hamburg, Germany: Hamburger Edition.

Konig, R., Scheepers, P., & Felling, A. (2001). Research on anti-Semitism: A review of previous findings and the case of the Netherlands in the 1990s. In A. Örkény & K. Phalet (Eds.), *Ethnic minorities and inter-ethnic relations in context: A Dutch-Hungarian comparison* (pp. 179–200). Singapore: Aldershot.

Kovács, A. (1999). Antisemitismus im heutigen Ungarn [Anti-Semitism in today's Hungary] *Jahrbuch für Antisemitismusforschung, 8*, 195–227.

Kovács, A. (2005). *A kéznél lévö idegen. Antiszemita elöitéletek a mai Magyarországon* [The foreigner at hand. Anti-Semitric prejudice in todays Hungary] Budapest: PolgArt.

Krichevsky, L. (1999). *Russian Jewish elites and anti-Semitism*. New York: American Jewish Committee.

Krzemiński, I. (Ed.) (1996). *Czy Polacy są antysemitami? Waniki badania sondażowego* [Are Poles anti-semitic? Results of a scientific survey]. Warszawa: Oficyna Naukowa.

Lin, M. H., Kwan, V. S. Y., Cheung, A., & Fiske, S. T. (2005). Stereotype content model explains prejudice for an envied outgroup: Scale of anti-Asian American stereotypes. *Personality and Social Psychology Bulletin, 31*, 34–47.

Living History Forum & Swedish National Council for Crime Prevention. (2004). *Intolerance. Anti-Semitic, homophobic, Islamophobic and xenophobic tendencies among the young*. Retrieved 9/28/2007, from http//intolerans.levandehistoria.se/article/article_docs/engelska.pdf.

Markovitz, A. S. (2003). European anti-Americanism and anti-Semitism. Similarities and differences. *Post-Holocaust and anti-Semitism, 16* 1–13.

Mayer, N. (2005), Transformations in French anti-Semitism. *Journal für Konflikt- und Gewaltforschung, 7*, 91–104.

Orla-Bukowska, A. (2004). Presenting and representing the shoah in the post-communist world. In D. J. Schaller, R. Boyadjian, & V. Berg (Eds.), *Enteignet – Vertrieben – Ermordet. Beiträge zur Genozidforschung* [Expropriated – expelled – murdered. Contributions to research in genocide] (pp. 319–347). Zurich, Switzerland: Chronos.

Raportul Comisiei Internationale privind studiera Holocaustului Romania. (2004). Retrieved 12/2/2004, from www.presidency.ro.

Schweizerische Gesellschaft für praktische Sozialforschung (GfS). (2000). *Einstellungen der SchweizerInnen gegenüber Jüdinnen und Juden und dem Holocaust* [Attitudes of the Swiss toward Jews and the holocaust]. Retrieved 6/26/2002, from www.gfs.ch/antsem.html.

Schweizerische Gesellschaft für praktische Sozialforschung (GfS). (2007). *Kritik an Israel von antisemitischen Haltungen unabhängig. Antisemitismus-Potenzial in der Schweiz neuartig bestimmt. Schlussbericht zur Studie "Anti-jüdische und anti-israelische Einstellungen in der Schweiz* [Criticism of Israel is independent of anti-semitic attitudes. A new study of anti-Semitism in Switzerland. Final version of the survey:"Anti-Jewish and anti-Israel attitudes in Switzerland]. Bern: unpublished study 3/28/2007.

Sidanius, J., & Pratto, F. (1999). *Social dominance: An intergroup theory of social hierarchy and oppression*. New York: Cambridge University Press.

Stola, D. (2003). Die polnische Debatte um den Holocaust und die Rückerstattung von Eigentum [The Polish discussion on the holocaust and the restitution of property]. In C. Goschler, & P. Ther (Eds.), *Raub und Restitution. "Arisierung" und Rückerstattung jüdischen Eigentums in Europa* [Robbery and restitution. "Aryanization" and Restitution of Jewish property in Europe] (pp. 205–224). Frankfurt, Germany: Fischer.

Tajfel, H., & Turner, J. C.. (1986). The social identity theory of intergroup behavior. In S. Worchel & G. Austin (Eds.), *Psychology of intergroup relations* (pp. 7–24). Chicago: Nelson.

Zick, A. (1997). *Vorurteile und Rassismus. Eine sozialpsychologische Analyse* [Prejudice and racism. A social psychological analysis]. Münster, Germany: Waxmann.

Zuroff, E. (2005). Eastern Europe: Anti-semitism in the wake of Holocaust-related issues. *Jewish Political Studies Review, 17*, 1–2.

WERNER BERGMANN is a sociologist and Professor at the Center for Research on Anti-Semitism, Technical University of Berlin. His fields of research are the sociology and history of anti-Semitism, xenophobia, and right-wing extremism; sociology of social movements and collective violence. His publications in English include *Anti-Semitism in Germany, The Post-Nazi Epoch since 1945* (1997), *Exclusionary Violence, Anti-Semitic Riots in Modern German History* (2002), *Pogroms* (2004).

The Syndrome of Group-Focused Enmity: The Interrelation of Prejudices Tested with Multiple Cross-Sectional and Panel Data

Andreas Zick*
University of Bielefeld

Carina Wolf
University of Marburg

Beate Küpper
University of Bielefeld

Eldad Davidov
GESIS-Central Archive for Empirical Social Research, University of Cologne

Peter Schmidt
University of Giessen

Wilhelm Heitmeyer
University of Bielefeld

Different types of prejudice are usually treated as separate constructs. We propose that they constitute a syndrome of group-focused enmity (GFE), that is, they are related to each other and share a common core that is strongly predicted by a generalized ideology of inequality. Furthermore, GFE components are supposed to

---

*Correspondence concerning this article should be addressed to Andreas Zick, University of Bielefeld, Institute for Interdisciplinary Research of Conflict and violence, Universitaetssr. 25, 33615 Bielefeld, Germany [e-mail: zick@uni-bielefeld.de].

The authors thank the Volkswagen Foundation, Freudenberg Foundation and Möllgaard Foundation for their financial support to the project on "Group-focused Enmity." We thank Tom Pettigrew and Uli Wagner for their helpful comments on an earlier draft of this article, and Jim Sidanius and Jorge Vala for their inspiring ideas on the topic at the International Workshop on "Group-focused Enmity" *have similar predictors and outcomes. An empirical test is presented using structural equation modeling on the syndrome, its causes, consequences, and structural stability over time. The study relies on three German cross-sectional probability samples (each* N = *2,700) and a related panel study (2002, 2003, and 2004). The idea of a GFE syndrome is strongly supported. Future research is discussed, as well as alternative approaches of a common prejudice factor.*

Components of Group-Focused Enmity (GFE)

In 1997, the European Union agreed on a struggle to put an end to prejudice and discrimination in article 13 of the Amsterdam Declaration: "the Council [...] may take appropriate action to combat discrimination based on sex, racial or ethnic origin, religion or belief, disability, age or sexual orientation." The focus on a range of different target groups of discrimination seems reasonable because different groups share a long history of disparagement and prejudiced believers are not limited to few but many groups. Already Allport noted: "One of the facts of which we are most certain is that people who reject one out-group will tend to reject other out-groups. If a person is anti-Jewish, he is likely to be anti-Catholic, anti-Negro, anti any out-group" (1954, p. 68). There is considerable empirical evidence that different types of prejudice are significantly interrelated. In addition, studies have repeatedly demonstrated that various kinds of prejudice are predicted by similar factors. For example, Adorno, Frenkel-Brunswik, Levinson, and Sanford (1950) showed that their proposed syndrome of the authoritarian personality was related to prejudice against several groups (see also Meloen, 1993). However, for the most part, prejudice toward particular out-groups have been analyzed in separate lines of research, where large probability samples of respondents were rarely employed.

This article takes a step beyond that. We propose a syndrome of GFE. In social science, a syndrome is a group of interrelated factors that together form a specific state or condition. The GFE syndrome encompasses prejudices toward different groups that are, within a stable structure, substantially interrelated over a period of time even though the level of approval can vary across time, cultures, and individuals. They are proposed to be interrelated because they all mirror a generalized devaluation of out-groups, that is, GFE. Second, we assume that the central underlying factor is an ideology of inequality that considers some social groups as unequal in value by "reasons," for example, of economic uselessness, lower levels of civilization, or abnormal sexual practices. Third, we assume that the GFE syndrome can be triggered by the same factors with comparable

---

in 2006. The fourth and fifth authors would like to thank Maria Rohlinger for insightful ideas and discussions during the spring seminar 2006 in Cologne, Germany. The fourth author also would like to thank the German Israeli Foundation (GIF) for their financial support.

consequences (e.g., discrimination). In other words, some personal and situational factors, like authoritarianism or even group relative deprivation (GRD), toward a certain group like labor migrants will predict different types of prejudices. Additionally, we assume that specific prejudices like anti-immigrant prejudices as components of GFE predict discrimination of other groups, like Jews and the homeless.

Prejudices as Components of a Syndrome of GFE

Although a meta-analytic test of the relationships between various prejudices is missing, evidence from numerous studies measuring the devaluation of various groups—most of which are only based on samples of convenience—supports our first contentions. For example, significant relations were found between prejudices of White Americans toward African Americans, homosexuals, and elderly persons (Bierly, 1985; Weigel & Howes, 1985). Substantial correlations showed up whether prejudices were operationalized as affective prejudices, as stereotyping, or as attitudes against equality enhancement (Whitley, 1999).

A few studies have explicitly presented evidence for generalized prejudice. Stangor, Sullivan, and Ford (1991) found generalized prejudices in the form of (negative) affective responses toward Americans, Whites, Asians, Jews, Blacks, Hispanics, Russians, Arabs, and homosexual persons. Heyder and Schmidt (2003) revealed a second-order factor (i.e., a higher level factor that accounts for the lower order factors) constituted by anti-Semitism, anti-immigrant sentiments, and in-group favoritism in a German national survey. Guimond, Dambrun, Michinov, and Duarte (2003) developed a reliable scale ($\alpha = .94$) of prejudices toward 17 ethnic out-groups in France. Bratt (2005) found attitudes toward five non-Western immigrant groups (Turks, Somalis, Pakistanis, Kosovo Albanians, Vietnamese) to be substantially related to a second-order factor among Norwegian adolescents. Ekehammar and his co workers (2004) reduced narrowed racism, modern sexism, and prejudice toward mentally disabled and homosexual persons to a single factor of generalized prejudice in Sweden. They argued that their results support Allport's (1954) idea of prejudice being a trait of personality. Similarly, Backström and Björklund (2007) showed that classical and modern racism, sexism, and classical and modern prejudices toward people with developmental disorders are represented by a general prejudice factor.

These results support our contention that various prejudices can be understood as components of a syndrome. We assume that all features that differentiate outgroups from the normative consensus of a dominant group can serve to indicate some sort of deviance (regarding, for example, the out-group's gender, sexual orientation, religious belief, or appearance), thereby confirming the normalcy of the in-group. Therefore, all prejudices toward any target group marked as different in a negative sense can become components of the syndrome. Prejudices can also be expressed by any group (dominant or subordinate, majority or minority), even though gaining dominance is more likely for members of a majority than a minority and prejudices usually serve the dominant group's intentions better (see Jost & Burgess, 2000).

Cultures offer a wide range of well-known out-groups. Some are marked as out-groups across cultures—such as those defined by gender, age, or physical deviance. Others are more cultural- or time-specific such as the Maghrébins in France. For our analyses, we posit nine constitutive components for a current German GFE syndrome. They reflect target groups of hate crimes claimed by the new German antidiscrimination law. (a) *Racism* is a strong support of racially legitimized inequality between groups. It asserts the idea of superiority of one group on the basis of biological or natural differences. Against the background of National Socialist ideology, racism is of special relevance in the German context. (b) *Sexism* is the devaluation of women characterized by the same underlying argumentation as racism, referring to natural differences. (c) *Xenophobia* is defined as the devaluation and rejection of immigrants. Several studies indicate that negative attitudes toward immigrants are widespread across Germany (Wagner, van Dick, & Zick, 2001). (d) *Anti-Semitism* is a deeply embedded prejudice toward Jews and Judaism, which is still shared among Germans in its classical form, but even more in its newer transformations (Zick & Küpper, 2005). (e) Since 9/11 *Islamophobia* is on the agenda across the Western world; it includes hostility toward Muslims and negative attitudes toward Islam. Both anti-Semitism and Islamophobia are prejudices toward different religious groups in Germany's predominantly Christian culture. (f) *Devaluation of homosexual persons* (gays and lesbians), (g) *Disabled*, and (h) *Homeless* persons all embrace negativity toward groups who are outside mainstream society. Even though they are not captured by the antidiscrimination law, homeless persons are considered as a particularly visible group systematically excluded from society in the public space, from welfare, in the housing and job market and have become victims of right-wing–motivated hate crimes. (i) Following Elias and Scotson (1965), the last component is the general *devaluation of newcomers* (e.g., new neighbors, colleagues, and classmates), seeking to uphold the precedent rights of the established.

Despite the fact that some target groups are more clearly defined, such as Jews and homosexual persons, while others, such as immigrants and newcomers, are defined rather vaguely, all of these GFE components incorporate group-based devaluation and reflect perceived inequality between groups.

A Common Core: The General Ideology of Inequality

We argue that several types of prejudice serve to maintain or enhance group status and to keep lower status groups in their inferior place (Blumer, 1958). A critical function of prejudices is to legitimize group-based inequality. We assume that several types of prejudices are not only related to each other but that also share a common core, namely a generalized devaluation of out-groups. We assume that this common core is strongly determined by an ideology of inequality. According to social dominance theory prejudices, like other legitimizing myths, rest on an individual's social dominance orientation (SDO), which is defined as "a very broad orientation expressing one's general endorsement of group-based inequality" (Sidanius, Pratto, & Levin, 1996, p. 387).

SDO should reflect an ideology of inequality, and if individuals accept this ideology, they tend to devalue multiple out-groups. However, which out-groups become targets of prejudice and discrimination depends on the options a specific society offers. Therefore, while means can vary between individuals according to their unique acceptance of the ideology of inequality, the syndrome's structure (i.e., the linkage of specific prejudices) is assumed to be ubiquitous within one society at a given time. The same is expected for the content of the single GFE components. However, research shows that the content of single GFE components like anti-Semitism or racism varies over time, and that the content of the structure varies between societies or cultures. Thus, while prejudice toward homosexual persons are supposed to be part of the GFE syndrome in Germany nowadays, it might not be part of a GFE syndrome in a more liberal country or it might, with increasing social acceptance of homosexuality, be excluded of the GFE syndrome in Germany, in the future. The components of the GFE syndrome (thus) depend on socially offered justifications for the agreement on prejudices, on norms to suppress them, but also on the degree of attention an individual pays to such option (see Crandall & Eshleman, 2003).

Common Causes and Outcomes

If a GFE syndrome does exist, it is reasonable to assume that the same personal and situational factors will predict different types of prejudices. Agnew, Thompson, and Gaines (2000) proved several distal and proximal factors to have an impact on a generalized negative attitude toward several out-groups. This article exemplifies a test of two empirically very powerful predictors that were available in the data set: authoritarianism as a personal factor and GRD as a perceived situational factor.

Since Adorno et al.'s (1950) famous study on *authoritarianism* and Altemeyer's (1981) modification into right-wing authoritarianism (RWA), numerous studies reveal that authoritarianism is strongly related to a great variety of prejudices. Substantial correlations have also been found between RWA and SDO (Duckitt, 2001; Sidanius & Pratto, 1999; Whitley, 1999). Ekehammer et al. (2004) showed that RWA and SDO predict generalized prejudice, but SDO has a stronger direct impact on generalized prejudice than RWA, and the impact of RWA is also indirectly transmitted by SDO.

Prejudice is also a consequence of situational influences such as an individual's perceived social position (Smith, 1981). Many studies show that especially GRD defined as the perceived disadvantage of one's own group in comparison to other relevant groups (Runciman, 1966) functions as an important predictor of prejudice (see Pettigrew et al., 2008).

Pursuing the idea of a GFE syndrome, we expect the impact of authoritarianism on specific prejudices to be mediated by a generalized ideology of inequality as a second-order factor explaining several types of prejudices—that is, authoritarianism influences single prejudices via their common core. As a more critical test of the GFE syndrome, we test the same assumption for GRD focused on immigrants.

We also expect different components of the GFE syndrome to have similar consequences such as the intention to discriminate out-groups (see Wagner, Christ, & Pettigrew, 2008). Traditionally, analyses show relations between prejudice and discrimination with respect to the same group (see Dovidio, Brigham, Johnson, & Gaertner, 1996; Schuetz & Six, 1996). We go beyond these findings and assume that GFE directly predicts discriminatory intentions toward different groups, even controlling for the direct link between prejudices toward a specific group and discriminatory intentions toward the respective group.

Empirical Tests of the Syndrome of GFE

To sum up, we claim that different types of prejudices constitute a syndrome of GFE. Thus, we expect that the nine GFE components are moderately to highly intercorrelated, and that they can be attributed to a single second-order factor labeled GFE. We presume that this factor is strongly predicted by the individual's acceptance of a generalized ideology of inequality. However, we do not anticipate that different types of prejudice are interrelated to an identical strength and contribute with the same weight as the common factor across time. The whole GFE syndrome should be predicted by authoritarianism and GRD, and in turn it should predict discriminatory intentions toward specific groups. Causes as well as outcomes show their influence via the second-order factor GFE.

Samples and Measures

Analyses were conducted within the German project on "Group-Focused Enmity" (Gruppenbezogene Menschenfeindlichkeit) headed by Heitmeyer (2002).

Data. Analyses are based on three samples representative of the German adult population (16 years and older) with no migration background of the respondents' parents or grandparents. Data were collected by a professional survey institute conducting standardized telephone interviews in 2002 (Study 1, $N = 2,722$), 2003 (Study 2, $N = 2,722$), and 2004 (Study 3, $N = 2,656$). In addition, data were derived from a 3-year panel study base on the survey 2002; 1,383 respondents were reinterviewed in 2003 (panel Wave 2) and 825 respondents in 2004 (panel Wave 3). Systematic panel mortality was negligible. Missing values were replaced with multiple imputations using expectation maximization estimates (Schafer & Graham, 2002). The "full" data set (two or three panel waves together) thus consists of $N = 2,648$ respondents.

Measures. The nine components of the GFE syndrome were measured by items successfully used in other surveys and/or pretested for our study. Items focused either the dominant or the subordinate group. Based on the pretests the best items were selected for the main surveys. Respondents indicated their agreement on a 4-point response scale (1 = *fully disagree*, 2 = *rather disagree*, 3 = *rather agree*, 4 = *fully agree*). See Table 1 for final items, means, standard deviations and intercorrelations.

In our basic data set, *xenophobia* was measured by eight items, *anti-Semitism* and *Islamophobia* by four items each (the latter was extended and improved in 2003), *devaluation of newcomers* and *racism* by three items each, and the devaluation of *homosexuals, disabled,* and *homeless* persons by two items each. *Sexism* was measured by only one item in 2002 but in the following measuring times with two items, as well. Three SDO items taken from Sidanius and Pratto (1999) (e.g., "Some groups of people are just more worthy than others.") measured the *ideology of inequality. Authoritarianism* employed four indicators based on Altemeyer (1981) (e.g., "Crime should be punished more harshly."). GRD was assessed by the single question: "If you compare the economic situation of Germans with that of the immigrants living in Germany, how well off are Germans by comparison?" *Intended discrimination of immigrants and Muslims* was measured by two items: "I would never buy a car from an immigrant." "I would have problems to move into an area in which many Muslims are living."

Hypotheses, Data Analyses, and Results

We performed the analysis in three steps encompassing a series of subanalyses: (a) Analyses of the internal structure of GFE, that is, analyses of interrelations between the GFE components and the second-order factor GFE, followed by a cross-validation in the other data sets, and finally estimation of the stability of the syndrome over time. (b) Tests of the nature of the second-order factor by estimating its relation to SDO. (c) Analyses of the causes and consequences of GFE. For greater clarity, we have presented each set of specific hypotheses and their corresponding analyses step by step (see also Table 2). Our analyses used the statistical program AMOS 5.

Internal Structure of GFE

Generalized prejudice as a second-order factor. According to our hypotheses, responses to the prejudice items toward nine different groups can be explained by nine first-order factors (racism, xenophobia, etc.) in each data set and at each point

Table 1. Means, Standard Deviations, and Intercorrelations of all Syndrome-Items (Data Base: Study 2)

	M (SD)	2	3	4	5	6	7	8	9	10	11	12	13	14	15	16	17	18
1. Sexism: Women should think stronger on the role as wives and mothers.	1.96 (.90)	.61	.34	.27	.26	.21	.23	.21	.26	.27	.14	.09	.18	.19	.23	.23	.05*	.04+
2. Sexism: It is more important for a wife to help her husband's career than to have one herself	1.86 (.86)	1.00	.33	.33	.26	.22	.24	.24	.29	.33	.18	.11	.21	.24	.23	.26	.04*	.02+
3. Devaluation of homosexuals: Marriages between two women or between two men should be permitted.	2.14 (1.17)		1.00	.50	.26	.24	.24	.23	.19	.18	.18	.14	.23	.26	.17	.18	−.01+	−.02+
4. Devaluation of homosexuals: It is disgusting when homosexuals kiss in public.	2.19 (1.10)			1.00	.27	.24	.32	.25	.18	.16	.30	.23	.26	.29	.21	.17	.06	.06
5. Anti-Semitism: As a result of their behavior, Jewish people are not entirely without blame for being persecuted.	1.68 (.83)				1.00	.60	.33	.35	.22	.32	.22	.13	.30	.31	.24	.28	.05*	.00+
6. Anti-Semitism: Jewish people have too much influence in Germany.	1.91 (.90)					1.00	.35	.32	.19	.25	.21	.12	.29	.31	.23	.31	.02+	−.01+
7. Xenophobia: There are too many foreigners living in Germany.	2.61 (1.01)						1.00	.57	.25	.30	.32	.23	.52	.49	.35	.36	.05*	.05*
8. Xenophobia: When jobs get scarce, the foreigners living in Germany should be sent (back) home.	2.13 (.93)							1.00	.28	.30	.30	.20	.44	.47	.29	.39	.06	.01+
9. Racism: German re-settlers should be better off than foreigners because they are of German origin.	1.82 (.83)								1.00	.34	.19	.12	.23	.25	.22	.36	.05*	.02+

Continued.

The Syndrome of Group-Focused Enmity

Table 1. *Continued.*

	M (SD)	2	3	4	5	6	7	8	9	10	11	12	13	14	15	16	17	18
10. Racism: It is right that Whites are leading in the world.	1.60 (.81)									1.00	.21	.10	.25	.30	.22	.29	.05*	.06
11. Devaluation of homeless people: Begging homeless should be chased away from the pedestrian zone.	2.28 (.98)										1.00	.45	.27	.25	.21	.22	.11	.08
12. Devaluation of homeless people: The homeless in the towns are unpleasant.	2.47 (.91)											1.00	.18	.14	.12	.14	.22	.23
13. Islamophobia: With so many Muslims in Germany, one feels increasingly like a stranger in one's own country.	2.04 (.98)												1.00	.45	.24	.31	.05*	.05*
14. Islamophobia: Immigration to Germany should be forbidden for Muslims.	1.99 (.90)													1.00	.25	.31	.05*	.00+
15. Devaluation of newcomers: Those who are new somewhere should be content with less.	2.56 (.96)																	.07	.07
16. Devaluation of newcomers: Those who have always been living here should have more rights than those who came later.	2.10 (1.01)																1.00	.04*	.04*
17. Devaluation of disabled people: Sometimes I feel uncomfortable in the presence of handicapped people.	1.96 (.94)																	1.00	.50
18. Devaluation of disabled people: Sometimes I am unsure how to behave in face of handicapped people.	2.67 (1.03)																		1.00

Note. *$p < .05$; +n.s.; all other $p < .01$.

Table 2. Overview Hypotheses and Strategy of Analyses

Hypotheses	Analyses	Database
I. Internal structure of GFE		
Generalized prejudice as second-order factor (with cross-validation)		
H1: Responses to the prejudice items toward nine different out-groups can be explained by nine first-order factors.	Second-order confirmatory factor analysis (CFA)	Main-Study 1, cross-section 2
H2: The first-order factors are explained by one second-order factor.	Cross-validation of the second-order GFE model	Cross-section 3, panel wave 2, panel wave 3
H3: H1 and H2 are true for all levels of education.	Multiple group analyses	Cross-section 2
Stability of GFE over time		
H4: Invariance in meaning of prejudice constructs over time is expected.	Autoregressive panel models tests for invariance of item factor loadings on first-order factors over time.	
H5: Invariance in the meaning of GFE over time is not expected.	Autoregressive panel models tests for invariance of first-order factor loadings on second-order factor GFE over time.	Main-Study 1, panel wave 2, panel wave 3
H6: (a) GFE at t1 predicts GFE at t2. GFE at t2 predicts GFE at t3. GFE at t1 does not predict directly GFE at t3. (b) The stability of the second-order factor of GFE over time is significantly positively different from zero.	Autoregressive panel models.	
II. Common core: Ideology of inequality		
H7: (a) The correlation between social dominance orientation and the second-order factor GFE differs from 1.00. (b) SDO is strong positive predictor of GFE.	(a) Simultaneous second-order CFA, correlation SDO and GFE = 1.00; (b) Regression coefficient SDO on GFE.	Cross-section 2
III. External validation: Common causes, common consequences		
H8: The effect of authoritarian orientation on eight prejudice components of GFE is fully mediated by the second-order factor of GFE.	SEM, mediation models.	Cross-section 2
H9: GRD predicts prejudice factors via the second-order factor of GFE.		
H10: The second-order factor of GFE predicts specific discriminatory attitudes.		

of time (H1). In turn, the nine first-order factors are explained by one second-order factor (GFE) in each data set and at each point of time (H2). This prediction requires the covariation among the nine first-order factors to be completely explained by the second-order factor of GFE. To make sure that respondents did not evaluate different out-groups distinctively just because of less complex cognitive abilities, which are related to education (Zaller, 1995), we tested H1 and H2 controlled for all levels of education (H3). Furthermore, we did not expect the meaning of the GFE components to vary depending on the level of education (metric invariance). Therefore, we postulate that the relationship between the GFE components and their indicators is the same across educational groups. Finally, it remains an open question as to whether the meaning or composition of the second-order GFE factor is the same across the different educational levels; that is, whether the loadings of the first-order prejudice factors on GFE are equal across these groups. However, we will also test for the invariance of the second-order factor GFE.

We tested H1 and H2 using second-order confirmatory factor analyses (CFA) on the bases of Study 1 and cross-sectional Study 2 and cross-validated the results in the other data sets (cross-sectional Study 3 and panel Wave 2 and 3).[1] In the first step, nine separate first-order CFAs were conducted for each prejudice component (except for sexism in Study 1, which was measured by only one item). The best two items per construct were selected on the basis of their factor loadings for a parsimonious model of GFE. Seventeen items in Study 1 and 18 items in cross-sectional Study 2 were the basis for the subsequent second-order CFA with GFE as a second-order factor hypothesized to explain the latent first-order prejudice constructs.

As predicted, the second-order CFA based on Study 1 and cross-sectional Study 2 clearly revealed separable first-order prejudice constructs explaining responses to the items (H1) and one second-order factor (labeled as GFE) explaining the intercorrelations of the different measures of prejudices. (H2). According to Hu and Bentler (1999) and to Marsh, Hau, and Wen (2004), the fit of the model is acceptable (for model fits see Figure 1 and Table 2). A test of the two panel models with data that included only individuals, who took part in all three waves, did not produce different results.

Nevertheless, two problems occurred. First, prejudice toward disabled people does not belong to GFE; the factor loading of the first-order construct on the second-order factor was rather low. Upon reexamination, we noted that prejudice toward disabled persons triggered negative intergroup emotions ("feel unsure"; "feel unpleasant/uneasy"), while the other measures were characterized

---

[1] A second-order factor analysis is a variation of factor analysis in which the correlation matrix of the common factors is itself factor analyzed to provide a second-order factor.

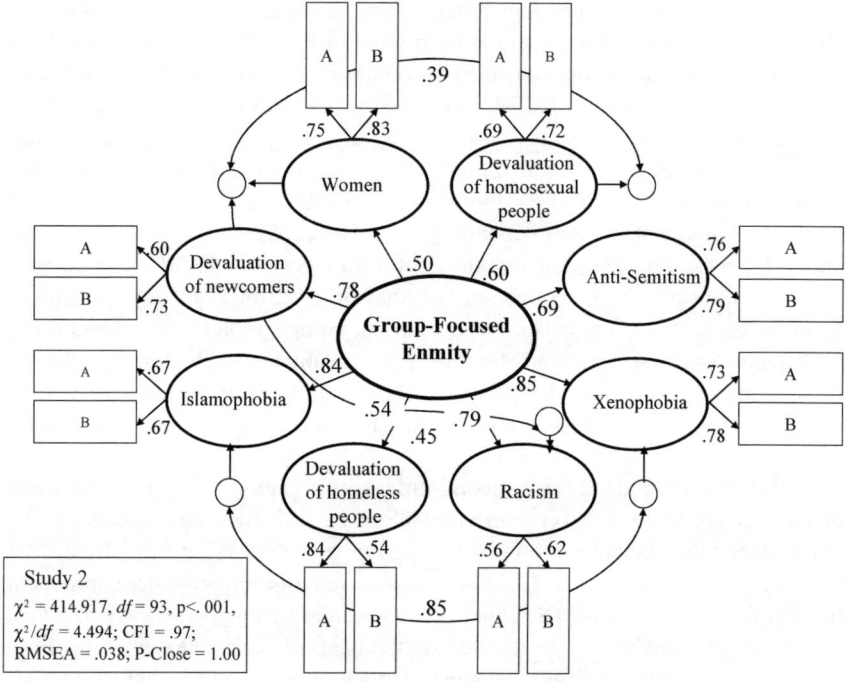

Fig. 1. The syndrome of GFE with first- and second-order factors (Study 2).

by cognitive beliefs. The different measure might explain the deviant structure. Therefore, we removed this component from further analyses.

A second problem involves the close relationships between some of the components as indicated in their residual correlations, concerning sexism and devaluation of homosexual persons, sexism and racism, and xenophobia and Islamophobia. For all of these intercomponent correlations the overlapping of content offers a possible explanation. Both sexism and the devaluation of homosexual persons stress conservative attitudes toward gender roles. They are also associated with similar stereotypes like those of feminity (Weinberger & Millham, 1979). However, the strong relationship between the two components may simply reflect that sexism is represented by only one item. A recalculation of the model using the panel studies of Wave 2 and 3 and the cross-sectional studies 2 and 3 including two items for sexism showed improved model fits by adding sexism into the CFA. Nevertheless, sexism still correlates directly with the devaluation of homosexual persons.

The strong relation between sexism and racism may be grounded in the similarity of the category and arguments used to legitimize inequality. Both categories are defined by biological or natural peculiarities and seek to legitimize status differences by nature. Xenophobia and Islamophobia might be strongly related because respondents may have had the same group of people in mind when answering. In panel Wave 3, respondents were asked which group they think of when considering immigrants in Germany. Roughly two thirds think of Turks, who are the largest group of immigrants in Germany and who are predominantly Muslim. Thus, we decided to allow direct correlations between the residuals in all three cases.

Hence, the cross-validation analyses and the following validation analyses have as their starting point a model with one second-order factor of GFE connecting eight syndrome components, of which three pairs are correlated via their residuals.

Cross-validation. We cross-validated both models in the three remaining data sets. The selected model with one second-order factor of GFE and no direct interrelations between the first-order constructs but three residual correlations fits best in all five data sets.

Based on cross-sectional Study 2, we next checked to determine if a second-order factor GFE can be found at different levels of education (H3). Furthermore, we tested whether the meaning of the different prejudice constructs and the second-order factor GFE is equal across different levels of education. Multi-group comparisons were conducted to contrast all three levels of education in the GFE second-order model. Good model fits were revealed in all three educational levels ($\chi^2 = 747.761$, $df = 279$, $p < .001$, $\chi^2/df = 2.68$, Comparative Fit Index (CFI) = .958, root mean square error of approximation (RMSEA) = .025).

The test for invariance of the prejudice factors and their second-order GFE, however, yielded mixed results. Global fit measures suggested to accept the strictest model assuming invariance in the meaning of prejudice factors and the second-order factor GFE across all levels of education (for a discussion of fit indices see Cheung & Rensvold, 2002; $\chi^2 = 747.761$, $df = 279$, $p < .001$, $\chi^2/df = 2.68$, CFI = .958, RMSEA = .025; invariance of prejudice factors: $\chi^2 = 777.272$, $df = 295$, $p < .001$, $\chi^2/df = 2.635$, CFI = .957, RMSEA = .025; invariance of second-order factor GFE: $\chi^2 = 1.926$, $df = 309$, $p < .001$, $\chi^2/df = 2.595$, CFI = .956, RMSEA = .024). Nevertheless, minor path differences occur. For example, the regression coefficients of anti-Semitism (.76 vs. .55) and the devaluation of homosexual persons (.64 vs. .45) on the second-order factor were higher for highly educated than for poorly educated respondents. The error variance of GFE was lower in the higher education group indicating that this group renders fewer chance responses (Zaller, 1995).

These results provide strong empirical evidence for a GFE syndrome. It holds for both high and low levels of education with equal meaning for the prejudice components. Patterns of GFE across educational groups were only slightly different.

Stability of GFE over time. Two features of general stability are especially relevant for this article: (a) the stability of construct meanings and (b) positional stability, that is, stability in the interindividual ranking of prejudiced attitudes over time. Mean differences are addressed elsewhere (Davidov, Schmidt, Wolf, & Heitmeyer, in press). Different types of prejudice are expected to be stable in their meaning over time; that is, the loadings of the items on their first-order prejudice factors should be invariant (H4). However, we do not expect the loadings of the prejudice factors on GFE to be invariant (H5), that is, we do not think the meaning of GFE is constant over time.

To examine positional stability, we predict that the GFE syndrome at time 1 (t1) will predict the syndrome at t2, which in turn will predict the syndrome at t3, while the GFE syndrome at t1 is not expected to predict the syndrome directly at t3 (H6a) after checking for t2. This is because the effect from GFE in 2002 (t1) to GFE in 2004 (t3) is expected to be completely mediated by GFE in 2003 (t2) (Jöreskog & Sörbom, 1977). Furthermore, we predict stability in the ranking of prejudiced attitudes over time, without knowing from prior work the exact stability coefficient (H6b). H4 to H6 are tested by specifying autoregressive models (Meredith, 1993) with three reference dates (2002, 2003, 2004). A panel model with only the 2003 and 2004 data was tested to take the new measures of sexism and Islamophobia into account.

Results. As there was only one sexism item in Study 1 the 2002 data had to be excluded from this test due to identification problems. The fit measures of the autoregressive panel model over three time points are satisfactory ($\chi^2 = 4653.414$ $df = 735$, $p < .001$, $\chi^2/df = 6.331$, CFI $= .926$, RMSEA $= .045$). As hypothesized, each GFE measure is significantly predicted by the preceding GFE measure without any direct path from GFE in t1 to GFE in t3 (H6a). The second-order GFE factor is highly stable over time (H6b). This means that those individuals showing relatively higher prejudices in t1 are again comparatively highly prejudiced at t2 and t3. The standardized regression coefficient of GFE in t1 on GFE in t2 is .93 and the regression coefficient of GFE in t2 on GFE in t3 is .96.

All first-order prejudice measures have high autocorrelations. That is, xenophobia in t1 is correlated with xenophobia in t2, which is again correlated with xenophobia at t3. These autocorrelations are all statistically significant (with the one exception of the autocorrelation between the measurement errors of the second Islamophobia item in points in t1 and t3).

The model also supported invariance across time for the prejudice measures ($\chi^2 = 4707.911$, $df = 749$, $p < .001$, $\chi^2/df = 6.286$, CFI $= .925$, RMSEA $= .045$). But there was no such support for invariance of factor loadings between the GFE components and the second-order factor GFE across time ($\chi^2 = 4909.633$, $df = 761$, $p < .001$, $\chi^2/df = 6.452$, CFI $= .922$, RMSEA $= .045$). Hence, as predicted, the meaning of prejudice constructs is equal across all three points in time whereas the composition or meaning of GFE varies across the three points in time (H4, H5). To sum up, the meaning of the prejudice constructs remained constant again.

Common Core of an Ideology of Inequality

Because the ideology of inequality is assumed to be a strong predictor of GFE, we expect a strong positive effect of the ideology of inequality, as measured by SDO, on the second-order GFE factor. This necessarily implies that the second-order factor GFE and SDO are two distinct concepts. If so, the correlation between GFE and SDO should be lower than 1. If the two were conceptually the same, the correlation would be equal to 1. In our test the correlation between GFE and SDO is extremely high ($r = .85$) but different from 1 (the fit of the model is reasonable: $\chi^2 = 784.099$, $df = 140$, $p < .001$, $\chi^2/df = 5.601$, CFI $= .955$, RMSEA $= .041$; the regression coefficient of SDO on GFE was .85). Nevertheless, CFA confirms divergent validity of SDO and GFE. Hence, as expected, SDO and GFE are two very closely linked but in the strict sense theoretically and empirically distinct concepts.

Common Causes and Consequences

We checked the relationships between the GFE syndrome and its determinants and consequences to establish construct validation. Because this is only a validation test we do not account for the detection of relationships between the different predictors GRD, authoritarianism, and SDO. Three hypotheses are relevant: First, we predict that GFE mediates the relationship between authoritarianism and the eight single prejudice components of the syndrome (H8). Second, we hypothesize that GRD focused on prejudice toward immigrants will have a significant effect not only on one type of prejudice but also on all measures of prejudice, and that this influence goes via GFE (H9). Third, we predict that GFE is positively related to discriminatory intentions. Not only will a specific component of GFE (e.g., xenophobia) explain specific forms of discrimination (e.g., intended discrimination against immigrants), but other prejudices will also help explain such intentions via the second-order factor GFE (H10). We expect GFE to completely mediate these effects of the prejudice factors on discriminatory intentions; thus, there should be no need in the model for any direct effects from the prejudice measures to discriminatory intentions.

We tested H8 and H9 by conducting structural equation modelings (SEMs) with the GFE factor as dependent variable and authoritarianism with three items as latent factor and GRD with one observed indicator as predictors. The models were specified only with direct paths from the predictors to GFE, but not to its components. Next, we checked whether additional paths were necessary due to the amount of the modification indices. The procedure in testing H10 was analogous with GFE as predictor variable and the latent construct discrimination against Muslims and immigrants (one item each) as dependent variables. To exclude spurious relationships, we checked for the effects of the demographic variables education, age, gender, and income in all three models.

Results. As predicted by H8, authoritarianism predicts GFE ($\beta = .82$) ($\chi^2 = 1477.381$, $df = 227$, $p < .001$, $\chi^2/df = 6.508$, CFI $= 924$, RMSEA $= .048$). However, model indices suggested an additional direct path from authoritarianism to sexism. Even though including this path did not substantially change the model fit, we have to state that GFE does not completely mediate the strong link between authoritarianism and sexism.

As H9 held, GRD predicts all the prejudice components via GFE ($\beta = .32$) with a reasonably good fit of the model ($\chi^2 = 831.174$, $df = 165$, $p < .001$; $\chi^2/df = 5.037$, CFI $= .949$, RMSEA $= .041$). Even though GRD was focused on the comparison between Germans and immigrants, no direct paths between GRD and xenophobia or Islamophobia were necessary. This means that GFE almost completely mediated the links between GRD and xenophobia and Islamophobia (see Figure 2). If the direct paths from GRD on xenophobia ($\beta = .15$) and Islamophobia ($\beta = .13$) are allowed, the effect of GRD on GFE is only slightly reduced

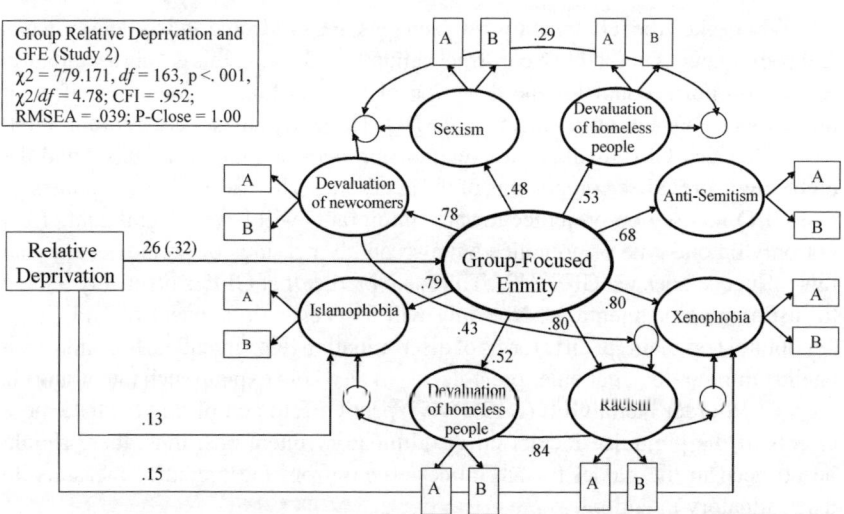

Note. The effect of relative deprivation on GFE without accounting for direct effects on attitudes toward Muslims and immigrants is in parentheses. The fit measures refer to the full model. All coefficients in the model are calculated holding the effect of age, education, gender, and income on GFE constant.

Fig. 2. Specific external validation: The influence of GRD on several prejudice elements is mediated by group-focused enmity.

($\beta = .26$) ($\chi^2 = 779.171$, $df = 163$, $p < .001$, $\chi^2/df = 4.334$, CFI $= .952$, RMSEA $= .039$).

As expected by H10, GFE determines directly and positively ($\beta = .79$) discriminatory intentions toward immigrants and Muslims ($\chi^2 = 939.591$, $df = 188$, $p < .001$, $\chi^2/df = 4.998$, CFI $= .946$, RMSEA $= .041$). However, if we introduce the direct paths from prejudice against the discriminated target groups, the effect of GFE on discrimination is strongly reduced ($\beta = .19$), but still significant and meaningful ($\chi^2 = 889.430$, $df = 186$, $p < .001$, $\chi^2/df = 4.782$, CFI $= .950$, RMSEA $= .039$).

To sum up, authoritarianism as a general predictor of prejudice affects only GFE directly and does not affect the specific prejudice factors directly—except for sexism. As a target-group-specific predictor of prejudice, GRD regarding immigrants does not only affect xenophobic and islamophobic attitudes, but also all of the other components of the syndrome via GFE. Moreover, the intended discrimination toward a specific target group is not only predicted by its respective prejudice component but also by GFE.

Conclusions and Questions

Even though each target group of prejudice and discrimination is unique and stereotypes of groups differ, they all share the fate of being victims. We successfully tested a syndrome of GFE that includes prejudice toward several out-groups related to one another, sharing a common factor, and possessing common predictors and consequences. Three German probability surveys and a 3-wave panel study empirically support these contentions and, with few exceptions, reveal a remarkable stability of these patterns over time.

As an exception, negative attitudes toward disabled people were not, as was hypothesized, closely interlinked to the other prejudices and to their common core, which may be ascribed to measurement reasons. Further research using other measures is needed.

Noteworthy is that sexism and prejudice toward newcomers are highly correlated with prejudice toward other groups (see as well Ekehammar, Akrami, Gylje, & Zakrisson, 2004) and the general GFE factor, even though both components do not focus on minorities in a narrow sense, and a large number of our respondents are themselves member of these groups. Like in other studies, sexism is nevertheless especially linked with prejudice toward homosexual persons (Weinberger & Millham, 1979). Models did not differ between men and women. Social dominance theory (Sidanius & Pratto, 1999) proposes that particularly dominant groups such as men, Whites, or "the established" support an ideology of inequality and prejudices to maintain and enhance group-based hierarchies. Moreover, Jost and Burgess (2000) argued that subordinate groups could favor hierarchies if they were motivated to justify the system. We think that subordinate groups such as women and newcomers support group-based hierarchies having other groups of even lower status in mind. The structure of the GFE syndrome within high and low status groups would be the same.

Our results suggest that the common factor of multiple prejudices is not identical but highly related to SDO, which presents an ideology of inequality. Again, this could be explained by measurement differences, since SDO is recorded by three items, which cover only *group-based dominance* and not *opposition to equality*. Alternatively, SDO may not reflect a generalized ideology of inequality, which would imply that the definition of SDO has to be reconsidered. In addition, other possible factors such as hate (cf. Brewer, 1999) might reflect the common core of prejudice even better. Additionally the syndrome-like pattern might be caused by other factors such as a misanthropic mood. Such general predicting factors can be explored by future research testing alternative interpretations of the common prejudice core GFE. But by all means, the strong ties of GFE and SDO stress that ideologies do play an important role. Even more critical from a theoretical point of view is the possibility that there is more than just one common core of prejudices. Some types of prejudice might form subpatterns within the syndrome being more highly related with each other and sharing a specific core.

Given our findings some theories on prejudice must be reconsidered, such as Young-Bruehl's (1996) proposition that there are only unique individual prejudices. Research also needs to focus not only on the similarities among different types of prejudices and highlight their relation, but also on peculiarities of particular prejudices. As an implication for intervention programs against prejudice and discrimination our findings suggest to address a variety of prejudices simultaneously and to study their linkage.

With changing conditions and political topics, new groups might become part of the syndrome, such as victims of AIDS, the elderly, the unemployed, or welfare recipients, while other groups may disappear. From a sociological perspective, variations within the GFE syndrome depend on the level of status threat. From an individual perspective, it can depend on the motive to allay feelings of insecurity. From a political perspective of power, it can depend on the changes in the relations between groups. Such processes are combined by the attempt to manifest social order as a basis of standards of normalcy and security motivated to maintain and establish superiority. An effective way to demonstrate power is to point to the supposed inferiority of weak groups as often initiated and mobilized by elite groups. The key role to avoid such processes seems to be the fight for social integration processes and a struggle to combat private and public ideologies of inequality.

References

Adorno, T. W., Frenkel-Brunswik, E., Levinson, D. J., & Sanford, R. N. (1950). *The authoritarian personality*. New York: Harper & Row.
Agnew, C. R., Thompson, V. D., & Gaines, S. O. Jr. (2000). Incorporating proximal and distal influences on prejudice: Testing a general model across outgroups. *Personality and Social Psychology Bulletin, 26*(40), 403–418.
Allport, G. W. (1954). *The nature of prejudice*. Cambridge, MA: Perseus Books.
Altemeyer, B. (1981). *Right-wing authoritarianism*. Winnipeq, Canada: University of Manitoba Press.
Backstrom, M., & Bjorklund, F. (2007). Structural modeling of generalized prejudice: The role of social dominance, authoritarianism, and empathy. *Journal of Individual Differences, 28,* 10–17.
Bierly, M. M. (1985). Prejudice toward contemporary outgroups as a generalized attitude. *Journal of Applied Social Psychology, 15,* 189–199.
Blumer, H. (1958). Race prejudice as a sense of group position. *Pacific Sociological Review, 1,* 3–7.
Bratt, C. (2005). The structure of attitudes toward non-western immigrant groups: Second-order factor analysis of attitudes among Norwegian adolescents. *Group Processes & Intergroup Relations, 8,* 447–469.
Brewer, M. B. (1999). The psychology of prejudice: Ingroup love and outgroup hate? *Journal of Social Issues, 55,* 429–444.
Cheung, G. W., & Rensvold, R. B. (2002). Evaluating goodness-of-fit indexes for testing measurement invariance. *Structural Equation Modeling: A Multidisciplinary Journal, 9,* 233–255.
Crandall, C. S., & Eshleman, A. (2003). A justification-suppression model of the expression and experience of prejudice. *Psychological Bulletin, 129,* 414–446.
Davidov, E., Schmidt, P., Wolf, C., & Heitmeyer, W. (in press). Level, change and social-structural determinants of group-focused enmity in Germany. *International Journal of Conflict and Violence.*
Dovidio, J. F., Brigham, J. C., Johnson, B. T., & Gaertner, S. L. (1996). Stereotyping, prejudice, and discrimination: Another look. In C. N. Macrae, C. Stangor, & M. Hewstone (Eds.), *Stereotypes and stereotyping* (pp. 276–322). New York: Guilford.
Duckitt, J. (2001). A dual-process cognitive-motivational theory on ideology and prejudice. *Advances in Experimental Social Psychology, 33,* 41–113.
Ekehammar, B., Akrami, N., Gylje, M., & Zakrisson, I. (2004). What matters most to prejudice: Big five personality, social dominance orientation, or right-wing authoritarianism? *European Journal of Personality, 18,* 463–482.
Elias, N., & Scotson, J. L. (1965). *The established and the outsiders: A sociological enquiry into community problems*. London: Cass.
Guimond, S., Dambrun, M., Michinov, N., & Duarte, S. (2003). Does social dominance generate prejudice? Integrating individual and contextual determinants of intergroup cognition. *Journal of Personality and Social Psychology, 84,* 697–721.
Heitmeyer, W. (2002). Gruppenbezogene Menschenfeindlichkeit. Die theoretische Konzeption und erste empirische Ergebnisse [Group-focused enmity. Theoretical conception and first empirical results]. In W. Heitmeyer (Ed.), *Deutsche Zustände, Folge 1* Vol. 1, (pp. 15–36). Frankfurt: Suhrkamp.
Heyder, A., & Schmidt, P. (2003). Authoritarianism and ethnocentrism in East- and West-Germany—does the system matter? In R. Alba, P. Schmidt, & M. Wasmer (Eds.), *Germans or foreigners? Attitudes toward ethnic minorities in post-reunification Germany* (pp. 187–210). New York: Palgrave Macmillan.
Jöreskog, K. G., & Sörbom, D. (1977). Statistical models and methods for analysis of longitudinal data. In D. J. Aigner, & A. S. Goldberger (Eds.), *Latent variables in socioeconomic research* (pp. 303–351). New York: Academic Press.
Jost, J. T., & Burgess, D. (2000). Attitudinal ambivalence and the conflict between group and system justification motives in low status groups. *Personality and Social Psychology Bulletin, 26,* 293–305.

Hu, L., & Bentler, P. M. (1999). Cutoff criteria for fit indexes in covariance structure analysis: Conventional criteria versus new alternatives. *Structural Equation Modeling: A Multidisciplinary Journal, 6*, 1–55.

Marsh, H. W., Hau, K. T., & Wen, Z. (2004). In search of golden rules: Comment on hypothesis-testing approaches to setting cutoff values for fit indexes and dangers in overgeneralizing. Hu and Bentler's (1999) findings. *Structural Equation Modeling: A Multidisciplinary Journal, 11*, 320–341.

Meloen, J. (1993). The F scale as a predictor of fascism: An overview of 40 years of authoritarianism research. In W. F. Stone, G. Lederer, & R. Christie (Eds.), *Strength and weakness. The authoritarian personality today* (pp. 47–69). New York: Springer-Verlag.

Meredith, W. (1993). Measurement invariance, factor analyses and factorial invariance. *Psychometrika, 58*, 525–543.

Pettigrew, T. F., Christ, O., Wagner, U., Meertens, R. W., van Dick, R., & Zick, A. (2008). Relative deprivation and intergroup prejudice. *Journal of Social Issues, 64*(2), 385–401.

Runciman, W. A. (1966). *Relative deprivation and social justice.* Berkeley: University of California Press.

Schafer, J. L., & Graham, J. W. (2002). Missing data: Our view of the state of the art. *Psychological Methods, 7*, 147–177.

Schuetz, H., & Six, B. (1996). How strong is the relationship between prejudice and discrimination? A meta-analytic answer. *International Journal of Intercultural Relations, 20*, 441–462.

Sidanius, J., & Pratto, F. (1999). *Social dominance: An intergroup theory of social hierarchy and oppression.* New York: Cambridge University Press.

Sidanius, J., Pratto, F., & Levin, S. (1996). Consensual social dominance orientation and its correlates within the hierarchical structure of American Society. *International Journal of Intercultural Relations, 20*, 385–408.

Smith, A. W. (1981). Racial tolerance as a function of group position. *American Sociological Review, 46*, 558–573.

Stangor, C., Sullivan, L. A., & Ford, T. E. (1991). Affective and cognitive determinants of prejudice. *Social Cognition, 9*, 359–380.

Wagner, U., van Dick, R., & Zick, A. (2001). Sozialpsychologische Analysen und Erklärungen der Fremdenfeindlichkeit in Deutschland [Social psychological analyses and explanations of hostility toward strangers in Germany]. *Zeitschrift für Sozialpsychologie, 32*, 59–79.

Wagner, U., Christ, O., & Pettigrew, T. F. (2008). Prejudice and group-related behavior in Germany. *Journal of Social Issues, 64*(2), 403–416.

Weigel, R. H., & Howes, P. W. (1985). Conceptions of racial prejudice: Symbolic racism reconsidered. *Journal of Social Issues, 41*, 117–138.

Weinberger, L. E., & Millham, J. (1979). Attitudinal homophobia and support of traditional sex roles. *Journal of Homosexuality, 4*, 237–246.

Whitley, B. E. Jr. (1999). Right-wing authoritarianism, social dominance orientation, and prejudice. *Journal of Personality and Social Psychology, 77*, 126–134.

Young-Bruehl, E. (1996). *The anatomy of prejudice.* Cambridge, MA: Harvard University Press.

Zaller, J. R. (1995). *The nature and origins of mass opinion.* Cambridge, MA: Cambridge University Press.

Zick, A., & Küpper, B. (2005). Transformed anti-Semitism? A report on anti-Semitism in Germany. *Journal für Konflikt- und Gewaltforschung, 7*, 50–92.

ANDREAS ZICK received a call to become Professor of Socialization and Conflict Research at the University of Bielefeld in Germany. Additionally, he manages the project "Group-Focused Enmity in Europe project." He received his PhD at the University of Marburg in 1996, worked from 1998 to 2003 as Assistant Professor at the University of Wuppertal, from 2004 to 2006 at the University of Bielefeld, and headed the Chair of Social Psychology at the University of Dresden (2006–2007) and Jena (2007–2008). His research interests focus on prejudice, acculturation, and intergroup relations.

CARINA WOLF has been a postgraduate in the graduate college of "Group-Focused Enmity" at the University of Marburg since 2004. Her research interest lies in intergroup relations, especially prejudice, and intergroup contact.

BEATE KÜPPER is Research Assistant at the University of Bielefeld and is managing an international project on "Group-Focused Enmity" in Europe. Currently, she is on the leave from Bielefeld to chair the Department of Social Psychology at the University of Dresden. She works on social status and dominance, and interpersonal relations in modernization processes.

ELDAD DAVIDOV is a Postdoctorate and Research Assistant at the Central Archive for Empirical Social Research at the University of Cologne. He is interested in economic and social inequality of immigrants, human values in Europe and structural equation modeling.

PETER SCHMIDT is Professor for Social Science Methodology in the Department of Political Science at the University of Giessen. His works on structural equation models, panel data, inter ethnic relations, national identity, and environmental behavior.

WILHELM HEITMEYER is Professor at the University of Bielefeld and Director of the Interdisciplinary Institute for Research on Conflict and Violence. In numerous projects, he worked on violence, right-wing extremism, social disintegration, and ethnic segregation.

Relative Deprivation and Intergroup Prejudice

Thomas F. Pettigrew*
University of California

Oliver Christ
Philipps University Marburg and Bielefeld University

Ulrich Wagner
Philipps University Marburg

Roel W. Meertens
University of Amsterdam

Rolf van Dick
Goethe University

Andreas Zick
University of Bielefeld

Using three diverse European surveys, we test the relationship between relative deprivation (RD) and anti-immigrant prejudice. We find that both group relative deprivation (GRD) and individual relative deprivation (IRD) are found primarily among working-class respondents who are politically alienated. We also find that GRD, but not IRD, serves as a proximal correlate of prejudice. IRD's effects on prejudice are largely mediated through GRD. In addition, GRD partially mediates the effects of such distal predictors of prejudice as education and family income. Finally, blaming the victim mediates in part the GRD link with prejudice. These

---

*Correspondence concerning this article should be addressed to Thomas Pettigrew, Department of Psychology, Social Sciences II, University of California, Santa Cruz, CA 95060 [e-mail: pettigr@ucsc.edu].

A preliminary version of this article was presented at the joint SPSSI—EAESP Conference at Grenada, Spain, May 23–26, 2001.

results lead to a socially situated path model of RD's effects on prejudice with public policy implications.

Relative deprivation (RD) is a social psychological concept par excellence. It postulates a subjective state that shapes emotions, cognitions, and behavior. It links the individual with the interpersonal and intergroup levels of analysis. It melds easily with other social psychological processes to provide more integrative theory—a prime disciplinary need (Pettigrew, 1991). Moreover, RD challenges conventional wisdom about the importance of absolute deprivation. And it has proven useful in a wide range of areas—from such internal states as stress and self-evaluation to such social phenomena as participation in collective behavior and intergroup prejudice (Walker & Smith, 2001). Indeed, the concept has now won acceptance throughout the social sciences, from criminology (Lea & Young, 1993) and economics (Duclos & Gregoire, 2002) to political science (Brown, 2004).

Samuel Stouffer, a sociologist and survey specialist, introduced the concept a half-century ago (Stouffer, Suchman, DeVinney, Star, & Williams, 1949). He fashioned RD to provide a post hoc explanation for several puzzling findings in his major study of the American soldier in World War II. These puzzles became famous in social science. Recall the greater satisfaction of the military police with slow promotions compared with the air corpsmen with rapid promotions. This finding offers an apparent puzzle only if we assume the wrong referent comparisons. Immediate comparisons, Stouffer reasoned, were the salient referents. The military police compared their promotions with other military police—not with air corpsmen whom they seldom encountered.

Since 1949, the RD idea slowly but steadily developed into a major concept that fits easily with a variety of social psychological theories—from social comparison and attribution theories to social identity theory (Crosby, 1976; Mark & Folger, 1984; Merton, 1957; Olson, Herman, & Zanna, 1986; Pettigrew, 1967; Runciman, 1966; Suls & Miller, 1977; Vanneman & Pettigrew, 1972; Walker & Pettigrew, 1984; Walker & Smith, 2001). Indeed, this article will provide an empirical demonstration of how RD joins with other theories to form a broader model of intergroup prejudice.

Runciman's (1966) distinction between different types of RD has proved vital to its development as a predictor of prejudice. He broadened the construct by carefully distinguishing between egoistic (individual) and fraternal (group) RD. People can decide whether they are personally deprived, that a social group to which they belong is deprived, or both. Repeated studies show that it is feelings of group RD (GRD), not individual RD (IRD), which directly promote political protest and prejudice (Pettigrew, 1964, 1967; Vanneman & Pettigrew, 1972; Walker & Mann, 1987; Walker & Smith, 2001).

Yet researchers often ignore Runciman's critical distinction (Walker & Pettigrew, 1984). For example, many have used interpersonal comparisons to predict collective behavior and prejudice (Long, 1975; Newton, Mann, & Geary, 1980; Useem, 1980). This confusion of levels explains many of the literature's negative RD results. Feeling deprived can invoke intergroup prejudice; but it does so primarily if one feels deprived on behalf of a relevant reference group. The strongest relationships between RD and dependent measures occur when the level of reference for both measures is the same. For prejudice, GRD captures the appropriate level.

Method

This article attempts to expand our understanding of the relationship of RD to prejudice by probing more deeply into Runciman's distinction between IRD and GRD. We will use three contrasting European data sets. First, we employ the extensive data-base provided by the European Union's 1988 Eurobarometer 30 survey (Pettigrew et al., 1998; Reif & Melich, 1991). This survey is one of the larger international studies of prejudice using probability samples in social science. Among other data, it drew seven national samples from France, West Germany, the Netherlands, and Great Britain. And the survey asked 3,796 adult, majority respondents in these four countries an array of both prejudice and RD questions.

Our second data source is a smaller, more focused survey of German youth (Schneider, 1994). It asked a sample of 794 East and West German teenagers of varying educational levels both IRD and GRD questions as well as their attitudes toward immigration and numerous ethnic groups.

For our third study, we employ a German national probability phone survey conducted in 2002 (GFE Survey; cf. Zick et al., 2008). This survey contains data on 2,722 adult respondents without a migration background, and it included a variety of prejudice and RD questions. Note the marked differences between our three data sets in terms of location, time, respondents' age, and items used to test RD and prejudice. Such differences provide a rigorous test for our ideas.

The Eurobarometer measures GRD by asking: "Would you say that over the last 5 years people like yourself in Britain have been economically a lot better off, better off, the same, worse off, or a lot worse off than most West Indians living here?" The survey taps IRD with the item: "Would you say that over the last 5 years you have been economically a lot better off, better off, the same, worse off, or a lot worse off than other British people like yourself?" Two scales of 10 items each in the Eurobarometer study assess blatant and subtle forms of prejudice (Pettigrew & Meertens, 1995). Researchers have successfully employed these scales in a great variety of nations and intergroup situations (Australia, Belgium, France, Germany, Great Britain, Italy, the Netherlands, Portugal, Spain, and the United States) (Arcuri & Boca, 1996; Hamberger & Hewstone, 1997; Hightower, 1997; Pedersen & Walker, 1997; Pettigrew, 1997; Pettigrew et al., 1998; Rattazzi & Volpato, 2001, 2003; Rueda & Navas, 1996; Six & Wolfradt, 2000; Vala, Brito, & Lopes, 1999;

Volpato & Rattazzi, 2000; Wagner & Zick, 1995; Zick, Wagner, van Dick, & Petzel, 2001).

The German youth study utilized more elaborate, multiple-item indicators of IRD and GRD styled for its sample of 14- to-18-year-old respondents. Four items tapped the individual form of RD by asking for comparisons with classmates, other Germans, other Germans of their region (east or west), and other German families of their region. Four additional items measured the group form of RD. They asked the young respondents to compare their present in-group situation with the other region's Germans and German families as well as with students of a different educational level.

The youth survey used two somewhat different prejudice indicators. A 1-to-10 favorability thermometer tapped feelings toward Turks. Five other items measured immigration attitudes. Agreement or disagreement was recorded for such statements as: "All foreigners not born in Germany should be sent back to the countries of their origin."

The GFE Survey contains one item each to measure IRD and GRD. Both questions are directly comparable to those of the Eurobarometer. The prejudice scale contains seven items concerning foreigners (e.g., "If jobs become scarce, foreigners should be sent back to their home countries."). These items are similar to the blatant scale in the Eurobarometer 30 analysis.

With these three contrasting data sets, we address five interrelated questions: (a) "Who are the relatively deprived?" (b) "Does RD serve as a proximal correlate of prejudice?" (c) "What is the relationship between IRD and GRD in the link with prejudice?" (d) "Does RD serve as a mediator of distal predictors of prejudice?" (e) "What are the critical additional variables operating in the RD–prejudice link?" From these analyses, we will present a socially situated, global model of RD's effects on prejudice.

Results

Who Are the Relatively Deprived?

Table 1 shows the social locations and personal characteristics of the relatively deprived respondents uncovered by the two RD forms in each of the three surveys. (The data in parentheses for the youth study are for the parents of the respondents.) In the Eurobarometer data, both those respondents indicating IRD and GRD are on average of lower socioeconomic status. They are less likely to own their own homes or apartments, and they tend to have limited family incomes. Not surprisingly, the adults in the Eurobarometer study regard themselves as of lower social status when they rate themselves as lower, working, middle, or upper class.

Also in the Eurobarometer data, older people tend to report IRD, while the less educated report GRD. However, there are no sex differences between the relatively

Table 1. Different Predictors Regressed on GRD and IRD

	Eurobarometer 30 (N = 3,796)		German Youth Survey (N = 794)		GFE Survey (N = 2,722)	
	GRD	IRD	GRD	IRD	GRD	IRD
Social location						
Age	.01	.08***	−.22**	−.03	−.11***	−.01
Education (of parents)	−.09***	−.02	(−.05)	(−.12**)	−.20***	−.06**
Social class (of parents)	−.12***	−.16***	(.07*)	(−.15**)	—	—
City size	.00	−.03	—[b]	—	−.02	−.05**
Family income	−.08***	−.15***	—	—	—	—
Sex[a]	.00	.00	.10**	.09*	.08***	.06**
Persons per room	—	—	.24**	.12**	—	—
Own home/apartment	−.05**	−.06***	—	—	—	—
Political alienation						
Political interest	−.07***	−.02	—	—	.02	−.05**
Political inefficacy	.09***	.14***	—	—	.14***	.18***
Social identity						
National pride	.03	−.08***	.13**	−.04	.11***	.05*
Euro. identity and Euro. pride	−.07***	−.02	—	—	−.05*	−.06**
R	.32	.36	.27	.26	.32	.24

Note. [a]Male = 1, female = 2. [b]Variable not measured.
* $p < .05$; ** $p < .01$; *** $p < .001$.

deprived and nondeprived in these data. The two groups share political alienation and tend to report somewhat less interest in politics in general and European politics specifically. Note how both IRD and GRD respondents in the Eurobarometer study score relatively highly on the scale measuring political inefficacy. Thus, they are significantly more likely than the nondeprived to agree with such items as: "Most people in power try to gain something out... of you" and "People who run the country are not really concerned with what happens to you." National identity, as indexed by a Eurobarometer item concerning national pride, tends to be lower among those reporting IRD. And thinking of yourself as a European is negatively related with GRD.

Although we must use somewhat different predictors, we repeat this analysis for the German youth study in Table 1. The respondents' sex, which was not a predictor in the adult Eurobarometer sample, rises to significance in this sample; the teenage girls report significantly more GRD and IRD than the boys. The social class indicators replicate the finding that the relatively deprived tend to be of lower social status. The variables measuring persons per room in households and the social class and education of parents all link lower status with RD save for GRD and parental social class. In the youth study, GRD respondents report more pride in being German.

We calculated a comparable analysis for the GFE Survey. As in the German youth study, those reporting GRD are younger, less educated, and more likely to be female. The shift of sign in the age and GRD relationship between the 1988 and 2002 adult surveys may reflect the rise of unemployment especially among the young throughout Western Europe during this period. Like the Eurobarometer results, both types of deprivation score higher on a political inefficacy scale. Moreover, the IRD and GRD respondents report more pride in being German but less pride in being European.

In summary, then, the three studies agree that both IRD and GRD are strongest among lower-status respondents. And the two adult studies show that both types of RD correlate with a sense of political inefficacy.

The Basic RD and Prejudice Relationships

Table 2 provides the correlations of the IRD and GRD measures with the five different measures of prejudice. The consistently larger coefficients for GRD than IRD in Table 2 were also found for each of the seven samples and four nations of the 1988 Eurobarometer data (not shown).

Table 2 also reveals how these first-order relationships hold up once the other RD measure is controlled, and then when an array of social variables are also controlled. Recall from Table 1 the relationships of IRD and GRD with the social location variables. Because we assume that all these variables had their causal influence prior to the formation of RD, we control for them in Table 2 in each data set.

Consistent with the extensive research of the past, Table 2 shows that it is GRD, not IRD, that is a primary correlate of prejudice. Note that controlling for GRD greatly reduces the IRD correlations with the various prejudice indicators; and they virtually disappear with one exception when the social location variables

Table 2. Relative Deprivation–Prejudice Correlations

	Eurobarometer 1988		German Youth Survey		GFE Survey Prejudice
	Blatant Prejudice	Subtle Prejudice	Antipathy Against Turks	Immigration Attitudes	
IRD	.12**	.06**	.02	.02	.19**
with controls for[a]:					
GRD	.03	.01	−.03	−.04	.15*
GRD and social variables	.00	−.01	−.05	−.07	.13**
GRD	.27***	.15**	.19*	.21*	.29**
with controls for[a]:					
IRD	.24**	.14**	.18*	.21*	.26**
IRD and social variables	.19**	.11**	.17*	.22*	.23**

Note. [a]The control variables are the social location variables of Table 1 for each sample, respectively.
* $p < .05$; ** $p < .01$.

are also controlled. By contrast, controlling for IRD only marginally reduces the GRD correlations; and they remain uniformly significant even after the social variables and IRD are controlled. The lone exception to these trends occurs in the GFE Survey results. Here the correlation of IRD with prejudice remains significant after controlling for GRD and the social location variables ($r = .13$). But the partial correlation of GRD is significantly stronger ($r = .23$). Table 2 also reveals that the RD relationships are consistently larger for blatant than subtle prejudice.

How Are IRD and GRD Related in Predicting Prejudice?

Researchers have advanced three possibilities: IRD and GRD are unrelated; they interact with GRD moderating the IRD effects; or GRD mediates the IRD effects on prejudice. We can test each of these proposals with our surveys.

Ellemers (2001) asserted "that there is no logical or self-evident connection between the two forms of deprivation." She noted that considerable research has shown that it is common for people to be satisfied with their personal situation while expressing considerable GRD (Crosby, Pufall, Snyder, O'Connell, & Whalen, 1989; Martin, 1981; Taylor, Wright, Moghaddam, & Lalonde, 1990).

While there may be no "logical or self-evident" reason why they are related, IRD and GRD consistently and positively relate to each other. They correlate .35 in the 1988 Eurobarometer data, and this relationship is only slightly reduced ($r = .29$; $p < .001$) when the six social location variables are controlled. Moreover, this aggregate finding holds true for each of the seven national samples. The extensive IRD and GRD measures of the German youth survey also correlate .25 and is .24 ($p < .01$) when the five location variables of Table 1 are controlled. The same can be found in the GFE Survey: IRD and GRD correlate .20 and the partial correlation is .17 ($p < .001$). In addition, Table 1 demonstrated the similarity of the correlates of IRD and GRD.

These results are consistent with earlier research. Both experimental and survey research have found IRD and GRD to be positively and significantly related. Though the fixed effect sizes from six relevant studies with 1,021 respondents are not homogeneous, the mean correlation weighted for sample size is highly significant, .41 (Cohen's $d = .89$; $p < .001$), with a range between .19 and .80 (Beaton & Tougas, 1997; Foster & Matheson, 1995; Guimond & Dube-Simard, 1983; Kawakami & Dion, 1993; Kelly & Kelly, 1994; Kooman & Frankel, 1992). When trimmed of two outliers to attain homogeneity, the mean r (.23) is reduced but remains statistically significant.

Foster and Matheson (1995) proposed an interactive model to connect the two RD types. Their hierarchical regression results show that the interaction between the two forms of deprivation added to the prediction of reported collective action beyond that of the main effects of IRD and GRD. Thus, GRD acts in their data as a moderator of the IRD effects, with those high in both types of deprivation showing an unusually strong effect. Hence, Foster and Matheson held "double deprivation" to be an especially potent motivator of collective action.

But this empirical demonstration is limited. The data are from a college sample of convenience of politically inactive Canadian females on one particular dependent variable measure. More extensive research using large probability adult samples, better indicators of RD, and an array of diverse dependent variables fail to support the interactive model (Tougas & Beaton, 2001; Vanneman & Pettigrew, 1972). Similarly, we failed to find significant moderator effects using IRD and GRD in all three of our European samples.

Tougas and Beaton (2001) showed there is often a spill-over effect from high levels of IRD to GRD. Clearly, IRD is not a necessary condition for GRD, but it can be a contributing factor. Tougas and her colleagues demonstrated that IRD does not directly predict such responses as support or resistance to affirmative action employment programs (Beaton & Tougas, 1997). In path analyses, however, IRD indirectly relates to such responses through its influence on GRD. In this indirect sense, then, Tougas and Beaton concluded that "the personal is political" with GRD acting as a mediator of IRD's effects.

However, Tougas and Beaton used a special sense of IRD. That is, the spill-over effect they demonstrate occurs when people compare themselves individually to a single out-group member. We test with our survey data their interesting resolution of the issue with the classic definition of IRD involving comparison with in-group individuals.

First, we have already noted that IRD and GRD are positively and significantly correlated throughout the research literature—a fact consistent with the Tougas and Beaton position. Next, we saw in Table 2 what happens when we apply partials for each type of RD. Controlling for GRD greatly reduces the IRD correlations with all four measures of prejudice. But controlling for IRD only marginally reduces the GRD correlations with prejudice.

Finally, we can estimate the degree of mediation that GRD exerts on the IRD–prejudice correlations (Preacher & Leonardelli, 2006; Sobel, 1982). In the Eurobarometer data for blatant prejudice, GRD mediates 73% of the IRD effect; for subtle prejudice, GRD mediates 84% of the IRD effect. Only trivial direct effects of IRD on the prejudice scores (.03) remain after the mediation is controlled (Fig. 1). In the German youth data for both prejudice indicators (antipathy against Turks and immigration attitudes), IRD has no significant link with prejudice to be mediated. We find comparable mediation effects in the GFE Survey (see Fig. 1); but in these data IRD retains a significant direct effect on prejudice (.15). In short, IRD's influence on prejudice occurs in part through its contribution to greater GRD. We believe these results lend support to the Tougas–Beaton mediating model.

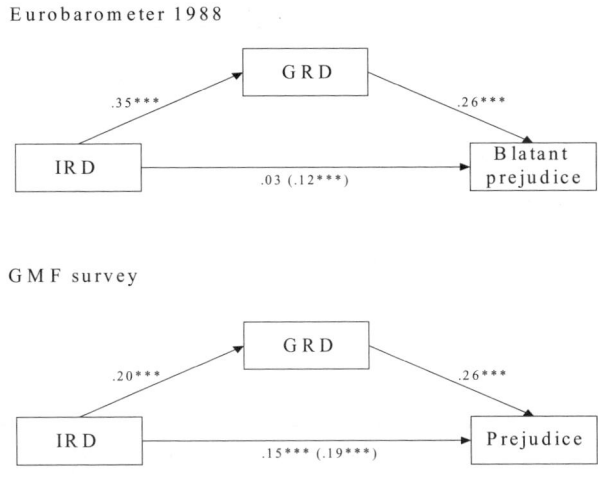

Fig. 1. Mediation effects of GRD on IRD – prejudice association (*** $p < .001$).

Moderating and Mediating the Effects of Distal Predictors of Prejudice

Moderator effects of GRD for social variable effects on prejudice are rare. Using the Aiken and West method (1991), we found only two moderator effects in the Eurobaromater data set, three in the German youth survey, and none in the GFE Survey. The two moderator effects of GRD in the Eurobarometer 88 are for political interest and political inefficacy. For those who score high in GRD, the negative associations between both political interest and political inefficacy with blatant prejudice are stronger. In the German youth survey, three moderator effects emerge for national pride, education, and age. That is, the effects of GRD on the prejudice measures are stronger for those who score high in national pride, have a low education, and are older.

It is far more common for GRD indicators to mediate the effects of social variables on prejudice. Consider the Eurobarometer results shown in Table 3. We see that for family income, subjective social class, political inefficacy, European identification, political interest, and education the mediation by GRD is substantial and highly significant. The German youth data reveal comparable mediation effects for the persons per room and national pride variables on both prejudice indicators. In the GFE Survey, GRD significantly mediates the effects on prejudice of seven predictors: political inefficacy, political interest, education, sex, national pride, city size, and age. GRD mediates only part of these predictors' effects on the five prejudice measures with direct effects remaining. Hence, GRD is providing partial mediation for these variables, but it is neither a necessary nor sufficient condition for these prejudice effects to occur. Other mediating factors are also operating.

Table 3. Percentage Mediated by Group Relative Deprivation in Prejudice[a]

	Eurobarometer 1988		German Youth Survey		
	Blatant Prejudice	Subtle Prejudice	Antipathy Against Turks	Immigration Attitudes	GFE Survey Prejudice
Persons per room	—[b]	—	7*	70***	
Own home/apartment	—	—	—	—	—
Family income	41***	65***	—	—	—
Social class	37***	48***	—	—	—
Political inefficacy	30***	17***	—	—	13***
Political interest	16***	14***	—	—	16***
European identity	14***	25***	—	—	10***
Education	10***	18***	—	—	21***
Sex	—	—	—	—	55***
National pride	5*	4*	5**	3**	9***
City size	—	—	—	—	11***
Age	5*	—	—	—	8***

Note. [a]The Sobel test was used for calculating statistical significance (Preacher & Leonardelli, 2006; Sobel, 1982). [b]"—" signifies that the variable was not measured or it had no significant relation with GRD or the prejudice indicator.
*$p < .05$; **$p < .01$; ***$p < .001$.

Mediating the Effects of GRD on Prejudice

Walker, Wong, and Kretzschmar (2001) proposed a model of RD that melds Folger's (1986) referent cognitions theory with Weiner's (1986) attributional theory of motivation and emotion. Their model's central contention is that causal attributions serve as important mediators of RD's effects.

We can make a rough test of these contentions with the Eurobarometer data. To mediate between GRD and the prejudice scales, we employ the following item: "There is a great deal of discrimination against Turks living here today that limits their chances to get ahead" (with *agree strongly* to *disagree strongly* responses). Reversing the scoring produces a measure of the denial of discrimination. Through the eyes of these majority respondents, such denial attributes intergroup problems to the minority itself—the widespread "blaming the victim" phenomenon. And, as Walker and his colleagues predicted, this single item serves to mediate a significant part of GRD's effect on blatant prejudice (25%; $Z = 10.838$, $p < .001$) in our large sample of Western Europeans.

Discussion

From these various empirical threads, we can now advance a broader model of RD's effects on prejudice (adapted from Pettigrew, 2001). Again employing the extensive Eurobarometer data, Figure 2 provides a path analytic model of how both IRD and GRD shape blatant prejudice within a larger social context. A comparable,

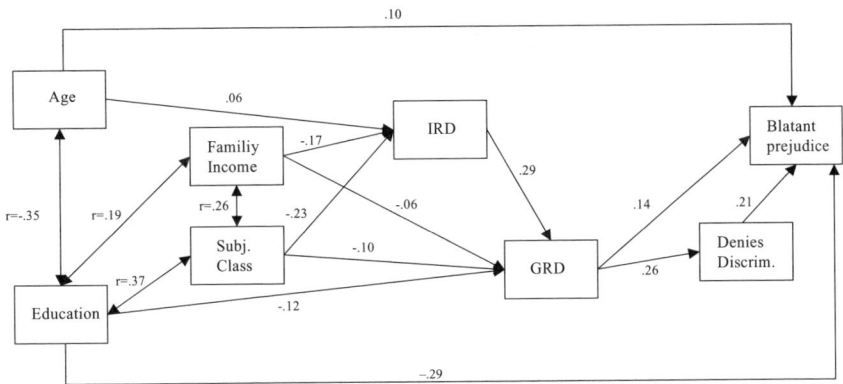

Note. EQS Normed Fit = .976; CFI = .979; Lisrel GFI = .994; Lisrel AGFI = .981; SRMR = .029; RMSEA = .042; $\chi^2 = 75.24$; $df = 12$; $N = 2,980$ (listwise deletion); all paths: $p < .01$.

Fig. 2. Model of RD and blatant prejudice; the Eurobarometer 1988; all paths significant.

though less robust, model also emerges when subtle prejudice is employed as the dependent variable.

Observe that age influences IRD, education influences GRD, and family income and subjective social class influence both RD forms. Note also that age and education have direct paths to blatant prejudice, while the effects of family income and subjective social class are mediated entirely though the two RD forms. Following Tougas and Beaton (2001), Figure 2 also shows that IRD has no significant direct effect on prejudice; it influences blatant prejudice by increasing GRD. Finally, observe that GRD's effects on blatant prejudice are mediated by the single item with which respondents deny discrimination against minorities.

Summary

Returning to our original questions, these analyses support the following conclusions concerning the relationship between RD and various indicators of intergroup prejudice.

(a) Who are the relatively deprived? Not surprisingly, the ranks of the relatively deprived—for both IRD and GRD—center among those of lower social class standing. They are most numerous among those who have restricted incomes, do not own their own homes or apartments, and live in smaller quarters. They are also more politically alienated. They pay less attention to politics and feel less politically efficacious than others.

(b) Does RD serve as a proximal correlate of prejudice? Runciman's (1965) distinction between IRD and GRD is crucial. IRD often does not directly relate to intergroup prejudice, while GRD routinely correlates positively with a variety of prejudice indicators in diverse samples. We show this often replicated finding with our three contrasting samples.

(c) What is the relationship between IRD and GRD in the link with prejudice? Theorists have advanced three proposals: IRD and GRD are unrelated; IRD and GRD interact in their relationship with prejudice; and GRD mediates IRD's effects. Our analyses reject the first two proposals and lend support to the third. Only GRD consistently correlates positively with prejudice; and it acts as a critical mediator of IRD's effects on prejudice.

(d) Does RD serve as a mediator of distal predictors of prejudice? Sociology typically specifies numerous distal predictors of prejudice—such as social class. Social psychology often sharpens such analyses by specifying the proximal variables at the individual level that mediate these broad effects of distal social variables.

GRD often serves as an important but not exclusive mediator of the distal effects on prejudice of a variety of social variables. In particular, we found that GRD significantly mediated such distal social predictors as social class and political inefficacy.

(e) What are the critical additional variables operating in the GRD—prejudice link? Many variables probably influence the positive relationship between GRD and intergroup prejudice. Our analysis, following the contentions of Walker and his colleagues (2001), focused on the role of attribution. Using the Eurobarometer data, we found that a significant part of the GRD's enhancement of prejudice is mediated by the denial of discrimination against the out-group and thus blaming intergroup problems on the out-group.

In sum, GRD plays a central role in social psychology's understanding of intergroup prejudice. The policy implications of this phenomenon are straightforward. Governmental policy needs to look beyond absolute deprivation in their populations and consider RD as well. Policy attempts to reduce group-linked discrimination and disparities are important; but such attempts are likely to threaten the privileged group and produce greater intergroup prejudice.

Such negative effects of needed governmental remediation must be anticipated and ameliorated by skillfully crafted social policies. At the structural level, attempts to improve the lives of minorities should be coupled with comparable attempts to improve the lives of the poorer segments of the majority. At the psychological level, most native Western Europeans do not realize that the influx of immigrants over the past half-century was absolutely necessary for the rapid rise in the continent's living standards over these years. Thus, policies to combat discrimination and improve the lives of the new immigrants should be tightly interwoven with efforts to make this economic fact widely understood.

References

Aiken, L. S., & West, S.G. (1991). *Multiple regression: Testing and interpreting interactions.* Newbury Park, CA: Sage.

Arcuri, L., & Boca, S. (1999). Posicionamentos politicos: Racismo subtil e racismo flagrante em Italia. [Political attitudes: Subtle racism and blatant racism in Italy]. In J. Vala (Ed.), *Novos racismos: Perspectivas comparativas* (pp. 61–75). Oeiras, Portugal: Celta Editora.

Beaton, A. M., & Tougas, F. (1997). The representation of women in management: The more, the merrier? *Personality and Social Psychology Bulletin, 23*, 773–782.

Brown, D. (2004). Why independence? The instrumental and ideological dimensions of nationalism. *International Journal of Comparative Sociology, 45*(3–4), 277–296.

Crosby, F. J. (1976). A model for egoistical relative deprivation. *Psychological Review, 83*, 85–113.

Crosby, F. J., Pufall, A., Snyder, R. C., O'Connell, M., & Whalen, P. (1989). The denial of personal disadvantage among you, me, and all other ostriches. In M. Crawford & M. Gentry (Eds.), *Gender and thought: Psychological perspectives* (pp. 79–99). New York: Springer-Verlag.

Duclos, J., & Gregoire, P. (2002). Absolute and relative deprivation and the measurement of poverty. *Review of Income and Wealth, 48*(4), 471–491.

Ellemers, N. (2001). Social identity and relative deprivation. In I. Walker & H. Smith (Eds.), *Relative deprivation: Specification, development and integration* (pp. 239–264). New York: Cambridge University Press.

Folger, R. (1986). A referent cognitions theory of relative deprivation. In J. M. Olson, C. P. Herman, & M. P. Zanna (Eds.), *Relative deprivation and social comparison: The Ontario symposium* (pp. 33–55) (Vol. 4). Hillsdale, NJ: Lawrence Erlbaum.

Foster, M. D., & Matheson, K. (1995). Double relative deprivation: Combining the personal and political. *Personality and Social Psychology Bulletin, 21*, 1167–1177.

Guimond, S., & Dube-Simard, L. (1983). Relative deprivation theory and the Quebec Nationalist Movement: The cognition-emotion distinction and the personal-group deprivation issue. *Journal of Personality and Social Psychology, 44*, 526–535.

Hamberger, J., & Hewstone, M. (1997). Interethnic contact as a predictor of blatant and subtle prejudice: Tests of a model in four West European nations. *British Journal of Social Psychology, 36*, 173–190.

Hightower, E. (1997). Psychosocial characteristics of subtle and blatant racists as compared to tolerant individuals. *Journal of Clinical Psychology, 53*, 369–374.

Kawakami, K., & Dion, K. L. (1993). The impact of salient self-identities on relative deprivation and action intentions. *European Journal of Social Psychology, 23*, 525–540.

Kelly, C., & Kelly, J. (1994). Who gets involved in collective action? Social psychological determinants of individual participation in trade unions. *Human Relations, 47*, 63–88.

Kooman, W., & Frankel, E. G. (1992). Effects of experienced discrimination and different forms of relative deprivation among Surinamese, a Dutch ethnic minority group. *Journal of Community and Applied Social Psychology, 2*, 63–72.

Lea, J., & Young, J. (1993). *What is to be done about law and order?* London: Pluto.

Long, S. J. (1975). Malevolent estrangement: Political alienation and political justification among black and white adolescents. *Youth and Society, 7*, 99–129.

Mark, M. M., & Folger, R. (1984). Responses to relative deprivation: A conceptual framework. *Review of Personality and Social Psychology, 5*, 182–218.

Martin, J. (1981). Relative deprivation: A theory of distributive justice for an era of shrinking resources. *Research in Organizational Behavior, 3*, 57–107.

Merton, R. K. (1957). *Social theory and social structure* (rev. ed.) Glencoe, IL: Free Press.

Newton, J. W., Mann, L., & Geary, D. (1980). Relative deprivation, dissatisfaction and militancy: A field study in a protest crowd. *Journal of Applied Social Psychology, 10*, 384–397.

Olson, J. M., Herman, C. P., & Zanna, M. P. (Eds.). (1986). *Relative deprivation and social comparison: The Ontario Symposium* (Vol. 4). Hillsdale, NJ: Lawrence Erlbaum.

Pedersen, A., & Walker, I. (1997). Prejudice against Australian Aboriginals: Old-fashioned and modern forms. *European Journal of Social Psychology, 27*(5), 561–587.

Pettigrew, T. F. (1964). *A profile of the Negro American.* New York: Van Nostrand.

Pettigrew, T. F. (1967). Social evaluation theory: Convergencies and applications. In D. Levine (Ed.), *Nebraska Symposium on Motivation, 1967* (pp. 241–311). Lincoln: University of Nebraska Press.

Pettigrew, T. F. (1991). Toward unity and bold theory: Popperian suggestions for two persistent problems of social psychology. In C. Stephan, W. Stephan, & T. F. Pettigrew (Eds.), *The future of social psychology* (pp. 13–27). New York: Springer-Verlag.

Pettigrew, T. F. (1997). Generalized intergroup contact effects on prejudice. *Personality and Social Psychology Bulletin, 23*, 173–185.

Pettigrew, T. F. (2001). Summing up: Relative deprivation as a key social psychological concept. In I. Walker & H. Smith (Eds.), *Relative deprivation: Specification, development and integration* (pp. 351–373). New York: Cambridge University Press.

Pettigrew, T. F., & Meertens, R. W. (1995). Subtle and blatant prejudice in Western Europe. *European Journal of Social Psychology, 57*, 57–75.

Pettigrew, T. F., Jackson, J., Ben Brika, J., Lemain, G., Meertens, R. W., Wagner, U., & Zick, A. (1998). Outgroup prejudice in Western Europe. *European Review of Social Psychology, 8*, 241–273.

Preacher, K. J., & Leonardelli, G. J. (2006). *Calculation for the Sobel test: An interaction calculation tool for mediation tests*. Retrieved August 21, 2006 from http://www.psych.ku/preacher/sobel.

Rattazzi, A. M. M., & Volpato, C. (2001). Forme sottili e manifeste di pregiudizio verso gli immigrati [Subtle and blatant forms of prejudice against immigrants]. *Giornale Italiano di Psicologia, 26*(2), 351–375.

Rattazzi, A. M. M., & Volpato, C. (2003). The social desirability of subtle and blatant prejudice scales. *Psychological Reports, 92*(1), 241–250.

Reif, K., & Melich, A. (1991). *Euro-barometer 30: Immigrants and out-groups in Western Europe, October-November 1988*. (ICPSR 9321). Ann Arbor, MI: Inter-University Consortium for Political and Social Research.

Rueda, J. F., & Navas, M. (1996). Hacia una evaluacion de las nuevas formas del prejuicio racial: Las actitudes sutiles del racismo [Toward an evaluation of the new forms of racial prejudice: The subtle attitudes of racism]. *Revista de Psicologia Social, 11*, 131–149.

Runciman, W. G. (1966). *Relative deprivation and social justice*. London: Routledge & Kegan Paul.

Schneider, S. (1994). *Vorurteile gegeneuber ethnischen Minderheiten in Ost und West* [Prejudice against ethnic minorities in the East and West.] Diploma thesis, Department of Psychology, Bochum University, Bochum, Germany.

Six, B., & Wolfradt, U. (2000, July 25). *Authoritarianism and some more social psychological traits: Structures and contingencies*. Paper presented at the International Congress of Psychology Conference, Stockholm, Sweden.

Sobel, M. E. (1982). Asymptotic intervals for indirect effects in structural equations models. In S. Leinhart (Ed.), *Sociological methodology 1982* (pp. 290–312). San Francisco: Jossey-Bass.

Stouffer, S. A., Suchman, E. A., DeVinney, L. C., Star, S. A., & Williams, R. M., Jr. (1949). *The American soldier: Vol. 1. Adjustment during army life*. Princeton, NJ: Princeton University Press.

Suls, J. M., & Miller, R. L. (Eds.). (1977). *Social comparison processes: Theoretical and empirical perspectives*. New York: Halsted Press.

Taylor, D. M., Wright, S. C. Moghaddam, F. M., & Lalonde, R. N. (1990). The personal/group discrimination: Perceiving my group, but not myself, to be a target for discrimination. *Personality and Social Psychology Bulletin, 16*, 254–263.

Tougas, F., & Beaton, A. M. (2001). Personal and group relative deprivation: Connecting the "I" to the "we." In I. Walker & H. Smith (Eds.), *Relative deprivation: Specification, development and integration* (pp. 119–135). New York: Cambridge University Press.

Useem, B. (1980). Solidarity model, breakdown model and the Boston anti-busing movement. *American Sociological Review, 45*, 357–369.

Vala, J., Brito, R., & Lopes, D. (1999). O racismo flagrante e o racismo subtil em Portugal [On blatant and subtle racism in Portugal]. In J. Vala (Ed.), *Novos racismos: Perspectivas comparativas* (pp. 31–59). Oeiras, Portugal: Celta Editora.

Vanneman, R. D., & Pettigrew, T. F. (1972). Race and relative deprivation in the urban United States. *Race, 13*, 461–486.

Volpato, C., & Rattazzi, A. M. M. (2000). Pregiudizio e immigrazione:. Effetti del contatto sulle relazioni interetniche [Prejudice and immigration: Effects of contact upon interethnic relations]. *Ricerche di Psicologia, 24*(3–4), 57–80.
Wagner, U., & Zick, A. (1995). The relation of formal education to ethnic prejudice: Its reliability, validity, explanation. *European Journal of Social Psychology, 25*, 41–56.
Walker, I., & Mann, L. (1987). Unemployment, relative deprivation and social protest. *Personality and Social Psychology Bulletin, 13*, 275–283.
Walker, I., & Pettigrew, T. F. (1984). Relative deprivation theory: An overview and conceptual critique. *British Journal of Social Psychology, 23*, 301–310.
Walker, I., & Smith. H. (Eds.). (2001). *Relative deprivation: Specification, development and integration.* New York: Cambridge University Press.
Walker, I., Wang, N. G., & Kretzschmar, K. (2001). Relative deprivation and attribution: From grievance to action. In I. Walker & H. Smith (Eds.), *Relative deprivation: Specification, development and integration* (pp. 288–312). New York: Cambridge University Press.
Weiner, B. (1986). *An attributional theory of motivation and emotion.* New York: Springer-Verlag.
Zick, A., Wagner, U., van Dick, R., & Petzel, T. (2001). Acculturation and prejudice in Germany: Majority and minority perspectives. *Journal of Social Issues, 57*(3), 541–557.
Zick, A., Wolf, H., Küpper, B., Davidov, E., Schmidt, P., & Heitmeyer, W. (2008). The syndrome of group-focused enmity: The interrelation of prejudices tested with multiple cross-sectional panel data. *Journal of Social Issues, 64*(2), 363–383.

THOMAS F. PETTIGREW is Research Professor of Social Psychology at the University of California, Santa Cruz. He received his PhD at Harvard University (1956) and taught there until 1980. From 1986 to 1991, he taught at the University of Amsterdam and conducted research on prejudice in the Netherlands. Pettigrew has published 10 books and more than 200 articles and reviews on prejudice and racism. His publications include *How to Think Like a Social Scientist* (1996) and chapters on intergroup relations in the *Annual Review of Psychology* (Pettigrew, 1998a) and the *Annual Review of Sociology* (Pettigrew, 1998b). He served as president of SPSSI (1967–68) and has twice been awarded the Society's Allport Prize for Intergroup Relations Research (with Joanne Martin in 1988 and Linda Tropp in 2003). He also received the Society for Experimental Social Psychology's Distinguished Scientist Award (2001), a Senior Fellowship at the Research Institute of Comparative Studies in Race and Ethnicity at Stanford University (2001), and a Fulbright New Century Scholar Fellowship for continued research on prejudice and discrimination against the immigrants of Western Europe (2003).

OLIVER CHRIST is a Lecturer for Methods at Philipps-University Marburg, Germany. Previously he was Lecturer in Social Psychology at the University of Marburg and Advisor for Survey Methodology at the University of Bielefeld, Germany. He earned his PhD in Social Psychology from Philipps-University, Marburg, Germany in 2005. His research interests lie in the field of intergroup relations, ethnic prejudice and social identity processes in organizations.

ULRICH WAGNER is Professor of Social Psychology and Director of the Center for Conflict Studies at Philipps-University Marburg in Germany. Dr. Wagner's research interests include intergroup relations, ethnic prejudice, and intergroup aggression. His publications include contributions to the analyses of survey data on ethnic prejudice and racism, as published in a special issue of the *Zeitschrift für Politische Psychologie [Journal of Political Psychology]* (Eds. Wagner & van Dick, 2001), an overview article in the *Zeitschrift für Sozialpsychologie [Journal of Social Psychology]* (Wagner, van Dick, & Zick, 2001) and original data analyses (e.g., Wagner, van Dick, Pettigrew, & Christ, 2003; Wagner, Christ, Pettigrew, Stellmacher, & Wolf, 2006). He heads the special graduate school addressing Group-Focused Enmity, sponsored by the Deutsche Forschungsgemeinschaft (German Science Foundation). For the academic year 2003–2004, Wagner was a Senior Fellow at the Research Institute of Comparative Studies in Race and Ethnicity at Stanford University.

ROEL W. MEERTENS is Professor of Social Psychology at the University of Amsterdam, the Netherlands. He received his PhD in Social Psychology at the University of Groningen in 1976. He has worked extensively in the area of intergroup relations, prejudice, and subtle racism. His publications include Pettigrew, T. F., and Meertens, R. W. (1995). Subtle and blatant prejudice in western Europe. *European Journal of Social Psychology, 25*, 57–75; Pettigrew, T. F., and Meertens, R. W. (1996) The verzuiling puzzle: Understanding Dutch intergroup relations. *Current Psychology, 15;* Meertens; R. W., & Pettigrew, T. F. (1997). Is subtle prejudice really prejudice? *The-Public-Opinion-Quarterly, 61*, 54–71.

ROLF VAN DICK earned his PhD from Philipps-Universität, Marburg, Germany. He is Professor of Social Psychology at the Department of Psychology, Johann Wolfgang Goethe-Universität Frankfurt, Germany, and also holds a part-time chair at Aston Business School, Birmingham, United Kingdom. His primary research interests are in the application of social identity theory in organizational settings (diversity, leadership, mergers). He is Associate Editor of the *European Journal of Work & Organisational Psychology* and incoming Editor-in-Chief of the *British Journal of Management*. Publications in the area of acculturation, prejudice and intergroup contact include: Van Dick, R., Wagner, U. Pettigrew, T. F., Christ, O., Wolf, C., Petzel, T., Smith Castro, V., & Jackson, J. S. (2004). Role of perceived importance in intergroup contact. *Journal of Personality and Social Psychology, 87*, 211–227.

ANDREAS ZICK is on the leave from the University of Bielefeld to chair the professorship for social psychology at the University of Jena. Additionally he manages the "Group-Focused Enmity in Europe" project. He received his PhD at the University of Marburg in 1996, worked from 1998 to 2003 as Assistant

Professor at the University of Wuppertal, from 2004 to 2006 at the University of Bielefeld, and was the Chair of Social Psychology at the University of Dresden from 2006 to 2007. His current research interests include migration as well as studies on prejudice, racism, and discrimination in Europe; right-wing extremism; social dominance; and the self-concept in social identity. He has published numerous articles and a monograph on prejudice and racism in Western Europe. His recent research investigates the link between immigration ideologies, dominance orientations, and racism (see, Zick, A., Ed., 1999, Special Issue: Authoritarianism, *Politics, Groups and the Individual*; Zick, A., Wagner, U., van Dick, R. & Petzel, T., 2001, Acculturation and Prejudice in Germany: Majority and Minority Perspectives, *Journal of Social Issues*).

Prejudice and Group-Related Behavior in Germany

Ulrich Wagner[*]
Philipps-University, Marburg

Oliver Christ
Philipps-University, Marburg

Thomas F. Pettigrew
The University of California

This article analyses the relationship of ethnic prejudice and discriminatory behavioral intentions in Germany. We utilize two representative surveys conducted in 2002 and 2004 (N = 2,722 and 1,383, respectively) as well as a longitudinal study with three annual measurement points (2002–2004; N = 825). Results show that prejudice is substantially correlated with the respondents' reports of their own discriminatory intentions (R = .33 to .49). Controlling for additional psychological variables, the cross-lagged, longitudinal analyses support the causal hypothesis that prejudice leads to discriminatory intentions. Additional influences on discriminatory intentions—intergroup threat and intergroup contact—are substantially mediated by ethnic prejudice. Thus, a practical implication of these results is that the reduction of intergroup threat and increment of intergroup contact may well lead to both reduced intergroup prejudice and to less discriminatory behavior.

Numerous studies document systematic discriminatory behavior of majorities against minorities, especially ethnic minorities. Crosby, Bromely, and Saxe (1980) have summarized studies on subtle forms of such discriminatory behavior in the United States. Klink and Wagner (1999) have presented comparable results for

---

[*]Correspondence concerning this article should be addressed to Ulrich Wagner, Philipps-University, Department of Psychology, Gutenbergstr. 18, 35032 Marburg, Germany [e-mail: wagner1@staff.uni-marburg.de].

Data collection was funded by a grant of the Volkswagen Stiftung and the Freudenberg Stiftung to Wilhelm Heitmeyer, University of Bielefeld (project "Group-Focused enmity"). The authors are grateful to Bernd Six and Andreas Zick for their comments on a first draft of the article.

Germany. Recent events of hate crimes, especially in Germany (Willems, 2002), are dramatic examples of such hostile intergroup behavior.

One possible origin of negative behavior directed toward out-group members is the attitude the discriminating person holds toward these out-groups. This does not imply that prejudiced attitudes are the only reason for discriminatory behavior (Allport, 1954). But the intensive scientific analysis of attitudes can only be justified if attitudes allow at least for a partial prediction of behavior (Eagly & Chaiken, 1993). Who would care about analyzing a person's attitudes or prejudices, if these concepts were neither indirectly nor directly connected to any kind of behavior? Attitude research and research on prejudice have always been based on the basic assumption that knowing a person's attitude toward a (social or nonsocial) object enables the researcher to predict future behavior directed toward this object. To name a few examples, researchers assumed that a person's attitude toward a certain product allows predicting his or her consumer behavior (Lavidge & Steiner, 1961), that citizens' political attitudes predict their voting behavior (Campbell, Converse, Miller, & Stokes, 1960), and that a person's prejudiced attitude helps to understand his or her discriminatory behavior against an out-group member (Dovidio, Kawakami, & Gaertner, 2002). From this perspective, attitude/prejudice research fits directly into the neo–behavioristic assumption that a real psychological perspective has to take the subjective elaboration of objectively defined stimuli into account in order to be able to make accurate predictions of behavior (Lewin, 1936).

These basic assumptions concerning attitudes and prejudice have historically been heavily debated. Based on a review of the then available empirical data, Wicker (1969) concluded that the attitude/prejudice–behavior relation is lower than expected if existing at all. This contention helps to explain why in the following years social psychological theorists started focusing more on moderators of the relation between attitudes and behavior (as measurement compatibilities (cf. Ajzen & Fishbein, 1977; for an overview see Eagly & Chaiken, 1993).

Recent meta-analytic summaries of the attitude/prejudice–behavior relation come to a less pessimistic view than those of the 1960s (Eagly & Chaiken, 1993). Based on the analysis of 60 independent studies, Schütz and Six (1996) found a mean correlation of $r = .36$ between prejudice and behavior and of $r = .45$ between prejudice and behavioral intentions. Dovidio, Brigham, Johnson, and Gaertner (1996) reported similar results based on a summary of 23 studies. Thus, these data show that prejudice and discriminatory behavior covary.

We will focus upon the prejudice–behavior relation once more, using data from an ongoing research project in Germany (Heitmeyer, 2002). The project's general aim is to determine societal developments in negative attitudes toward various minorities in Germany and to identify individual and societal causes of these trends. These two aims attain practical and political relevance only if we can assume that hostile attitudes toward a society's minority groups are related to behavior—be it to individual behavior or to the institutional and societal treatment of minorities.

This article analyzes the prejudice–behavior relationship on the basis of extensive survey data. If these data show that the reported prejudice–behavior relation can also be generalized to our German samples, we will ask three additional research questions. Much of the research on the prejudice–behavior relationship is experimental (Dovidio, Gaertner, Nier, Kawakami, & Hodson, 2004). For these experimental results, the question of causality is clear. But the high internal validity is often achieved at the expense of external validity; that is, the generalization of the results to situations other than the experimental context. For correlational data (LaPiere, 1934), the reverse problem emerges. In particular, the question of causality often remains open, an artifact can thus not be ruled out. The correlation may result from the influence of a third variable—such as education—that is negatively related both with prejudice and with behavior (Wagner & Zick, 1995). Thus, *our first research question is whether the prejudice–behavior relation remains valid if we control for influences of reasonable third variables.*

Even after controlling for possible confounds, correlational data typically do not allow for tests of causality. We argue that prejudice is a cause of discriminatory behavior. The alternative is that discriminatory conducts cause a change in the attitude toward the out-group, as proposed by dissonance theory (Cooper, Mirabile, & Scher, 2005). Therefore, *our second research question is whether prejudice really predicts behavior in a strictly controlled longitudinal cross-lagged design.*

Research has shown that discriminatory behavior is dependent on certain independent variables other than prejudice. For example, Semyonov, Raijman, and Yom-Tov (2002) showed that feelings of intergroup threat go along with an increase in discriminatory behavior against foreign workers in Israel. Craig (2002) presented evidence that hate crimers conducting violence against ethnic out-group members usually did not have contact with their targets previous to their aggression. This supports the hypothesis that intergroup contact and intergroup aggression are negatively correlated. If, as proposed here, prejudice is an important causal precondition for discriminatory behavior, one can assume that the effects of intergroup threat and intergroup contact on discriminatory behavior are mediated by prejudiced attitudes. *Our third research question addresses the influence of intergroup threat and intergroup contact on discriminatory behavior and of how far this effect is mediated by contingent variations in prejudice.* The empirical demonstration of such mediation would also support our assumption of a causal effect from prejudice on discriminatory behavior.

Method

Our analyses are based on three data sets: For Studies 1 and 2, we used two telephone surveys representative for the adult (16 years or older) German population with no migration background (German citizens whose parents and grandparents were born in Germany). The surveys were conducted during the summers of 2002 (Study 1, $N = 2{,}722$) and 2004 (Study 2, $N = 1{,}383$[1]) and focused on preconditions, phenomenology, and consequences of group-focused enmity, that is, attitudes toward many different minority groups in Germany (see Heitmeyer, 2002), including foreigners living in Germany. The 2002 sample was also the basis of a panel survey we used in Study 3. A random selection of 825 respondents from the 2002 sample was reinterviewed in the summers of 2003 and 2004. We thus obtained a panel with three measuring points.

In none of the studies did missing data exceed 5%. In all studies maximum likelihood algorithms were used to handle missing data (Enders, 2001; Schafer & Graham, 2002). Regression analyses in Studies 1 and 2 were calculated with SPSS 12. We therefore used the expectation maximization method/imputation, which is implemented in SPSS Missing Value. In Study 3, we performed structural equation modeling using Mplus 3.13 (Muthen & Muthen, 2006). In Mplus, full information maximum likelihood (FIML) is implemented to handle missing data. Enders and Peugh (2004) demonstrated that both of these methods yield comparable results.

Two items measured prejudice. Respondents were asked if they thought: "too many foreigners live in Germany" and "foreigners should be sent back to their home country if jobs become scarce."[2] Respondents answered these and the following items on a 4-point Likert-type scale (from *fully agree* to *fully disagree*). Intercorrelations of the two items were r (Study 1) $= .59$, r (Study 2) $= .59$, and in Study 3, t1: $r = .61$; t2: $r = .66$; t3: $r = .63$.

We analyzed three "behavioroid" indices of discrimination (Aronson, Brewer, & Carlsmith, 1985), that is, discriminatory behavior was operationalized as behavioral intentions. Two items assess avoidance tendencies and one taps aggressive behavior (Mackie, Devos, & Smith, 2000): "I would never buy a car from a foreigner"; "I would have problems moving into a district where many foreigners live"; and "If others take too much space, one should show them by the use of violence who is master in one's house." Even though the last item does not directly focus on foreigners as a target group, it is embedded in a battery of items addressing foreigners. Thus, it is clear from the context that the item implies aggression against foreigners. The items were used as three separate behavioroid indicators,[3]

---

[1] The original sample size is $N = 2{,}656$. However, only a random half of the sample responded to the intergroup contact indicators. Because we used these contact indicators, all analyses are based on this subsample.

[2] One could argue that the second of these two prejudice indicators is closer to behavior than the first one and that this might explain a co variation of the attitude and behavior indicators used here. However, the mean correlation of both prejudice items with all behavior indicators used in the three studies is identical (mean $r = .35$).

[3] Using confirmatory factor analyses, we tested both the 2002 and for the 2004 data to see if the two prejudice (loading on one latent factor) and the three behavioroid indicators can be separated from a single factor solution. In both data sets the four separated factors model (2002: $\chi^2 = 5.85$, $df = 2$, p

because the intercorrelations among these items were relatively low (buy car and move into district, r [Study 1] = .35; r [Study 2] = .40; r [Study 3, t1] = .32; buy car and use of violence, r [Study 1] = .21; r [Study 2] = .24; r [Study 3, t1] = .19; move into district and use of violence, r [Study 1] = .27; r [Study 2] = .28; r [Study 3, t1] = .31).

Variables that might affect the prejudice–behavior relationship were controlled in Studies 1 and 2. Several studies have demonstrated that higher education goes along with lower prejudice (Wagner & Zick, 1995), therefore respondents' education was measured with a 5-point scale representing the respondents' highest formal educational degree (1 = *no degree* to 5 = *university degree*). Earlier analyses have shown that both prejudice and hate crimes are more prevalent in the eastern part of Germany, the former German Democratic Republic, than in West Germany, the former Federal Republic (Wagner, van Dick, Pettigrew, & Christ, 2003). Consequently, the place of residence was controlled for (West = 1, East = 2). A strong focus on national identity or a strong national identification often contributes to out-group derogation, as well (cf. Jackson, 2002; Tajfel & Turner, 1979). We therefore controlled for it with two items (e.g., "I am proud to be German"—answering format as above, r [Study 1] = .60, r [Study 2] = .59). A further important variable is authoritarianism as a general personality variable that centers on submissive deference to authorities, a rigid adherence to cultural conventions, and a general aggressiveness toward nonconformity (Adorno, Frenkel-Brunswik, Levinson, & Sanford, 1950; Altemeyer, 1988). Authoritarianism was measured with three items, for example, "Delinquents should be punished more severely," α (Study 1) = .75, α (Study 2) = .75. Social dominance orientation (SDO; Sidanius & Pratto, 1999) also represents general convictions about the world, in this case normative expectations about the appropriateness of hierarchical relations between groups. SDO was operationalized with three items, for example, "The groups that have a low status position in our society should stay there," α (Study 1) = .61, α (Study 2) = .61.

According to Stephan and Renfro (2002), intergroup threat should correlate with both out-group prejudice and discriminatory behavior. They differentiate between group threat, perceived threat to the in-group as a whole, and individual threat, threat directly related to oneself. Threat was measured only in Study 2, using four items each for group and individual threat (e.g., "The foreigners living here threaten our culture," for group threat, $\alpha = .85$; and "The foreigners living here threaten my personal safety," for individual threat, $\alpha = .85$). Intergroup contact (cf. Pettigrew & Tropp, 2006) was assessed by three items in Study 1 and four items

---

$< .001$, Comparative Fit Index (CFI) = 1.00, root mean square error of approximation (RMSEA) = .027; 2004: $\chi^2 = 13.73$, $df = 2$, $p < .001$, CFI = .99, RMSEA = .065) is superior to the one factor model (2002: $\chi^2 = 98.32$, $df = 5$, $p < .001$, CFI = .96, RMSEA = .083; 2004: $\chi^2 = 60.16$, $df = 5$, $p < .001$, CFI = .96, RMSEA = .089). χ^2-difference test is highly significant for both data sets (2002: $\Delta\chi^2 = 92.47$, $df = 3$, $p < .001$; 2004: $\Delta\chi^2 = 46.43$, $df = 3$, $p < .001$).

Table 1. Correlations of Prejudice with Behavioroid Indicators in Study 1 ($N = 2{,}722$) and Study 2 ($N = 1{,}383$)

	Behavioroid Indicators					
	Buy Car		Move into District		Use of Violence	
	Study 1	Study 2	Study 1	Study 2	Study 1	Study 2
Prejudice	.33***	.37***	.45***	.49***	.35***	.36***

***$p < .001$.

in Study 2, for example, "How many of your friends and good acquaintances are foreigners?" (α [Study 1] = .55, α [Study 2] = .66). The means, standard deviations and intercorrelations of these measures are presented in the appendix (Table A for Study 1 and 2, and Table B for Study 3).

Results

Simple correlations of prejudice and the behavioroid measures are presented in Table 1 for Studies 1 and 2. As can be seen, these correlations approach those reported in the meta-analysis of Dovidio et al. (1996) and Schütz and Six (1996). Thus, we establish that the substantial covariation of prejudice and behavioral intentions exists in our German data as well.

To test whether the covariation of prejudice and behavioroid indicators is an artifact of third variable influences, the relationship was introduced into a multiple regression that controlled for confounding variables and—to control also for all possible moderations—their interactions with prejudice. Table 2 delivers the data for Studies 1 and 2. Table 2 reveals that numerous variables have an effect on the behavioroid indicators in addition to prejudice—age, sex, education, residence in West versus East Germany, authoritarianism, social dominance orientation, collective threat, and intergroup contact. But the interactions reveal few systematic effects. The major exception is the interaction of sex and prejudice on the use of violence. This interaction indicates that the use of violence by females corresponds less strongly with their prejudice than is the case with males—a finding that may well relate to females' stronger avoidance of physical aggression (Krahé, 2001). The primary result, however, is, that the prejudice–discrimination relationship remains highly significant even after controlling for 10 variables and 10 interactions displayed in Table 2.

These results indicate that the prejudice–behavioroid covariation is not an artifact created by third variable influences. This raises the next question of causal sequence. To test this relation, we conducted three separate cross-lagged analyses for each of the three behavioroid indices using the data of Study 3. To test directionality of the link between prejudice and the behavioroid indicators, we tested a set of nested cross-lagged models for each of the three behavioroid items. In the first model A, only the cross-lagged relations from prejudice on the behavioroid

Table 2. Simultaneous Regressions on the Three Behavioroid Indicators in Study 1 ($N = 2,722$) and Study 2 ($N = 1,383$)

	Buy Car		Move into District		Use of Violence	
	Study 1	Study 2	Study 1	Study 2	Study 1	Study 2
1. Age		.09***	.06**	.08**	.09***	.17***
2. Sex (1 = male)	−.05**				−.17***	−.17***
3. Education			.08***	.10***		
4. West-East (1 = West)	.08***	.14***				.07**
5. National identification						
6. Authoritarianism			.08**			
7. SDO	.13***	.11***	.09***	.07**	.18***	.19***
8. Individual threat	—	.14***	—		—	
9. Collective threat	—	.11***	—	.32***	—	.16***
10. Contact	−.08***	−.11***	−.11***	−.07**		
Interactions						
1. By prejudice						
2. By prejudice					−.07***	−.09***
3. By prejudice			−.04**			
4. By prejudice						
5. By prejudice						
6. By prejudice						
7. By prejudice			−.06**	−.08**		
8. By prejudice						
9. By prejudice						
10. By prejudice						
Prejudice	.23***	.15***	.34***	.23***	.19***	.11***
R^2	.15	.24	.25	.34	.22	.28

Note. Only significant β weights are presented.

items were allowed. In model B, only the reverse cross-lagged paths from the behavioroid indicators on prejudice were specified. In model C, bidirectional causations were allowed, and in model D all cross-lagged paths were constrained to zero. Only for the behavioroid indicator "Buy a car from a foreigner," model C showed best model fit as compared to the other cross-lagged models. For the other two behavioroid indicators, model A had the best fit to the data indicating a unidirectional causal flow from prejudice to behavioral intention. Figure 1 shows the results for the use of violence dependent variable.

In these longitudinal path analyses, prejudice is a latent variable and each of the behavioroid variables is a single indicator. Path coefficients correspond to β-coefficients, while the cross-lagged coefficients were calculated after controlling for the autocorrelations of the prejudice and behavioral indicators over time. The results of the cross-lagged paths are clear. Prejudice measured at time 1 (t1) and time 2 (t2) has a significant influence on willingness to use violence at t2 ($\beta = .27, p < .001$) and t3 ($\beta = .28, p < .001$). In sharp contrast, willingness to use violence has no effect on prejudice, neither on t2 nor on t3 prejudice scores.

This consistent pattern of results strongly supports the hypothesis that prejudice acts as a cause for proviolence. The data patterns for the other two behavioroid

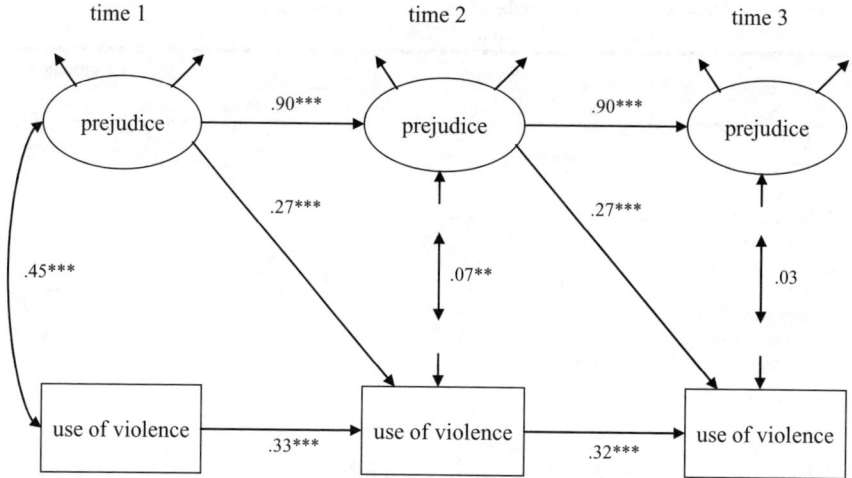

Note. Autocorrelations of errors of the prejudice indicators are not included in the figure.
$\chi^2 = 71.99$, $df = 23$, $p < .001$, CFI $= .98$, RMSEA $= .05$, standardized root mean square residual (SRMR) $= .03$; $*p < .05$; $**p < .01$; $***p < .001$; Equality constraints are set for autoregressive parameters of both constructs and factor loadings of prejudice indicators over time.

Fig. 1. Results of a cross-lagged analysis of the relationship between prejudice and behavior, here use of violence (Study 3, $N = 825$).

measures are very similar (move into a district t1–t2: prejudice-move $\beta = .27$, $p < .001$; t2–t3: prejudice-move $\beta = .27$, $p < .001$; buy a car t1–t2: prejudice-buy $\beta = .26$, $p < .001$; buy-prejudice $\beta = .05$, $p < .05$.; t2–t3: prejudice-buy $\beta = .26$, $p < .001$; buy-prejudice $\beta = .05$, $p > .05$). Thus, all three cross-lagged analyses support the view that prejudice has a causal influence on behavioral intentions (for all models, CFI $> .98$, RMSEA $= .04–.06$, and SRMR $= .03$).

As demonstrated in Table 2, additional factors predict the behavioroid indicators. Respondents' age and their social dominance orientation constitute rather distal personality concepts for the explanation of prejudice. But perceived collective threat and intergroup contact are more proximal determinants of discrimination that vary in accordance with situational influences. Thus, the relation of these proximal predictors is of particular relevance if one is interested in the implications of these results for the prevention of discriminatory behavior.

To get deeper insight into the causal relationship of collective threat, contact, prejudice, and behavioral intentions, we calculated several path models on the basis of Study 2 (recall that Study 1 contained no indicators of threat). Results are presented in Figure 2.

The data fit well with a model where the effects of collective threat and contact on behavioral intentions are largely mediated by prejudice, thus indicating again the causal role of prejudice for discrimination.

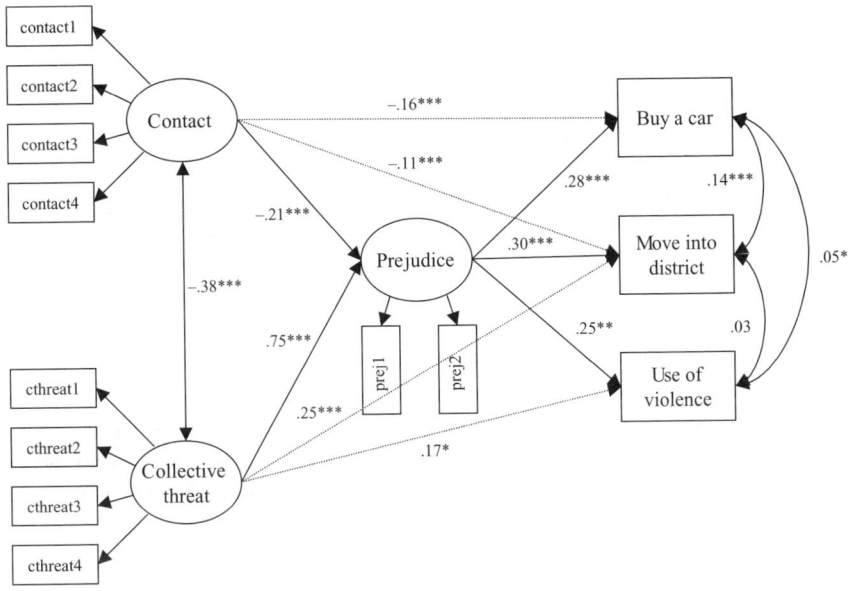

Note. Disturbances and error variances are not included in the figure.
$\chi^2 = 179.28$, $df = 53$, $p < .001$, CFI = .98, RMSEA = .041, SRMR = .021; $*p < .05$; $**p < .01$; $***p < .001$.

Fig. 2. A causal model of the relationship between threat, contact, prejudice and behavior (Study 2, $N = 1383$).

Discussion

Prejudice and behavioral intentions are closely related to each other not only in North America but also in Germany. Our data show that respondents' prejudice scores allow a prediction of their self-reported behavioral intentions—both avoidance tendencies and aggressive discriminatory acts. This relationship remained significant even after the influence of a large array of confounding variables was controlled for. The longitudinal data indicated that prejudice functions as the cause in this relationship while behavioral intentions are the consequence. Additionally, mediation analyses showed that the effects of intergroup threat and intergroup contact on discrimination were mediated by prejudiced attitudes. Thus, the data suggest that prejudice is an important determinant of discriminatory behavior toward out-groups.

From the perspective of preventing discriminatory behavior, the effects of intergroup threat and intergroup contact on prejudice and intergroup behavior are of special relevance. Perceived threat and contact are sensitive to situational changes. Collective threat reinforces prejudice and discriminatory behavior, while intergroup contact reduces prejudice and avoidance behavior. Hence, any systematic intervention that focuses on changing perceived group threat or contact will probably shape both negative intergroup attitudes and behavior. Therefore, systematic contact programs and information strategies to reduce intergroup threat are prime candidates for such intervention procedures (cf. Wagner, Christ, & van Dick, 2002).

Our results derive from survey data. Hence, the prejudiced attitudes and the behavioroid indicators were based on verbal reports. Further research must probe to what extent these results can be replicated with other methods, especially actual behavioral indicators (for the relation of behavioral intentions and behavior, see Sheeran, 2002).

We distinguished between two dimensions of discriminatory behavior: avoidance of the out-group and physical aggression against the outgroup. Mackie, Devos, and Smith (2000) demonstrated that avoidance tendencies coalesce with the negative intergroup emotions of fear and contempt, while aggressive behavior toward the out-group covaries with anger and irritation (see also Smith, 1993). We had no appropriate indicators of intergroup emotions in the available data that would allow for such a differentiation in the predictor variable prejudice. Further research should consider these emotions, as it might well uncover even stronger correlations between prejudiced attitudes and discriminatory behavior.

References

Adorno, T. W., Frenkel-Brunswik, E., Levinson, D. J., & Sanford, R. N. (1950). *The authoritarian personality*. New York: Harper & Row.
Ajzen, I., & Fishbein, M. (1977). Attitude behavior relations: A theoretical analysis and review of empirical research. *Psychology Bulletin, 84*, 888–918.
Allport, G. W. (1954). *The nature of prejudice*. Reading, MA: Addison-Wesley.
Altemeyer, B. (1988). *Enemies of freedom*. San Francisco: Jossey-Bass.
Aronson, E., Brewer, M., & Carlsmith, J. M. (1985). Experimentation in social psychology. In G. Lindzey & E. Aronson (Eds.), *Handbook of social psychology* (pp. 441–486). Hillsdale, NJ: Lawrence Erlbaum.
Campbell, A., Converse, P., Miller, W., & Stokes, D. (1960). *The Amercian voter*. New York: Wiley.
Cooper, J., Mirabile, R., & Scher, S. J. (2005). Actions and attitudes: The theory of cognitive dissonance. In M. C. Green & T. C. Brock (Eds.), *Persuasion: Psychological insights and perspectives* (pp. 63–79). Thousand Oaks, CA: Sage.
Craig, K. M. (2002). Examining hate motivated aggression. A review of the social psychological literature on hate crimes as a distinct form of aggression. *Aggression and Violent Behavior, 7*, 85–101.
Crosby, F., Bromley, S., & Saxe, L. (1980). Recent unobtrusive studies of Black and White discrimination and prejudice: A literature review. *Psychological Bulletin, 87*, 546–563.
Dovidio, J. F., Brigham, J. C., Johnson, B. T., & Gaertner, S. L. (1996). Stereotyping, prejudice, and discrimination: Another look. In C. N. Macrae, S. Stangor, & M. Hewstone (Eds.), *Stereotypes and stereotyping* (pp. 276–319). New York: Guilford.
Dovidio, J. F., Gaertner, S. L., Nier, J. A., Kawakami, K., & Hodson, G. (2004). Contemporary racial bias: When do good people do bad things. In A. G. Miller (Ed.), *The social psychology of good and evil* (pp. 141–167). New York: Guilford.
Dovidio, J. F., Kawakami, K., & Gaertner, S. L. (2002). Implicit and explicit prejudice and interracial interaction. *Journal of Personality and Social Psychology, 82*, 62–68.

Eagly, A. H., & Chaiken, S. (1993). *The psychology of attitudes.* Fort Worth, TX: Harcourt Brace Jovanovich.
Enders, C. K. (2001). A primer on maximum likelihood algorithms available for use with missing data. *Structural Equation Modeling, 8*, 128–141.
Enders, C. K., & Peugh, J. L. (2004). Using an EM covariance matrix to estimate structural equation models with missing data: Choosing an adjusted sample size to improve the accuracy of inferences. *Structural Equation Modeling, 11*, 1–19.
Heitmeyer, W. (2002). Gruppenbezogene Menschenfeindlichkeit. Die theoretische Konzeption und erste empirische Ergebnisse [Group-focused enmity. The theoretical conception and first empirical results]. In W. Heitmeyer (Ed.), *Deutsche Zustände. Folge 1* (pp. 15–34). Frankfurt, Germany: Suhrkamp.
Jackson, J. W. (2002). Intergroup attitudes as a function of different dimensions of group identification and perceived intergroup conflict. *Self and Identity, 1*, 11–33.
Klink, A., & Wagner, U. (1999). Discrimination against ethnic minorities in Germany: Going back to the field. *Journal of Applied Social Psychology, 29*, 402–423.
Krahé, B. (2001). *The social psychology of aggression.* East Sussex, UK: Psychology Press.
LaPiere, R. T. (1934). Attitudes vs. action. *Social Forces, 13*, 230–237
Lavidge, R., & Steiner, G. A. (1961). A model for predictive measurements of advertising effectiveness. *Journal of Marketing, 25*, 59–62.
Lewin, K. (1936). *Principles of topological psychology.* New York: McGraw-Hill.
Mackie, D. M., Devos, R., & Smith, E. R. (2000). Intergroup emotions: Explaining offensive action tendencies in an intergroup context. *Journal of Personality and Social Psychology, 79*, 602–616.
Muthén, L. Kl., & Muthén, B. (2006). *Mplus user's guide* (4th ed.). Los Angeles, CA: Muthén & Muthén.
COMP: for the "e" in "Muthen" pls show accent acute over the "e" 4X // italicize "mplus user's guide"
Pettigrew, T. F., & Tropp, L. R. (2006). A meta-analytic test of intergroup contact theory. *Journal of Personality and Social Psychology, 90*, 751–783.
Schafer, J. L., & Graham, J. W. (2002). Missing data: Our view of the state of the art. *Psychological Methods, 7*, 147–177.
Schütz, H., & Six, B. (1996). How strong is the relationship between prejudice and discrimination? A meta-analytic answer. *International Journal of Intercultural Relations, 20*, 441–462.
Semyonov, M., Raijman, R., & Yom-Tov, A. (2002). Labor market competition, perceived threat, and endorsement of economic discrimination against foreign workers in Israel. *Social-Problems, 49*, 416–431.
Sheeran, P. (2002). Intention-behavior relations: A conceptual and empirical review. In W. Stroebe & M. Hewstone (Eds.), *European review of social psychology* (Vol. 12, pp. 1–36). Chichester, UK: Wiley.
Sidanius, J., & Pratto, F. (1999). *Social dominance.* Cambridge, UK: Cambridge University Press.
Smith, E. R. (1993). Social identity and social emotions: Toward new conceptualizations of prejudice. In D. M. Mackie & D. L. Hamilton (Eds.), *Affect cognition, and stereotyping* (pp. 297–315). San Diego, CA: Academic Press.
Stephan, W. G., & Renfro, C. L. (2002). The role of threat in intergroup relations. In D. M. Mackie & E. R. Smith (Eds.), *From prejudice to intergroup emotions* (pp. 191–207). New York: Psychology Press.
Tajfel, H., & Turner, J. C. (1979). An integrative theory of intergroup conflict. In W. G. Austin & S. Worchel (Eds.), *The social psychology of intergroup relations* (pp. 33–47). Monterey, CA: Brooks/Cole.
Wagner, U., Christ, O., & van Dick, R. (2002). Die empirische Evaluation von Präventionsprogrammen gegen Fremdenfeindlichkeit [The empirical evaluation of prevention programs against prejudice]. *Journal für Konflikt- und Gewaltforschung, 4*, 101–117.
Wagner, U., van Dick, R., Pettigrew, T. F., & Christ, O. (2003). Ethnic prejudice in East- and West-Germany: The explanatory power of intergroup contact. *Group Processes and Intergroup Relations, 6*, 23–37.
Wagner, U., & Zick, A. (1995). The relation of formal education to ethnic prejudice: Its reliability, validity and explanation. *European Journal of Social Psychology, 25*, 41–56.

Wicker, A. W. (1969). Attitude versus action: The relationship of verbal and overt behavioral responses to attitude objects. *Journal of Social Issues, 25*, 41–78.

Willems, H. (2002). Rechtsextremistische, antisemitische und fremdenfeindliche straftaten in deutschland: Entwicklungen, Strukturen, Hintergründe [Right wing, anti-Semitic and prejudiced crimes in Germany: Development, structure and causes]. In T. Grimke & B. Wagner (Eds.), *Handbuch Rechtsradikalismus* (pp. 141–157). Opladen, Germany: Leske & Budrich.

ULRICH WAGNER is Professor of Social Psychology and Director of the Center for Conflict Studies at Philipps-University Marburg in Germany. Dr. Wagner's research interests include intergroup relations, ethnic prejudice, and intergroup aggression. His publications include contributions to the analyses of survey data on ethnic prejudice and racism, as published in a special issue of the *Zeitschrift für Politische Psychologie* [*Journal of Political Psychology*] (Eds. Wagner & van Dick, 2001), an overview article in the *Zeitschrift für Sozialpsychologie* [*Journal of Social Psychology*] (Wagner, van Dick, & Zick, 2001) and original data analyses (e.g., Wagner, van Dick, Pettigrew, & Christ, 2003; Wagner, Christ, Pettigrew, Stellmacher, & Wolf, 2006). He heads the special graduate school addressing Group-Focused Enmity, sponsored by the Deutsche Forschungsgemeinschaft [German Science Foundation]. For the academic year 2003–2004, he was a Senior Fellow at the Research Institute of Comparative Studies in Race and Ethnicity at Stanford University.

OLIVER CHRIST is a Lecturer for Methods at Philipps-University Marburg, Germany. Previously he was lecturer in social psychology at the University of Marburg and advisor for survey methodology at the University of Bielefeld, Germany. He earned his PhD in Social Psychology from Philipps-University, Marburg, Germany in 2005. His research interests lie in the field of intergroup relations, ethnic prejudice, and social identity processes in organizations.

THOMAS F. PETTIGREW is Research Professor of Social Psychology at the University of California, Santa Cruz. He received his PhD at Harvard University (1956) and taught there until 1980. From 1986 to 1991, he taught at the University of Amsterdam and conducted research on prejudice in the Netherlands. Pettigrew has published ten books and more than 300 articles and reviews on prejudice and racism. His publications include *How to Think Like a Social Scientist* (1996) and articles on intergroup relations in the *Annual Review of Psychology* (Pettigrew, 1998a) and the *Annual Review of Sociology* (Pettigrew, 1998b). He served as president of SPSSI (1967–1968) and has twice been awarded the Society's Allport Prize for Intergroup Relations Research (with Joanne Martin in 1988 and Linda Tropp in 2003). He has also received the Society for Experimental Social Psychology's Distinguished Scientist Award (2001), a Senior Fellowship at the Research Institute of Comparative Studies in Race and Ethnicity at Stanford University (2001), and a Fulbright New Century Scholar Fellowship for continued research on prejudice and discrimination against the immigrants of Western Europe (2003).

Appendix

Table A. Means, Standard Deviations and Intercorrelations of Measures of Study 1 and Study 2

	M (SD) Study 1	M (SD) Study 2	1	2	3	4	5	6	7	8	9	10	11	12	13
1. Prejudice	2.28 (0.87)	2.41 (0.88)	1	.33***	.45***	.35***	.52***	.45***	−.31***	.35***	.22***	.17***	.08***	−.30***	—
2. Buy car	1.84 (0.96)	1.91 (1.00)	.37***	1	.35***	.21***	.23***	.25***	−.21***	.15***	.18***	.08***	−.01	−.13***	—
3. Move into district	2.47 (1.05)	2.63 (1.07)	.49***	.40***	1	.27***	.31***	.27***	−.27***	.22***	.17***	.16***	.02	−.12***	—
4. Use of violence	1.49 (0.75)	1.65 (0.85)	.36***	.24***	.29***	1	.31***	.33***	−.16***	.22***	.11***	.18***	−.12***	−.19***	—
5. Authoritarianism	3.08 (0.73)	3.13 (0.70)	.58***	.28***	.33***	.30***	1	.37***	−.24***	.43***	.26***	.17***	.05***	−.39***	—
6. SDO	1.63 (0.60)	1.61 (0.58)	.40***	.26***	.27***	.35***	.35***	1	−.19***	.26***	.09***	.14***	.05***	−.23***	—
7. Contact	2.13 (0.76)	1.98 (0.62)	−.37***	−.29***	−.29***	−.22***	−.30***	−.17***	1	−.22***	−.40***	−.32***	−.09***	.18***	—
8. National identification	3.10 (0.73)	3.06 (0.75)	.31***	.13***	.20***	.19***	.40***	.23***	−.19***	1	.12***	.28***	.04***	−.24***	—
9. West/East	—	—	.17***	.21***	.08**	.12***	.22***	−.01	−.34***	.09**	1	.04	.02	−.05*	—
10. Age	45.94 (16.26)	45.47 (15.79)	.12***	.16***	.15**	.23***	.17***	.14***	−.28***	.23***	.03	1	.04*	−.23***	—
11. Sex	—	—	.12***	.02	.08***	−.11***	.12***	.01	−.15***	.06*	−.01	.03	1	−.05*	—
12. Education	—	—	−.34***	−.13***	−.12***	−.16***	−.35***	−.25***	.18***	−.26***	.02	−.21***	−.08**	1	—
13. Individual threat	—	1.56 (0.59)	.51***	.29***	.35***	.28***	.36***	.33***	−.15***	.17***	.03	−.07**	.01	−.19***	1
14. Collective threat	—	2.03 (0.68)	.66***	.35***	.51***	.37***	.47***	.40***	−.31***	.24***	.66***	.01	.10***	.11***	−.28***

Note. Intercorrelations for Study 1 above the diagonal and for Study 2 below the diagonal.
*** $p < .001$; ** $p < .01$; * $p < .05$.

Table B. Means, Standard Deviations and Intercorrelations of Measures for Study 3

	M (SD)	2	3	4	5	6	7	8	9	10	11	12
1. Prejudice (t1)	2.49 (0.85)	.75***	.72***	.31***	.32***	.30***	.44***	.43***	.42***	.38***	.36***	.32***
2. Prejudice (t2)	2.51 (0.84)	1	.78***	.31***	.35***	.34***	.42***	.49***	.47***	.37***	.42***	.36***
3. Prejudice (t3)	2.56 (0.83)		1	.31***	.37***	.37***	.44***	.47***	.49***	.37***	.38***	.36***
4. Buy car (t1)	1.83 (0.96)			1	.38***	.41***	.32***	.30***	.29***	.19***	.20***	.22***
5. Buy car (t2)	1.92 (0.97)				1	.48***	.36***	.48***	.24***	.24***	.24***	.27***
6. Buy car (t3)	1.97 (0.98)					1	.35***	.41***	.47***	.22***	.19***	.24***
7. Move into district (t1)	2.49 (1.05)						1	.63***	.59***	.31***	.26***	.27***
8. Move into district (t2)	2.47 (1.01)							1	.58***	.31***	.32***	.28***
9. Move into district (t3)	2.57 (0.98)								1	.27***	.28***	.26***
10. Use of violence (t1)	1.76 (0.92)									1	.47***	.46***
11. Use of violence (t2)	1.82 (0.89)										1	.43***
12. Use of violence (t3)	1.81 (0.87)											1

*** $p < .001$.

Viewing Intergroup Relations in Europe through Allport's Lens Model of Prejudice

Walter G. Stephan[*]
University of Hawaii

This article employs Allport's (1954) lens model of the causes of prejudice to analyze the articles in this issue of the Journal of Social Issues. *The lens model specifies that historical, socio cultural, personality, and situational factors contribute to prejudice. The articles in this issue examine a number of variables at each of these levels of analysis, and many employ multilevel designs in which variables at more than one level are examined within the same study. Suggestions for future research on intergroup relations in Europe are offered including conducting more comparative and multilevel studies and creating comprehensive theories that integrate different levels of analysis. Some implications of the findings of these studies for intergroup relations programs are also discussed.*

Europe has the highest concentration of stable democracies on the planet. It also has the highest number of former colonial powers. And, in the last century, two of the bloodiest wars in the history of the world were fought on its territory. It is divided by nationality, region, language, ethnicity, religion, political ideology, and social class. It is experiencing waves of immigration from its former colonies and elsewhere (see Zick, Wagner, & Pettigrew, 2008). These and countless other threads have combined to create a complex tapestry of intergroup tensions that threaten the attempts to create a unified Europe. The surface manifestations of these intergroup tensions can be seen across Europe. In recent years, there have been deadly acts of domestic terrorism, ethnic cleansing, riots, protests, vandalism of places of worship, acts of violence against individuals, and the ubiquitous graffiti that serves as a newspaper of discontent. The articles in this issue analyze these complex intergroup tensions using a variety of theories and analytical approaches in a range of different countries. They display a robust and sophisticated interest in understanding the well springs of these tensions.

---

[*]Correspondence concerning this article should be addressed to Walter G. Stephan, 2097 Aliali Place, Honolulu, HI 96821 [e-mail: gstepha@nmsu.edu].

This issue of the *Journal of Social Issues* helps us to understand not only the problems that confront Europe, but also the fundamental nature of intergroup hostility and its causes. Although some of the findings presented in these articles apply only to the European context (e.g., the concept of luso–tropicalism in Portugal), others may prove to be more universal (e.g., the importance of anger and threat, as well as perceptions of relative deprivation and cultural dissimilarity). After all, Europe is undergoing many of the same transformations as other societies around the world as local economies become globalized and technology revolutionizes everyone's life. Europe also confronts many of the same challenges as other societies such as global warming and the depletion of natural resources. The people of Europe, along with those in most of the rest of the world, have lived with a relatively stable set of traditions for centuries. Social change was always occurring, but at a gradual pace. Now they find themselves buffeted by rapid social change. Rapid social change disrupts the existing social equilibrium and spawns perceptions of uncertainty, injustice, relative deprivation, and threat, which, as the articles in this issue show, are fertile breeding grounds for prejudice, intolerance, and discrimination.

These articles can be seen as steps along the path to the creation of a comprehensive, empirically based theory of intergroup relations. All these articles can be viewed within the framework of the lens model of prejudice suggested by Allport (1954) more than half a century ago. Some articles focus on just one level of this model, but others employ multilevel techniques that Allport would have envied.

Allport (1954) argued that there are five basic categories of antecedents of prejudice, ranging from more distal factors (e.g., historical and socio cultural antecedents) to more proximal factors (e.g., situational, personality, and phenomenological antecedents). With respect to historical factors, Allport noted, "any pattern of prejudice existing in any part of the world receives marked illumination when it is examined from the historical point of view." Socio cultural factors refer to the "social context in which prejudice attitudes develop" (p. 211). In Allport's view, such factors include cultural traditions and values, the social class structure of the society, competition for scarce resources, values related to pluralism, and the size and relative population density of different groups. According to Allport, situational factors include not only the basic elements of the contact hypothesis (equal status contact, which is supported by authority figures and involves the pursuit of common interests and a common humanity), but also other aspects of situational contexts that promote prejudice, including whether or not the contact is voluntary, how superficial it is, whether or not group categories are salient, and where the contact takes place. By *personality factors*, Allport meant personality traits such as authoritarianism, aggressiveness, high levels of anxiety or guilt, and self-esteem. For the purposes of this article, I will expand this category to include a wider range of individual difference variables. I will ignore phenomenological factors (which refer to individuals' perceptions of their immediate situation) because none of these articles refers to them. Although Allport focused primarily on prejudice, the articles in this issue examine an array of outcome variables, including behavioral intentions, support for discrimination, and actual behavior. Thus, I will be using a slightly altered version of Allport's model to frame my discussion of the articles in this issue.

The Articles in This Issue

The rise of the political right in Belgium is the focus of the article by Billiet and de Witte (2008). Realistic group conflict theory is used as a basis for making predictions in this study. They show that the socio cultural factor of socioeconomic status (SES) influences voting patterns in Flemish Belgium. Specifically, lower SES is associated with voting for a right-wing political party. At the individual difference level, both the perception that immigrants pose a threat and a strong Flemish identity predict voting for the right-wing party. Right-wing authoritarianism and political alienation played less significant roles in voting for this party. This study is notable for focusing on an actual behavior. The theme of identity issues and the associated feelings of threat also play a central role in the next article in this issue.

The article by Coenders, Lubbers, Scheepers, and Verkuyten (2008) focuses on the socio cultural level of analysis using social structural factors and the ideological social context as predictors of support for discrimination against immigrants in the Netherlands. Like Billet and de Witte (2008), they employ realistic group conflict theory, arguing that broad-scale socio cultural factors such as rising levels of unemployment influence the attitudes of individual members of the society. Because they found that rising rates of unemployment, rather than the actual levels of unemployment, increased support for discrimination, it is likely that perceptions of impending group conflict, rather than actual current levels of conflict, determine attitudes toward immigrants. This, of course, is a fundamental tenet of social psychology—that perceptions often matter more than reality in determining attitudes and behavior.

Coenders et al. (2008) also included an interesting individual-level historical factor concerning immigration rates during the period when the Dutch participants in their study were coming to maturity. They find evidence that experiences during these formative years established the attitudes of a lifetime. In addition, they discuss a change in the socio cultural climate in the Netherlands from an orientation of multiculturalism with respect to immigration to one of assimilation. The authors frame the immigration issue in terms of social identity theory, arguing that immigrants are now seen as a threat to Dutch identity. Historically, the Dutch were tolerant when the number of immigrants was relatively small, but the increase in immigration has threatened the Dutch society and led to a negative reaction to immigrants. They also show experimentally that an orientation of assimilation (rather than multiculturalism) leads to prejudice.

Attitudes toward immigrants were also the focus of the next article, which addressed the attitudes of the Portuguese toward Black immigrants from its former colonies (Vala, Lima, & Lopes, 2008). They rely on a value-related socio cultural-level concept taken from the anthropologist Gilberto Freyre to understand the relatively positive attitudes of the Portuguese toward these immigrants. This concept, luso–tropicalism, embodies an openness toward people from other cultures. It was an integral aspect of the Portuguese approach to colonialism, especially in Brazil. They also rely on the concept of *luso–tropicalism* to interpret the finding that in Portugal, but in no other European country, national identity and attitudes toward immigrants are unrelated.

In other analyses, their survey data show that perceiving differences between Portuguese citizens and Black immigrants predicted negative attitudes toward immigrants and a willingness to discriminate against them. Employing a sample of Blacks living in Portugal, they found that perceived differences between themselves and White Portuguese citizens predicts perceptions of being discriminated against by White Portuguese citizens. They also measured perceived racial and cultural differences at the individual difference level and used them to predict discrimination. Unlike most of the articles in this issue, the Vala et al. (2008) article focuses on why one European country may differ from the others in one aspect of intergroup relations, and in doing so, they cite the unique cultural history and values of Portugal as a cause. However, the finding that perceived differences in cultural values predict discrimination may well be universal across cultures.

Although some problems such as immigration are shared by all of the countries of Europe, others are more local such as the long-term hostility between Catholics and Protestants in Northern Ireland. The study by Tam, Hewstone, Kenworthy, and Cairns (2008) focuses on the role that forgiveness may play in reducing the chances of future sectarian violence in Northern Ireland. Their studies focus exclusively on the individual level of analysis. They present evidence suggesting that anger toward the other group and a tendency to perceive them as less than human (infrahumanization) may be barriers to forgiveness. In a separate study, they show that negative responses to extremist out-groups are associated with an unwillingness to forgive the out-groups, distrust of the out-groups, and a tendency to behave aggressively to the out-groups. In contrast, the ability to empathize with the out-groups is positively related to forgiveness. It was also found that positive contact with the out-groups increased empathy while decreasing anger and infrahumanization.

Taken together, their findings suggest that at the individual difference level, certain emotion-related responses to the out-group (anger toward the out-group, low empathy for the out-group, and an unwillingness to ascribe subtle human emotions to the out-group) as well as some specific cognitions (negative attitudes toward extremist groups) may impede improved intergroup relations (forgiveness).

In contrast, positive personal contact can improve intergroup relations. Among the notable features of this study are its use of implicit measures of prejudice and its focus on the pathways toward improved intergroup relations.

Minescu, Hagendoorn, and Poppe (2008) give us a glimpse into a seldom studied set of societies and their intergroup relations issues—the Federation of Republics of the former Soviet Union. They rely on social identity theory to examine how individuals' identification with different levels of a nested social hierarchy affects stereotypes toward ethnic Russians and people from the ethnic groups after whom the former Soviet Republics were named. People in these Republics can either identify with the Republics themselves or they can identify with the more encompassing Federation of Republics. The results indicated that ethnic Russians who identified with the Republics in which they lived had more positive stereotypes of the people after whom the Republics were named than ethnic Russians who did not identify with the Republics. In contrast, members of the ethnic groups after whom the Republics were named had more positive stereotypes of Russians if they identified with the Federation of Republics than if they did not identify with the Federation. Thus, in-group members who identified with the governmental unit that was most closely associated with the out-group (for ethnic Russians, this means identifying with the Republics, while for people after whom the Republics were named, this means identifying with the Federation) had more favorable stereotypes of the out-group.

These findings add a new twist to the idea that identifying with superordinate groups improves intergroup relations. These findings suggest that when people identify with a superordinate group that grants legitimacy to an out-group, their views of the out-group will be favorable. In this study, it was also found that perceived competition with the out-group produces negative stereotypes. Although economic competition was measured at the individual level of analysis, it refers to socio cultural level phenomena (the actual level of competition among social groups in a society). Like so many articles in this issue, this study employed survey methods, but they achieved truly impressive response rates.

Bergmann (2008) provides us with an overview of anti-Semitism in Europe from the 1990s to the present. The picture he paints is not pretty. He argues that the fundamental underlying cause of anti-Semitism is a perceived threat to national identity. However, he also finds evidence that a number of other factors may play a role in anti-Semitism. Specifically, the specter of the Holocaust lies behind anti-Semitism in all of the European countries that were affected by the Holocaust (e.g., Germany, Austria, Poland, Russia, Ukraine, Lithuania, Slovakia, and Romania). He also argues that anti-Zionism, focused principally on the Israelis' treatment of the Palestinians, plays a role in anti-Semitism. In addition, there is some resentment toward the Jews among people who feel that Jews are exploiting the Holocaust to exact restitution. There continues to be an element of conspiracy thinking regarding the supposed economic and political power wielded by the Jews that contributes to anti-Semitism. Authoritarianism and conservative political attitudes also predict anti-Semitism. However, religious issues per se and SES are not strong predictors of anti-Semitism, nor is the percentage of Jews in a given country. Given the low percentage of Jews in most European countries, Bergmann (2008) argues that in Europe anti-Semitism exists despite the absence of Jews. This article nicely integrates factors at several levels of analysis. There is strong evidence of the role of historical factors in causing anti-Semitism (the Holocaust). Similarly, there is considerable evidence for socio cultural factors (nationalism, anti-Zionism, and differences in cultural values) as causes of anti-Semitism. And, a number of individual difference variables (authoritarianism, beliefs in conspiracies, stereotypes, and feelings of guilt or resentment) also contribute to anti-Semitism.

In the article by Zick, Wolf, Küpper, Davidov, Heitmeyer, and Schmidt (2008), the central argument is that in Germany a constellation of related prejudices exists toward a variety of subordinate groups (Blacks, Jews, immigrants, women, Muslims, homosexuals, and the homeless). They label this constellation "group-focused enmity" and relate it to the findings of Allport (1954) and many others that attitudes toward various out-groups are often correlated. They found considerable support for the group-focused enmity syndrome in three large-scale surveys in Germany. They make an argument at the socio cultural level that this syndrome reflects an ideology of inequality based on a strong correlation between group-focused enmity and social dominance orientation. In addition, group-focused enmity was predicted by authoritarianism and group-based relative deprivation (Germans feeling deprived with respect to the treatment of immigrants). Moreover, they found that group-focused enmity was related to a willingness to discriminate against immigrants. Thus, this study finds that two individual difference variables predict prejudice, and prejudice predicts willingness to discriminate. The basic findings of this study are potentially ominous because if prejudices toward different groups are interlinked, it may be especially difficult to change them.

Pettigrew, Christ, Meertens, Wagner, van Dick, and Zick (2008) studied the relationships between relative deprivation and blatant prejudice using the multinational Eurobarometer survey and two additional surveys in Germany. As has been found in other studies, it was group-relative deprivation, not individual-relative deprivation, which was most closely associated with prejudice. However, they also demonstrated that individual-relative deprivation has an effect on prejudice that is mediated by its relationship with group-relative deprivation. The individual difference variables of group identity (national pride) and political alienation moderated the relationship between group-relative deprivation and prejudice. Their study is particularly useful in helping to understand the types of people who are most likely to be prejudiced and who, therefore, should be the focus of the efforts to improve intergroup relations. They also suggest that for people who are politically alienated and have a strong national identity, it is their feelings of relative deprivation that should be addressed.

The study by Wagner, Christ, and Pettigrew (2008) examined the relationship between prejudice toward foreigners and discrimination in Germany using individual-level variables. Of particular note was a three-wave panel survey that provided strong correlational evidence for a causal link between prejudice and discrimination against foreigners. This article also indicated that the individual difference variables of authoritarianism, social dominance orientation, and perceived threat were related to a willingness to discriminate against foreigners. Furthermore, they found that positive intergroup contact was associated with less discrimination against foreigners. In addition, this study found that the relationship of collective threat and contact to discrimination was mediated by prejudice. These findings suggest that to change these patterns of discrimination, it may be useful to focus on increasing positive intergroup contact and reducing perceptions of threat since that will change prejudice, which will reduce discrimination.

Viewing These Articles through Allport's Lens Model

If we apply Allport's (1954) lens model of prejudice to these articles, we see that each of his four primary domains of variables is well represented. At the historical level, there is Bergmann's (2008) analysis of the historical origins of anti-Semitism in Europe, particularly the role the Holocaust has played in present-day attitudes toward the Jews. The article by Tam et al. (2008) concerns a deeply rooted religious conflict between Catholics and Protestants in Northern Ireland. In addition, several articles review the impact of historical factors on attitudes toward immigrants from former colonies. This is especially true for the article by Coenders et al. (2008) that traces the transition from an inclusive multicultural orientation toward immigration in the Netherlands to an orientation seeking assimilation of immigrants. Indeed, as Allport recognized, prejudice must always be considered in its historical context. Some other articles in this issue might have been strengthened by a greater consideration of such historical issues, at least for readers who are not Europeans. For example, what is it about the German past that leads to the emergence of a particular constellation of groups that constitute the group-focused enmity syndrome. More generally, what other historical factors helped to shape attitudes toward religious, ethnic, cultural, and racial out-groups in Europe? In particular, what roles do its history of Western philosophy, Christianity, capitalism, colonialism, democracy (communism in Eastern Europe and the former Soviet Union), and institutionalized structural inequality play in the evolution of intergroup relations in Europe?

The contemporary socio cultural climate was the focus of several articles. The article by Vala et al. (2008) emphasized the value that the Portuguese place on being nonprejudiced and empathizing with people who differ from them. Zick et al. (2008) cite an ideology of inequality that influences attitudes toward diverse out-groups in German society. Bergmann (2008) argues that anti-Semitism in Europe is based, to a large degree, on the feeling that national identity is threatened by the Jews. In addition to such cultural values and identity issues, this level of analysis also includes macrolevel societal variables such as SES and its relationship to prejudice (Pettigrew et al., 2008) and unemployment rates as a potential cause of anti-immigrant prejudice (Coenders et al., 2008). Other social indicators at this level of analysis that might be profitably examined for their effects on prejudice include actual value differences between groups, the role of language, differential birth rates, crime statistics, educational achievement levels, residential segregation, and intermarriage rates. In addition, governmental polices that can affect intergroup relations such as those affecting health care, social welfare, housing, the legal system, and education also fall into this level of analysis.

These articles focused less on Allport's situational factors than on the other factors. Although Billiet and de Witte (2008) refer to threats from immigrants, and Minescu et al. (2008) refer to perceived competition with out-groups for jobs, neither of these variables refers specifically to situational context factors that influence prejudice during interactions between groups. The amount and valence of contact were examined in several studies (Tam et al., 2008; Wagner et al., 2008), but again these were measured as individual difference variables, rather than as situational context variables. Because prejudice, intolerance, discrimination, and related phenomena are highly dynamic in nature and their expression depends greatly on situational context factors, they should not be ignored if the goal is a comprehensive understanding of negative intergroup relations.

Perhaps, because so many of the authors are social psychologists, these articles rely most heavily on variables measured at the individual difference level. Several studies (Bergmann, 2008; Billiet & de Witte, 2008; Pettigrew et al., 2008; Zick et al., 2008) examine right-wing authoritarianism or social dominance orientation (Wagner et al., 2008; Zick et al., 2008). Indices of social identity were measured in several studies (Minescu et al., 2008; Pettigrew et al., 2008). Tam et al. included measures of anger, infrahumanization, and empathy in their studies. The studies of anti-Semitism cited by Bergmann (2008) examined stereotypes, guilt, beliefs in conspiracies, and political attitudes among other variables. Measures related to political alienation were obtained in two studies (Billet & de Witte, 2008; Pettigrew et al., 2008). Two studies examined (Pettigrew et al., 2008; Zick et al., 2008) and two included measures of threat (Billet & de Witte, 2008; Wagner et al., 2008). And Vala et al. (2008) examined perceived value differences between groups. The sheer number of these variables suggests that it would be helpful to have a theory capable of integrating them.

Although few of these individual difference measures are new to the intergroup relations literature, the findings showing that they affect prejudice in Europe add to the growing evidence that they are common, if not universal, causes of prejudice. It would be of great interest to know if there were individual difference variables that were more strongly predictive of prejudice in Europe than elsewhere, and if there were variables that were related to prejudice in some countries of Europe, but not in others. For instance, Vala et al. (2008) find that national identity is not related to prejudice in Portugal, as it is in all of the other European countries where this relationship has been examined.

These articles deserve to be celebrated for the wide diversity of dependent measures they employ. Although they include standard measures of attitudes toward out-groups (e.g., immigrants, Jews), they also include attitudes toward discrimination, willingness to discriminate, behavioral intentions, and actual behavior (voting in Flanders). In addition, they include variables that are rarely studied, such as forgiveness of the out-group and the beliefs of victims of discrimination concerning the attitudes of the dominant group (Vala et al., 2008). The Pettigrew et al. (2008) study included a unique measure of the degree to which the respondents denied there was prejudice against an out-group. Another highlight of several of these studies was the use of mediational analyses. Wagner et al. (2008) found that prejudice mediated the relationship of both threat and contact with discrimination. Pettigrew et al. (2008) found that group-relative deprivation mediates the relationship between individual-relative deprivation and prejudice. This type of information can be valuable in designing interventions to improve intergroup relations because it indicates which variables these programs should emphasize to be the most effective.

The diversity of methodologies was also a notable feature of many of these studies. In particular, these studies employed survey methods much more extensively than American intergroup relations researchers commonly do. There were national surveys, multipanel surveys (Pettigrew et al., 2008), comparative cross-national surveys (Bergmann, 2008; Minescu et al., 2008), and pan-European surveys, where the data from many European countries were integrated. In addition, there were studies that incorporated implicit measures of attitudes (Tam et al., 2008), experiments (Coenders et al., 2008), and parallel studies of victims and dominant groups (Vala et al., 2008). One of the striking features of these diverse studies is that a number of them sought to combine levels of analysis, especially socio cultural variables (e.g., SES, immigration rates, unemployment rates, cultural differences, and economic competition) and individual difference variables (authoritarianism, social dominance orientation, social identity, stereotypes, guilt, anger, etc.). In general, the authors of these articles seem more comfortable drawing on both the sociological and psychological approaches to intergroup relations than are most American intergroup relations theorists and researchers. This type of combined approach offers the promise of a more complete understanding of the origins of intergroup relations problems than using either approach in isolation.

Some Implications of These Articles

The articles in this issue of the *Journal of Social Issues* present us with valuable insights into the current state of intergroup relations in Europe. What is the path forward toward a more complete understanding of the causes of intergroup relations problems in Europe and elsewhere? On the basis of the studies in this issue of the *Journal of Social Issues*, I would argue that more comparative studies (like those cited by Bergmann, 2008) are needed in the future to help us to understand what common factors create negative intergroup relations across European countries and what factors are unique to specific countries (e.g., luso–tropicalism in Portugal). More multilevel studies are needed to examine societal-level variables at the same time that they include individual-level variables—all the while being mindful of the historical and situational contexts. In order to conduct such multilevel studies, more effort will need to be put into developing theories and hypotheses that spell out the relationships among variables at different levels of analysis.

In addition, studies that examine the variations among European nations along cultural dimensions and the ways in which these variations are related to the patterns of intergroup relations within these countries might also be beneficial. For example, cultural dimensions such as individualism–collectivism (Hofstede, 1980; Triandis, 1995), power distance (Hofstede, 1980), and cultural tightness–looseness (Triandis, 1995) may be related to intergroup relations within and among countries. It would also be useful to have studies that provide information on which intergroup problems pose the greatest threat to Europe's future.

Ultimately, it would be invaluable if social scientists could develop a comprehensive overview of intergroup relations problems in Europe. This overview would include causal factors that are common across countries and those that are unique to specific countries. There would be some indication of which of these factors is most important and which is of less importance. It could also indicate how these factors moderate or mediate one another. It should reflect a deep historical understanding of the origins of these factors both locally and across Europe. Furthermore, such an overview could indicate which types of problems are the most grave and where these problems are most prevalent. In addition, this overview could indicate what types of individuals and which social categories of people hold the most negative attitudes. These types of information would be useful to both policy makers and practitioners in guiding their efforts to improve intergroup relations.

Social scientists can also play an important applied role in actively counteracting prejudice and discrimination in European and other countries. The primary levels of analysis at which social scientists can have an impact on applied intergroup relations are the socio cultural, situational, and individual difference levels. History cannot be changed, although it can certainly be taught in ways that improve intergroup relations, as multicultural education programs in the United States and elsewhere have shown (Banks & McGee-Banks, 2004). At the socio cultural level of analysis, psychologists could serve as advisors to government agencies that have an impact on educational, economic, housing, legal, health, and social welfare policies. They could also assist with the efforts at reconciliation among social groups, where this is needed, and help with the development of conflict resolution centers. In addition, their services would be beneficial in the design of mass media programs and community campaigns to improve intergroup relations. The studies in this issue suggest that such programs might have a more beneficial impact if they sought to promote the values of equality and diversity in order to offset the negative effects of the ideology of inequality and concerns about threats to national identity from immigrants. Likewise, programs that explode conspiracies concerning the Jews could help to reduce anti-Semitism. In addition, it might be well to place special emphasis on changing the attitudes and behaviors of individuals with politically conservative attitudes because it appears that they have the most negative relations with out-groups. The fact that people with lower SES and low status tend to be more prejudiced indicates that structural reforms that promote greater economic equality are also needed and social scientists may be able to contribute to formulating policies to achieve this goal.

At the individual difference and situational levels, social scientists can help to design, implement, and evaluate programs created to improve intergroup relations in educational, work, government, and community settings. The studies in this issue suggest that in Europe it would be important for these programs to try to change hierarchical belief systems, the tendency to view out-groups as less than human, issues of political alienation, perceived group deprivation, the assumption of value differences between groups, and perceptions of threat from outgroups. On the positive side, these studies suggest that empathy for out-groups and identifying with superordinate groups valued by out-groups can improve intergroup relations. Finally, promoting intergroup contact under optimal conditions would clearly improve intergroup relations.

One approach to modifying the individual difference variables found to be important in the studies reported in this issue would be to adapt intergroup programs developed elsewhere for use in the European context. For instance, intergroup dialogue programs and various programs for use in educational settings have shown great promise in the United States and elsewhere (Nagda, Tropp, & Paluck, 2006; Stephan & Vogt, 2004). Similarly, numerous co existence programs have been developed in Israel; some of which could be adapted for use in Europe (Hertz-Lazarowitz, Zelniker, Stephan, & Stephan, 2004; Weiner, 1998). There are, as well, many intergroup programs now in use in Europe that deserve to be more widely disseminated, and social scientists could play an important role in this process by evaluating them and publicizing the results.

It should be clear that the findings of basic research, which are well represented in this issue, have important implications for the practice of improving intergroup relations in European and other countries. Unfortunately, communication among theorists, researchers, and practitioners has been limited because of differences in their disciplinary backgrounds, the settings in which they work, the absence of cross-disciplinary journals, and a range of other factors. Theorists and researchers not only need to create more integrated theories, they also need to make greater efforts to present this information in venues and formats that are most likely to be useful to practitioners. This issue of the *Journal of Social Issues* represents an important step in that direction.

References

Allport, G. W. (1954). *The nature of prejudice*. Reading, MA: Addison-Wesley.

Banks, J. A., & McGee-Banks, C., Eds. (2004). *Handbook of research on multicultural education* (2nd ed.). San Francisco: Jossey-Bass.

Bergmann, W. (2008). Anti-semitic attitudes in Europe in a comparative perspective. *Journal of Social Issues*, 64(2), 343–362.

Billiet, B., & de Witte, H. (2008). "Everyday racism" as predictor for "political racism" in Flemish Belgium. *Journal of Social Issues*, 64(2), 253–267.

Coenders, M., Lubbers, M., Scheepers, P., & Verkuyten, M. (2008). More than two decades of changing ethnic attitudes in the Netherlands. *Journal of Social Issues*, 64(2), 269–285.

Hertz-Lazarowitz, R., Zelniker, T., Stephan, C. W., & Stephan, W. G., Eds. (2004). Improving Arab-Jewish relations in Israel: Theory and practice in coexistence education programs [Special issue]. *Journal of Social Issues*, 60(2).

Hofstede, G. (1980). *Culture's consequences*. Beverly Hills, CA: Sage.

Minescu, A., Hagendoorn, L., & Poppe, E. (2008). Types of identification and intergroup differentiation in the Russian Federation. *Journal of Social Issues*, 64(2), 321–342.

Nagda, R. A., Tropp, L. R., & Paluck, E. L. (Eds.). (2006). Reducing prejudice and promotiong social inclusion: Integrating research, theory, and practice in intergroup relations [Special issue]. *Journal of Social Issues*, 62(3)

Pettigrew, T. F., Christ, O., Meertens, R. W., Wagner, U., van Dick, R., & Zick, A. (2008). Relative deprivation and intergroup prejudice. *Journal of Social Issues*, 64(2), 385–401.

Stephan, W. G., & Vogt, W. P. (Eds.). (2004). *Education programs for improving intergroup relations: Theory, research and practice*. New York: Teachers College Press.

Tam, T., Hewstone, M., Kenworthy, J., & Chairns, E. (2008). Contemporary research on sectarianism in Northern Ireland: Intergroup forgiveness, trust, and implicit bias. *Journal of Social Issues*, 64(2), 303–320.

Triandis, H. C. (1995). *Individualism and collectivism*. Boulder, CO: Westview.

Vala, J., Lima, M., & Lopes, D. (2008). Black immigrants in Portugal: Luso-tropicalism and prejudice. *Journal of Social Issues*, 64(2), 287–302.

Wagner, U., Christ, O., & Pettigrew, T. F. (2008). Prejudice and group-related behavior in Germany. *Journal of Social Issues*, 64(2), 403–416.

Weiner, E. (1998). *The handbook of interethnic coexistence*. New York: Continuum.

Zick, A., Wagner, U., & Pettigrew, T. F. (2008). Introduction to prejudice and discrimination in Europe. *Journal of Social Issues*, 64(2), 417–429.

Zick, A., Wolf, C., Küpper, B., Davidov, E., Heitmeyer, W., & Schmidt, P. (2008). The syndrome of group focused enmity: A theory on devaluation and inequality and its empirical test. *Journal of Social Issues*, 64(2), 363–383.

WALTER G. STEPHAN received his PhD in psychology from the University of Minnesota in 1971. He has taught at the University of Texas at Austin and at New Mexico State University, where he currently holds the rank of Professor Emeritus. He has published articles and book chapters on attribution processes, cognition and affect, intergroup relations, and intercultural relations. He, along with his co-authors, has been the recipient of the Klineberg and Allport Awards, which are given by the Society for the Psychological Study of Social Issues. His recent publications include "The Road to Reconciliation" in A. Nadler, T. E., Malloy, and J. D. Fisher (Eds.), "The Social Psychology of Intergroup Reconciliation" (New York: Oxford University Press) "Intergroup Threat Theory" (with O. Ybarra and K. Rios-Morrison) in T. Nelson (Ed.), *Handbook of Prejudice* (Hillsdale, NJ: Lawrence Erlbaum).

Erratum

In Volume 64, Issue 1 of the *Journal of Social Issues* figure 1 in the article "Exploring the Roles of Extracurricular Activity Quantity and Quality in the Educational Resilience of Vulnerable Adolescents: Variable- and Pattern-Centered Approaches" by Stephen C. Peck, Robert W. Roeser, Nicole Zarrett, and Jacquelynne S. Eccles should have appeared as below:

Eighth-Grade Lifespace Configurations

			Eighth-Grade Self Profiles							
			S-I	S-II	S-III	S-IV	S-V	S-VI	S-VII	Total
Eighth-Grade World Profiles	W-I	Count	50	12	4	10	0	0	1	77
		ASR	11.2	1.7	-2.9	-1.2	-4.2	-3.0	-2.5	
	W-II	Count	23	5	21	9	10	2	0	70
		ASR	3.4	-.8	2.9	-1.2	-.7	-2.0	-2.8	
	W-III	Count	32	6	24	37	6	0	0	105
		ASR	3.5	-1.5	1.6	4.8	-3.4	-3.6	-3.5	
	W-IV	Count	43	25	25	54	12	4	1	164
		ASR	3.0	2.5	-.7	5.4	-3.8	-3.5	-4.2	
	W-V	Count	13	4	29	25	24	5	2	102
		ASR	-1.4	-2.1	3.1	1.8	1.7	-1.8	-2.7	
	W-VI	Count	4	2	15	10	20	3	6	60
		ASR	-2.3	-1.7	1.6	-.3	3.3	-1.3	.2	
	W-VII	Count	6	12	21	16	24	10	3	92
		ASR	-3.0	1.1	1.5	-.2	2.3	.3	-2.1	
	W-VIII	Count	6	11	12	10	24	16	12	91
		ASR	-3.0	.7	-1.1	-1.8	2.3	2.6	1.3	
	W-IX	Count	3	14	8	11	13	20	9	78
		ASR	-3.4	2.5	-1.7	-1.0	-.2	4.9	.7	
	W-X	Count	5	5	9	5	26	7	18	75
		ASR	-2.6	-1.0	-1.3	-2.7	4.0	-.2	4.5	
	W-XI	Count	1	4	6	0	18	25	34	88
		ASR	-4.3	-1.8	-2.7	-4.6	.7	6.1	9.8	
	W-XII	Count	1	3	6	2	6	11	12	41
		ASR	-2.6	-.6	-.5	-2.2	-.5	3.7	4.4	
Total		Count	187	103	180	189	183	103	98	1043

In the article "When Predictions Fail: The Case of Unexpected Pathways Toward High School Dropout," on page 175, the correct author order is:

Linda S. Pagani – Université de Montréal
Christa Japel – Université de Québec á Montréal
Frank Vitaro – Université de Montréal
Richard E. Tremblay – Université de Montréal
Simon Larose – Université Laval
Pierre McDuff – Université de Montréal

Also, on the front cover and Editorial Advisory Board of Volume 64, Issue 1 of the *Journal of Social Issues* Marcella Boynton's name was misspelled.

Author Services

www.blackwellpublishing.com/bauthor

Blackwell Publishing is committed to providing the best possible service to journal authors.

Production tracking:

- Track articles through production to publication online and in print
- Check article status online
- Receive e-mail alerts at key stages of production

Benefits for all authors include:

- Author guidelines by journal
- How to submit an article
- How to link to articles on Blackwell Synergy
- FAQs on all aspects of the publishing process and more

Blackwell Publishing

Visit the Author Services website at
www.blackwellpublishing.com/bauthor

HELL IS THE PLACE WHERE NOTHING CONNECTS — T.S. ELIOT

reliable reference linking, powered by CrossRef

Linking to and from this journal is powered by CrossRef. CrossRef links millions of articles and chapters, from thousands of publications, from hundreds of publishers. So your reference linking works. Permanently. Take a tour at **www.crossref.org**. And make sure all your published work is CrossRef-enabled.

CROSSREF.ORG | THE CITATION LINKING BACKBONE

40 SALEM STREET, LYNNFIELD MA 01940 • 781-295-0072